Language Con
the Future of I

This book reflects on the future of the English language as used by native speakers, speakers of nativized New Englishes, and users of English as a lingua franca (ELF). The volume begins by outlining the current position of English in the world and accounts for the differences among native and nativized varieties and ELF usages. It offers a historical perspective on the impact of language contact on English and discusses whether the lexicogrammatical features of New Englishes and ELF are shaped by imperfect learning or deliberate language change. The book also considers the consequences of writing in a second language and questions the extent to which non-native English-speaking academics and researchers should be required to conform to 'Anglo' patterns of text organization and 'English Academic Discourse.' The book then examines the converse effect of English on other languages through bilingualism and translation. This volume is essential reading for students and scholars in English language, sociolinguistics, language acquisition, and language policy.

Ian MacKenzie formerly taught translation at the University of Geneva. He is the author of *English as a Lingua Franca: Theorizing and Teaching English* (2014), *Paradigms of Reading: Relevance Theory and Deconstruction* (2002), and a number of English-language teaching coursebooks.

Routledge Studies in Sociolinguistics

For a full list of titles in this series, please visit www.routledge.com

9 **Gender Representation in Learning Materials**
International Perspectives
Edited by Abolaji S. Mustapha and Sara Mills

10 **The Sociolinguistics of Voice in Globalising China**
Dong Jie

11 **The Discourse of Powerlessness and Repression**
Life Stories of Domestic Migrant Workers in Hong Kong
Hans J. Ladegaard

12 **The Discourse of Sport**
Analyses from Social Linguistics
Edited by David Caldwell, John Walsh, Elaine W. Vine and John Juneidini

13 **Social Media Discourse, (Dis)Identifications and Diversities**
Edited by Sirpa Leppänen, Elina Westinen and Samu Kytölä

14 **Care Communication**
Making a Home in a Japanese Eldercare Facility
Peter Backhaus

15 **Heritage Language Policies around the World**
Edited by Corinne Seals and Sheena Shah

16 **The Politics of Translingualism**
Jerry Won Lee

17 **Living Languages and New Approaches to Language Revitalisation Research**
Tonya N. Stebbins, Kris Eira and Vicki L. Couzens

18 **Language Contact and the Future of English**
Ian MacKenzie

Language Contact and the Future of English

Ian MacKenzie

Routledge
Taylor & Francis Group
LONDON AND NEW YORK

First published 2018
by Routledge

2 Park Square, Milton Park, Abingdon, Oxfordshire OX14 4RN
52 Vanderbilt Avenue, New York, NY 10017

Routledge is an imprint of the Taylor & Francis Group, an informa business

First issued in paperback 2020

Library of Congress Cataloging-in-Publication Data
Names: MacKenzie, Ian, 1954– author.
Title: Language contact and the future of English / by Ian MacKenzie.
Description: New York : Routledge, [2017] | Series: Routledge studies in sociolinguistics; 18 | Includes bibliographical references and index.
Identifiers: LCCN 2017051258 | ISBN 9781138557222 (hardback : alk. paper) | ISBN 9781315150758 (ebk.)
Subjects: LCSH: Languages in contact. | English language—Variation—English-speaking countries. | English language—English-speaking countries. | English language—Study and teaching—Foreign speakers. | Lingua francas. | Sociolinguistics.
Classification: LCC P130.5 .M23 2018 | DDC 427—dc23
LC record available at https://lccn.loc.gov/2017051258

ISBN: 978-1-138-55722-2 (hbk)
ISBN: 978-0-367-59362-9 (pbk)

Typeset in Sabon
by Apex CoVantage, LLC

Contents

Preface

As everybody knows, because journalists keep telling us, non-native (or L2) speakers of English vastly outnumber the language's native (or L1) speakers. As virtually everybody knows (here we must exclude the few applied linguists who seek to deny this), the immense majority of non-native speakers—that is, people who did not acquire the language naturally in childhood—tend to use it differently from its native speakers, especially monolingual ones. Given the huge, and increasing, number of L2 speakers of English, the question arises whether their usages will have an influence on the varieties of English spoken and written as a native language. In this book I attempt to answer that question and come up with—spoiler alert!—a largely negative answer. Indeed in the penultimate chapter I suggest that English may be having a greater effect on other languages as a result of both direct and mediated contact (particularly through translation) than other languages are having on native English by way of second-degree language contact through non-native English, or English used as a lingua franca (ELF). I also consider the consequences of writing in a second language, which the majority of academic researchers are now obliged to do, and whether this will—or should—influence the standard forms of academic discourse in English.

This book ranges widely over theories of language acquisition and learning, language change, language contact, bilingualism, contrastive rhetoric, linguistic relativity, and translation. Readers hoping for an analysis of a custom-made corpus, and such delights as ANOVAs, chi-square tests, and left-skewed Gaussian distributions, will unfortunately be disappointed. The same might also apply to anyone who disapproves of introspection, speculation, and indeed opinion. But I trust that this book will engage readers interested in the past, present, and future of English, as well as in theories of how languages are learned and used, and how and why they change.

Abbreviations

BLC	Basic language cognition
BNC	British National Corpus
CLIL	Content and language integrated learning
CoCA	Corpus of Contemporary American
EAD	English Academic Discourse
EFL	English as a foreign language
EIL	English as an International Language
ELF	English as a lingua franca
ELFA	The English as a Lingua Franca in Academic Settings corpus
ELT	English-language teaching
ENL	English as a native language
ESL	English as a second language
HLC	Higher language cognition
ICE	International Corpus of English
L1	First language
L2	Second language
LaRa	*Lingua receptiva*
NNEST	Non-native English-speaking teacher
NNS	Non-native speaker
NS	Native speaker
SAE	Standard Average European
SLA	Second language acquisition
SOV	Subject—object—verb
SVO	Subject—verb—object
TEFL	Teaching English as a foreign language
TESOL	Teaching English to speakers of other languages
VOICE	The Vienna-Oxford International Corpus of English
VSO	Verb—subject—object

Acknowledgements

A fairly complete plan of this book unexpectedly surfaced in my mind, as these things do, while I was slowly cycling up a Swiss mountain, shortly after I finished my book about English as a lingua franca (2014). I was able to write a large part of it in New York during a sabbatical semester kindly granted by my former employer, the Faculty of Translation and Interpreting of the University of Geneva. Yes, former employer—this book and the following one are my odes to early retirement!

Many alterations were made to the manuscript after Kirsten Stirling drew my attention to a lack of sundry things described in Chapter 6 as necessary ingredients of 'English Academic Discourse'—structure, clarity, cohesion, transitions, and the like. Effusive thanks are in order.

Thanks are obviously also due to Routledge commissioning editor Elysse Preposi. I am also beholden to three anonymous reviewers for their useful suggestions. One of them even included the very generous—and possibly exaggerated!—*faux*-Voltairean maxim: 'I disapprove of what you say, but I will defend to the death your right to say it.'

Chapter 4 includes material from 'Will English as a Lingua Franca Impact on Native English?,' which appeared online in *Varieng* in 2015. Chapter 5 includes material from 'ELF and the Alternatives,' published in the *Journal of English as a Lingua Franca* in 2014. Chapter 6 includes material from 'Rethinking Reader and Writer Responsibility in Academic English,' published in the *Applied Linguistics Review* in 2015. These articles also benefitted, as per usual, from the comments of journal editors and anonymous reviewers.

A key claim in Chapter 6 draws on an Internet forum reply to a question of mine by Ernst-August Gutt. Thanks also go to Tim Parks, who told me about the Dutch novel quoted at the beginning of Chapter 6. Parks's *New York Review of Books* blogs about translation and the Anglicization of literature inspired the third part of Chapter 7. Vincent Renner and Geneviève Bordet provided useful references for Chapters 6 and 7.

I'll dedicate this one to Arthur Guinness, Chasselas, and Pinot noir—and to Arsène, in remembrance of times long past. Or perhaps, as this book is appearing in a series on sociolinguistics, to the linguist (a staunch believer in the Language Acquisition Device and the Tooth Fairy) who informed me that 'you don't have to be stupid to be a sociolinguist, but it helps,' and that 'sociolinguistics is dinner table conversation.' *Bon appétit!*

1 Introduction
English Today

This book is about something that no one actually *knows* anything about: the future of the English language. And like the man said, it's difficult to make predictions, especially about the future![1] But it is of course possible to extrapolate from past and present states of the language and attested sociolinguistic patterns. Historical linguists regularly invoke the uniformitarian principle, according to which natural processes and mechanisms that operated to produce language change in the past are almost certainly also occurring today (Labov 1972: 161; Lass 1997: 28–9). We may also expect them to continue to operate, making the present the key to the future as well as the past. Writing about the future of a language is necessarily highly speculative—although maybe not more speculative, and possibly even *less* speculative, than some work on a language's past[2]—but at least the uniformitarian principle provides a grounding for one's speculations.

Specifically this book is about whether the kinds of English used by non-native speakers—who greatly outnumber the language's native speakers—are likely to have an effect on the major varieties of native English, as is widely argued by theorists of English as a lingua franca lingua franca or ELF (e.g. Seidlhofer 2003; Mauranen 2012). Given that the differences between the English spoken by non-native and native users are to a large extent the result of first language (L1) interference—or, stated more neutrally, crosslinguistic interaction—this is a matter of language contact. And where language contact is concerned, I am unfortunately beguiled by Thomason and Kaufman's (1988) bold claim that '[a]s far as the strictly linguistic possibilities go, any linguistic feature can be transferred from any language to any other language' (p. 14), overriding any supposed internal structural constraints, because 'it is the sociolinguistic history of the speakers, and not the structure of their language, that is the primary determinant of the linguistic outcome of language contact' (p. 35). In this instance it would be the transfer of features from other languages to native English via the intermediary of non-native English. But (my beguilement notwithstanding) I will argue that the overall social context of interaction between non-native and native speakers of

English does not favour the transfer of many morphosyntactic, lexical, phonological, or other features.

1.1 Synopsis

In this introductory chapter, which revisits some points from my previous book, *English as a Lingua Franca: Theorizing and Teaching English*, I sketch the current role of English in the world, including its use as a native language, as a nativized second language in many multilingual countries (largely former British colonies in Africa, Asia, and Oceania), and as a lingua franca, or a language of wider communication, in many other parts of the world. I also defend the utility (indeed the reality) of the concept of the native speaker, or more accurately, the concept of native-like competence, defined in terms of a shared knowledge of lexis, phonology, morphology and syntax, and appropriate style shifting—the use of standard and non-standard social and contextual variants in a given speech community (Croft 2000). First and second language acquisition necessarily take place in very different ways, which lead to different ways of using language. This psycholinguistic or cognitive fact in no way diminishes the legitimacy of second language (L2) speakers. Non-native uses of English can be viewed as *different* from native uses rather than *deficient*: it is evident that the usages of any given community speaking a native or nativized variety of English are not necessarily appropriate (or even meaningful) in cross-cultural communication using English as a lingua franca.

In Chapter 2 I discuss theories of second language acquisition (SLA), centring on the effects of prior L1 learning on an L2, especially the replication of entrenched L1 constructions. This has been variously described in terms of transfer, interference, interlanguage, fossilization, approximative systems, and so forth. More recent work has shown how the language use of bi- and multilingual speakers *always* differs from that of monolinguals, while giving a neutral or even a positive account of the effects of crosslinguistic interaction. Such approaches are applicable to the nativized postcolonial 'New Englishes,' in which some of the fossilized 'errors' of early generations of speakers have developed into stable, conventionalized features of a new variety, and to English used as an international lingua franca, where it makes little sense to describe users as deficient native speakers, as in orthodox SLA theory.

In Chapter 3 I discuss conflicting accounts of language change, including those that attribute it to languages themselves, rather than their speakers, and those that attribute changes to active human agency and, often, the effects of language contact. I argue that adult language users can indeed make conscious and deliberate changes to the way they use a language in pursuit of enhanced expressivity, in an attempt to be optimally comprehensible, and sometimes (although clearly not in the case of

ELF) to follow the dictates of prescriptivists. This process is rather more apparent in ELF than in native English, and it appears likely that some ELF users have effected conscious, deliberate changes to native usages for reasons of clarity and communicative effectiveness, choosing to disregard some of the more incongruous and idiosyncratic elements of English lexicogrammar. The aggregate result of such intentional and purposeful choices can indeed be language change.

Chapter 4 offers a historical perspective on the effects of language contact on English, beginning with contact between the Anglo-Saxons and the indigenous British Celtic population and later with Scandinavian invaders. This contact is believed to have had a major impact on English, including both additions to the language and simplifications resulting from imperfect learning by post-adolescents and adults. But although population movements and adult acquisition had major effects on languages in the past, when literacy was limited, today changes are inhibited by education and by print (and its digital successors). I look at the standard models of innovation and diffusion, and the psycholinguistic and sociolinguistic mechanisms—accommodation, expressivity, prestige, and so on—that could lead to (or prevent) common lexicogrammatical features of L2 English being propagated among native English speakers. Of course contact between native and non-native varieties of English is more like dialect contact than ordinary language contact. The influence of other languages only manifests itself via varieties of L2 English, and many of the standard factors of language contact are inapplicable (the extent of bilingualism, diglossia, the societal roles of two different languages, etc.). The only pertinent parameters are duration and intensity of contact and attitudes towards the forms of speech involved.

In Chapter 5 I consider the scope and limitations of potential alternatives to the use of English as the world's lingua franca, including multilingualism (and consequently interpreting and translation), receptive multilingualism, and codeswitching or language mixing, as well as Mandarin Chinese, which some people consider a candidate for a future worldwide lingua franca.

Chapter 6 turns to academic English. To be widely read, or indeed to be published at all, researchers are increasingly obliged to write in English. But does this require L2 English users to conform to the dominant linear, deductive, 'Anglo' pattern of text organization (which can safely be called 'English Academic Discourse')? Or should they be free to transfer rhetorical patterns from their L1s—such as inductive and indirect styles of writing and end-weighted forms of argumentation—into articles written in English? Given that most academic writing in English is for an international audience, a strong case can be made for non-native English-speaking researchers (or their English translators)—and indeed native English-speaking writers too—being free to adopt a range of styles, or some sort of heterogeneous hybrid, depending on their perceptions of their readers' expectations. On the other hand, different languages have different grammatical structures, which result in different discourse patterns, so what seems natural and appropriate in one language is not necessarily so, or necessarily possible, in another. There are always gains and losses involved in writing in different languages, and in translation, as equivalence of meaning is only partial. Writing in another language inevitably changes what one wants to 'say.'

All round the globe there is a millennia-old history of language contact and bi- or multilingualism leading to lexicogrammatical change, or more specifically, replication, and today in many parts of the world the dominant language providing the model for replication is English. Increasing bilingualism with English, and the crosslinguistic interaction this entails, as well as extensive translation from English, are leading to English having a growing impact on the lexicon, syntax, and discourse structures of many other languages. Although translation can transfer ideas across cultures, and enhance the target language and its literary forms, after a certain point, too many calques of terminology, phraseology, and syntactic patterns can begin to impoverish a borrowing language. A parallel development is that more and more European writers, particularly novelists, appear to be deliberately simplifying their style and avoiding local cultural references to facilitate translation into English, hoping thereby to access the global market. In Chapter 7 I analyze these trends and attempt to relativize the consequences of crosslinguistic interaction with English from a historical perspective. Chapter 8 is a short conclusion.

1.2 Native, Nativized, and Non-Native Englishes

Following Braj Kachru (1985), and despite more than three decades of critiques, it has become conventional to talk about the 'three circles' of English. The countries in which the language is used and transmitted to children as the mother tongue of the majority of the population make up the inner circle, while the countries in which English has an institutionalized second language role in a multilingual setting constitute the outer circle. The rest of the world (almost without exceptions), in which English is taught, learnt and used as a foreign (or additional or auxiliary) language, for communication with speakers from all three circles, is the expanding circle (although today expanded would be more accurate). There are approximately 400 million native English speakers and 430 million outer circle L2 speakers (Crystal 2003: 65–7), and probably a billion or more expanding circle speakers of varying levels of proficiency (Crystal 2008). Alternative terms for the inner, outer, and expanding circles are English as a native language (ENL), English as a second language (ESL), and English as a foreign language (EFL) countries.

Kachru's classification, which is based more on sociopolitical criteria than linguistic ones, is clearly not without its problems, as there are countries that are difficult to place in a particular circle. For example, in South Africa—which Kachru (1992b: 356) simply left out of the country names on his well-known diagram of the different circles—there are native speakers of English but also many non-native ones: as Bruthiaux (2003: 163) points out, it would be more accurate to talk about White South African English, used as an L1, and Black South African English, generally used as an L2. Moreover, about half the native speakers of English speak South African Indian English, 'a variety that is distinct from both White and Black South African Englishes as well as from mainland Indian varieties.' Similarly about 20% of Canadians are Francophone, and another 20% have L1s other than English and French, which means that there are also a lot of L2 speakers of English in Canada. There are also differing proportions of speakers of other first languages in the United States, Australia, New Zealand, Scotland, Wales, Ireland, and England.

In the multilingual outer circle countries (such as Nigeria, Kenya, India, Singapore, the Philippines, Fiji, etc.), English is largely learned at school; has an official, high-status, second language role; and is often used by an economic elite—in most cases 'at best between 20% and 30% of the total population' (Mufwene 2010: 57)—as a lingua franca for intra-national (and often inter-ethnic) communication in politics, administration, education, the media, and so on. For some educated people in these countries, although English is not, chronologically, their first language, is it their primary or dominant language—'the one they use most, and perhaps are most comfortable and fluent in for many or even most purposes' (Trudgill 1995: 314). Once upon a time the localized varieties of English spoken in these countries were described as fossilized interlanguages—for example, Selinker (1972: 216) described Indian English as an interlanguage 'with regard to English'—but they are now more often called New Englishes, a term used in book titles by Pride (1982) and Platt et al. (1984). Kachru (1983) pointed out that so-called 'New' Indian English is actually older than Australian English, but I will still use the term New Englishes in preference to Kachru's preferred term, World Englishes, which logically includes *all* varieties, including British English, and Schneider's (2007) term Postcolonial Englishes, which includes American and Australian English, and so on.[3]

Unlike expanding circle learners, who might only use English in the classroom, and encounter it as a foreign language in the media (in song lyrics, on the Internet, etc.), learners of New Englishes tend to have considerable exposure to the local variety of the language. It is often used in schools as a medium for the teaching of other subjects, and there may be local English-language media (television, radio, newspapers, books, etc.). There will probably be frequent opportunities to acquire and use the language in a variety of situations in everyday life so that local patterns of usage become entrenched in individual speakers' minds and conventionalized in the community. English may also be used at home in codeswitching or in a diglossic relation with a local language: there are increasing numbers of native English-speaking households in supposedly outer circle Singapore, and to a lesser extent in India, East and West Africa, and elsewhere.[4]

The postcolonial New Englishes are now generally described as being endonormative, which is to say that they have largely stabilized, developed their own local norms, and do not look to an external source of authority (see Hickey 2012). Schneider (2007) proposes a 'dynamic model' showing how New Englishes pass through different evolutionary phases. In a grossly simplified version, over the course of time the settlers' English picks up cultural terms from the local population; increasing numbers of the local population become bilingual with English; the settlers' ties with the mother country weaken and inter-ethnic contacts increase; the settlers and the indigenous population accommodate to each other's uses of English, leading to phonological and structural innovations, largely due to transfer from local languages; particularly useful elements are selected from the 'feature pool' (Mufwene 2001: 14) of linguistic choices; and eventually a stable, nativized, endogenous variety of English emerges, with characteristic local features of grammar, lexis, and phraseology and a standard and recognizable pronunciation that is transmitted from one generation to the next.[5] The nativized variety is codified with the writing of dictionaries and grammars, and so on, but in the course of time differentiation may occur, with the birth of regional dialects and ethnic and social varieties. The term 'nativized' is important: without it, the children who learn and use English as their first language in multilingual countries like India, Singapore, Nigeria, and so on would have to be described as native speakers of a non-native variety, an obvious terminological absurdity.

Both Kachru's three circles model and Schneider's dynamic model largely neglect class differences, and other commentators point out that there is a considerable gap between middle-class varieties of New Englishes and simpler, basilectal varieties spoken in the same countries (Mesthrie and Bhatt 2008: 36). In fact, many speakers are competent in a 'slice' of a continuum running from a Creolistic 'basilect' through a number of 'mesolects' to a standardized 'acrolect' and vary their speech depending on their interlocutors, the formality of the situation, and so on (pp. 39–40).

In the expanding circle, where English has generally not been 'nativized,' it is often used in business and commerce, tourism, diplomacy, international law, higher education and scientific research, entertainment, popular culture and sport, and so on, although the proportion of English speakers and proficiency levels differ hugely from country to country. In the Netherlands and the Nordic countries, for example, the proportion of proficient, educated users of English is probably greater than in many outer circle countries, and Graddol (2006: 110) reports, without giving a source, that Kachru has revised his model and now proposes that the inner circle should be thought of as the group of highly proficient speakers of English (maybe half a billion strong) who have 'functional nativeness' regardless of which circle they come from. Around this circle are other concentric ones with speakers of lessening proficiency.[6]

Besides using a localized variety of English in their home countries, many outer circle speakers also participate in international interactions with speakers from the other circles, and indeed there is extensive overlap between widespread lexicogrammatical features found in the New Englishes and in the English of speakers from expanding circle countries (Williams 1987). For people working in international teams, whether Bangladeshi and Indonesian domestic workers in the Emirates, or highly qualified professionals in multinational companies or in organizations such as the UN, the G20, ASEAN, the WTO, CERN, and so on, the outer/expanding circle distinction is probably otiose.[7]

Expanding circle speakers were traditionally described as using English as a foreign language (EFL).[8] This term is progressively giving way to English as a lingua franca (ELF). ELF can be defined as '[a]ny use of English among speakers of different first languages for whom English is the communicative medium of choice, and often the only option' (Seidlhofer 2011: 7). This definition does not exclude the usages of native English speakers in ELF interactions, or those of speakers of nativized outer circle varieties, but most research into ELF focuses on the bi- or multilingual speakers of the expanding circle (see, e.g., Seidlhofer 2001, 2011; Jenkins 2007; Prodromou 2008; Kirkpatrick 2010; Mauranen 2012).[9]

If English is used as a lingua franca, it is no longer related to a particular target culture in which certain ways of speaking and behaving are appropriate. Rather than imitating the lexicogrammatical norms of a particular variety of native (or indeed nativized) English, ELF speakers (are said to) adopt ways of speaking (with their bi- or multilingual English-speaking interlocutors) that aid mutual intelligibility and successful communication. Seidlhofer (2009)—who describes ELF as 'the prevailing reality of English,' at least 'from the global perspective' (p. 237)—highlights the way ELF speakers 'assert and communicate their own identities,' 'how they use the language creatively and "subversively" rather than mimicking native speakers of English' (p. 239), and how 'ELF innovations' are 'evidence of the sense of ownership of the language' (p. 240). 'Communities of practice' (Wenger 1998) of ELF speakers are said to develop their own norms rather than depending on the norms of inner circle English varieties.

Corpus evidence[10] shows that this gives rise to a great deal of linguistic variation and the use of non-standard morphology, lexis, phraseology, and syntax, or what Widdowson (2003: 48–9) describes as 'the *virtual* language, that resource for making meaning immanent in the language which simply has not hitherto been encoded.' Using a metaphor from software development, House (2013: 59–60) describes ELF as 'a kind of "open source phenomenon," a resource available for whoever wants to take advantage of the virtual English language, on which ELF is based.'

As suggested above, according to this account, ELF is *different* from English as a native language but not *deficient* or inferior (Seidlhofer 2011: 120). Thus the difference between ELF and the older concept of EFL (English as a foreign language) is an outlook or an attitude: whereas EFL learners make *mistakes* (or commit errors), ELF users show a lot of *variation*, and the conventional accounts of imperfect learning found in SLA theory are not applicable (see Chapter 2). This argument echoes Kachru's (1992a: 62) distinction between 'deviations' in the New Englishes and mistakes in EFL. Whatever their level of proficiency, ELF speakers are described as *users* and not *learners*.[11]

Because ELF speakers are, like outer circle speakers, by definition bi- or multilingual, their use of English is likely to be influenced by crosslinguistic transfer from their mother tongue or dominant language as well as other languages they speak (again see Chapter 2). As Ferguson (2009: 129) puts it, ELF can be viewed 'as a fluid cluster of communicative practices where speakers draw on a wide, not clearly bounded range of linguistic features—some standard, some non-standard, and others not English at all (at least according to the conventional view).' Crosslinguistic interaction often results in similarities (the same transfer features, comparable accents, etc.) in the English used by speakers of the same L1. Mauranen (2012: 29) has coined the useful term 'similects' to describe the hybrid, L1-influenced varieties of English that come into contact with each other in ELF.[12] These are in some ways analogous to New English varieties (because the same L2 learning mechanisms are involved), but because expanding circle speakers rarely use English with their compatriots, these varieties do not undergo focusing or stabilize around endogenous norms like the nativized varieties. Similects *can* be described (preferably with a large place given to transfer features), and they are increasingly being labelled as 'varieties' or 'Englishes,'[13] but in this book I will only attempt to describe (in very broad strokes) the reified entity 'ELF.'

Typical contact situations involve speakers of two different languages who either use a mixture of the two or choose one of them in which to communicate so that some speakers are using an L2. Mauranen (2012: 30) characterizes ELF, in which everyone is speaking the 'same' L2, as 'second-order language contact,' a contact between hybrids which 'come together much like dialects in contact.' Some lexicogrammatical forms that are found in many similects have diffused into common usage (in a kind of koinéization), thereby lessening the variation to be found in ELF. These are mostly reconceptualizations (and simplifications) of the more incongruous and idiosyncratic elements of English grammar—those that differ from the majority of natural languages, and which appear bizarre, and therefore difficult to learn, to most L2 English speakers (see what follows).

There was a time when ELF researchers entertained 'the possibility of a codification of ELF with a conceivable ultimate objective of making it a feasible, acceptable and respected alternative to ENL in appropriate contexts of use' (Seidlhofer 2001: 150). But conjectures about codification have largely given way to 'a much more processual, communicative view of ELF,' in which the interest lies less in formal innovations per se than in the 'underlying significance' of forms and the functions they fulfil in ELF interactions (Seidlhofer 2009: 241). As Berns (2009: 196) puts it, echoing the modernist architectural slogan, in a lingua franca, 'form follows function.' However, because my interest lies in the potential influence of non-native varieties of English on native varieties (which are *another* 'prevailing reality of English'), I am necessarily interested in particular formal features.

Lexicogrammatical features found in many ELF similects include the use of the progressive rather than the present simple with stative verbs and verbs with habitual meaning (*I'm believing, is belonging to*); the conflation of the present perfect and the past simple with definite past time reference (*I have seen/saw her yesterday*); the use of the present simple rather than the present perfect to express continuing time spans (*He works here for/since three years*); very variable use of prepositions, especially dependent prepositions following verbs, nouns, or adjectives (*accumulate to*, *an interest on*, *interested for*); very variable article use (or non-use), including the use of articles with abstract nouns (*the nature*, *the society*); the frequent use of plurals with nouns that are uncountable in native English (*advices*, *equipments*, *feedbacks*); and verb complementation patterns that differ from those of native English, with the *to* infinitive frequently used as a complement in place of the gerund (see Chapter 3).[14] Most of these uses are also widespread in the nativized New Englishes, whose speakers are likely to find exactly the same features of native English grammar to be incongruous and idiosyncratic.[15]

All in all, grammatical accuracy, at least according to native English norms, does not seem to be a priority in ELF interactions. Many non-standard forms probably go unnoticed—and anyway, as improvizing jazz soloists like to say, 'It's not a mistake if you play it twice!'—but the more useful ones tend to be picked up and reused as speakers accommodate to each other's uses. As Mauranen (2012: 123) says, in ELF, structural features 'tolerate a good deal of turbulence without disrupting communication.' Mauranen even suggests that '[t]he variability of structure in use and the frequency of non-standard structural features would appear to call into question the significance of structure to successful communication' (p. 130).

ELF corpora such as ELFA and VOICE also reveal a reasonable amount of inexact lexis—approximations of established English words that are recognizably close to target forms, including regularized past-tense forms (*bringed*, *drawed*, *feeled*), the seemingly random use of negative suffixes (*disbenefits*, *intransparency*, *unrespect*), inventions by way of creative (or erroneous) use of suffixes (*all-embracive*, *devaluarized*, *disturbant*, *controversiality*, *maternalist*, *maximalize*, *plagiate*, *proletariatic*), backformations (*colonizators*, *introducted*, *standardizate*), truncations (*automously*, *phenomen*, *significally*), and so on (see MacKenzie 2014b, Ch. 5). There are also word-forms transferred from other languages known by the speaker (*homogene*, *phenomene*, *prognose*, *performant*, *sportive*). The corpora show that most of these words are used by speakers showing a high level of fluency in English who sometimes also use the standard form in another speech-turn.

These and many other non-standard words found in ELF corpora result from word formation processes that are widely attested in both native English and the nativized New Englishes (see Bauer 1983; Plag 2003; Biermeier 2008). Mauranen (2012) describes such approximations as involuntary, resulting from 'fuzzy processing' (p. 41) and the 'less deeply entrenched memory representations' involved in an L2 (p. 37), and argues that 'a complex environment like ELF seems to require stretching the tolerance of fuzziness wider than usual' (p. 42), giving rise to overproductive derivational morphology and exploitation of the virtual language.

In the ELFA and VOICE data, although interlocutors occasionally use the Standard English version of a non-standard word they have just heard in their next speech-turn (an embedded correction), they are more inclined to let them pass, if indeed they are noticed. The co-texts of non-standard words like those listed show that 'none caused any noticeable reactions in their extended contexts' (Mauranen 2012:103) or provoked any ripples or breakdowns in communication.

The logic of approximation resulting from the absence of entrenched schemas clearly applies to phraseology as much as to lexis (see MacKenzie 2014b, Ch. 6). As Mauranen says, 'speakers use sequences which approximate conventionalised, phraseological units, but in ways that do not quite match the target,' but—importantly—although 'ELF speakers tend to get them slightly wrong,' they 'also get them approximately right' (p. 144). In approximate versions of frequent multi-word units, the non-standard elements 'get embedded in the larger schematic unit, which is sufficiently conventionalised to be recognisable as a unit in a given function.' ELF corpora reveal versions of recognizable native English expressions, often using different articles and prepositions (*by the time being*, *in accordance to*, *on the long run*). Speakers also use semantic or lexical approximations, such as *divide and govern*, *a hen and egg thing*, *lift an eyebrow*, *small and middle business*, *a streak of good luck* (examples from ELFA and Prodromou 2008: 222).

When non-standard forms and linguistic anomalies *do* (temporarily) hinder comprehension, Firth (1996: 243) suggests that ELF users often adopt the 'let it pass' principle: that is, 'when faced with problems in understanding the speaker's utterance'—as long as the problems are 'non-fatal'—the hearer 'lets the unknown or unclear action, word or utterance "pass" on the (common-sense) assumption that it will either become clear or redundant as talk progresses.' Let it pass is just one of a number of cooperative strategies described by ELF researchers. Kirkpatrick (2010: 127–36), analyzing data from southeast Asian speakers, describes several more, including listening to the message (i.e., disregarding non-standard forms); requesting repetition and clarification when it is clear that a word is too important to let pass; spelling out a word if pronunciation seems to be a problem; making things explicit, including changes of topic; repeating a phrase (both self- and other-repetition); speaker paraphrase or self-rephrasing (adjusting form rather than meaning); participant prompting; participant paraphrase; and lexical anticipation and lexical suggestion (offering a word if the speaker hesitates or appears to stumble over a long word).

As well as using cooperative pragmatic strategies such as these, ELF speakers—like virtually all speakers of all languages—tend to accommodate to and converge with their interlocutors' ways of speaking, adjusting their accent, lexis, grammar, phraseology, and so on. This is a countervailing force to the inherent variability of ELF. In an L1, very slight variations of lexis, syntax, phonology, prosody, and so on can be meaningful, and different speech variants usually carry social significance and are associated with certain localities, social groups, and text types. In ELF much of this (native-like) information is either lacking or disregarded, and accommodation may be more related to ensuring comprehensibility, although of course successful ELF users vary their speech according to their communicative goals and to what is appropriate for specific interlocutors in any given interaction.

The foregoing characterization of ELF communication makes it sound like rather hard work. As Mauranen (2012: 7) says, 'The cognitive load in ELF is unusually heavy on account of the variety and unpredictability of language parameters: interlocutors' accents, transfer features, and proficiency levels,' although Schneider (2012: 87–8) suggests that in some types of ELF communication—'contexts where interaction remains stable in similar constellations over a longer period'—the 'stabilizing effects of mutual accommodation between the speakers and speaker groups involved' may lead to 'increased conformity via negotiation' and, ultimately, the kind of 'stable communal varieties' found in New Englishes. But it is easy to overestimate the formal differences between ELF and native English. Both ELF and the nativized, postcolonial New English varieties have largely appropriated the grammatical core of the major varieties of native English, at least in their written forms, and there is also a great deal of lexis common to all varieties. Consequently the claim that native English speakers will need 'an additionally acquired language system' to 'communicate successfully in ELF settings where [. . .] they are no longer the norm providers' (Cogo and Jenkins 2010: 275) is exaggerated—more interculturally competent speakers obviously do adapt their speech, using the subconscious accommodation skills most speakers develop; less interculturally competent speakers do not, or not so much. Yet there remain deep-seated differences between native and non-native speakers, which are the subject of the next section.

1.3 Native and Non-Native Speakers

The conventional tripartite division of English(es) into native, nativized, and non-native varieties is explicitly underwritten by what for most people is an intuitive distinction between native and non-native speakers, even though this has increasingly been challenged in recent years. Everyone naturally acquires a native language or languages by mere exposure; further languages are easy to acquire during childhood but much harder to master after puberty. As Beckner et al. (2009: 11) put it, the ultimate level of attainment for 'even the most diligent L2 learner [. . .] is usually considerably below what a child L1 acquirer achieves.' This is not news; as Trudgill (2011: 35) says, the inability of most adults to learn languages perfectly is a 'well-known fact, obvious to anyone who has been alive and present in normal human societies for a couple of decades or so.'[16] There are, of course, innumerable examples of highly proficient adult language learners; I grew up in an extended family full of such people and have spent much of my working life surrounded by many more. And yes, here's the obligatory reference to Conrad, Nabokov, and Beckett.[17] But even highly successful adult learning is not 100% native-like. Despite a great deal of research attempting to disprove this, Hyltenstam and Abrahamsson (2000: 155) insist that 'no single post-puberty learner with native-like behaviour in the L2 has been described.' There are evidently cognitive reasons why this is the case, which are of interest to most language teachers, not to mention language learners themselves.

Canagarajah (2007: 923) discusses radically multilingual communities in Africa, South Asia, South America, the Polynesian Islands, and elsewhere, where simultaneous childhood acquisition makes it hard to identify a native language, and he questions whether languages are actually 'separated from each other, even at the most abstract level of grammatical form.' In Europe, however, it is much more usual to talk about people, including bi- and multilinguals, as coming from specific linguacultural backgrounds and speaking fairly well-delineated and 'focused' languages, even though most European languages are *Ausbau* languages, or languages by extension, parts of geographical dialect continua that have been constituted as separate languages for political, social, cultural, and historical reasons as much as (or more than) linguistic ones (Saussure 1916/1986: 202; Trudgill 2002: 112).[18] For example, George Steiner (1998: 120), who has 'no recollection whatever of a first language,' and possesses 'equal currency in English, French, and German,' has no doubt that these are separable languages. Steiner believes that the same holds true in cases of societal bi- or multilingualism, as in Friuli, the Val d'Aosta, the Basque country, and so on. (This is from a book about translation, and a sense of the overall separateness of languages is clearly helpful when translating from one to another.) Steiner also has an orthodox sense of native and non-native languages: 'What I can speak, write, or read of other languages has come later and retains a "feel" of conscious acquisition.'

Exactly *why* post-puberty learners do not acquire native-like fluency is open to debate. Lenneberg (1967) posited a 'critical period' for language acquisition, a limited developmental phase during which it is possible to acquire a language to native-like levels, after which this ability declines. This is said to be a function of biological maturation: neural plasticity (or lack of cortical specialization) in early childhood, followed by the progressive lateralization of cerebral functions (or the specialization of the left hemisphere of the brain for language functions) thereafter, and perhaps the 'dismantling' of language learning neural circuitry because of metabolic costs (Pinker 1994: 294–5). After puberty, L2 learning is no longer automatic and takes 'conscious and labored effort' (Lenneberg 1967: 176). Adult learners have to reflect on language structure and employ explicit, analytical, problem-solving capacities, and only those with a high level of verbal analytical ability will reach near-native competence in a second language (DeKeyser 2000).

Many subsequent researchers, including Bialystok and Hakuta (1994) and Hakuta et al. (2003), have argued that there is no evidence of a dramatic decline of L2 learning capacity after a fixed maturational point around puberty but rather a steady linear decline, from around age 6 or 7 to 16 or 17 and beyond. Childhood is described as a sensitive or optimal period rather than a critical one. Another argument is that there are different critical periods for different L2 skills and that different age effects account for the decline in learners' abilities to acquire native-like accents, native-like grammar, native-like semantics, and so on. For example, Scovel (1988) states that no-one will acquire a native accent if first exposed to an L2 after the age of 12, and Long (1990: 274) says acquiring native-like morphosyntax requires exposure to the L2 before 15. All in all, Abrahamsson and Hyltenstam (2009: 290) suggest that 'nativelike L2 proficiency in individuals with low starting ages is considerably less common than has been assumed earlier.'

One of the better-known attempts to demonstrate the difference between native and non-native 'grammars' is Coppieters's (1987) study of *near*-native users of French who had learned the language as adults and could not normally be distinguished from French native speakers by mistakes or the use of a restricted range of words and constructions. Coppieters nevertheless found that the near-native speakers had different intuitions from native speakers (who have essentially acquired slightly more complex 'rules') and different interpretations of many basic structures and contrasts of French grammar. These differences do not surface in readily detectable forms in the speakers' use of the language but require elaborately devised tests involving grammaticality judgments. Sorace (1993) obtained analogous results in a study of adult English and French near-native speakers of L2 Italian.

On the contrary Birdsong (1992) found that 15 out of a group of 20 advanced native speakers of English, who had begun learning French as adults, 'fell within the range of native speaker performance on a challenging grammaticality task, and several of these 15 participants deviated very little from native norms' (Birdsong 1999: 9). Birdsong and Molis (2001: 235) also report 'modest evidence of nativelike attainment among late learners' of English. Birdsong consequently rejects the critical period hypothesis. Similarly White and Genesee (1996) found no significant differences in grammaticality judgments about English between a group of near-native Francophone speakers of English who began learning the language after the age of 12 and a smaller group of native speakers, while Ioup et al. (1994) report two adult learners of Arabic attaining performance levels close (but not identical) to native norms. But, as Hyltenstam and Abrahamsson (2000, 2003) point out, all these researchers only find native-like performance in restricted aspects of the learners' L2 and tend to hedge their claims (e.g., Birdsong's subjects 'deviated very little from native norms,' but deviate they did).

Furthermore, tests involving 'native norms' are usually restricted to the standard language, even though native speakers invariably have a (variable!) 'communicative competence' (Hymes 1972) that includes non-standard forms as well as standard ones. As Croft (2000: 58) puts it,

> The difficult-to-acquire nativelike ability to use a language is not simply mastery of grammatical details, but also mastery of the choice of appropriate variants of a linguistic variable, and mastery of the shifting currents of social values of the speech community that affect the choice. Nativelike ability includes nativelike ability to vary and shift one's language use appropriately.

Native speakers 'use several, possibly all, variants of a linguistic variable' (two or more ways of saying 'the same thing'), and 'use them consistently in ways that reflect the variable's social functions' (p. 51), thereby giving rise to what Weinreich et al. (1968: 101) describe as 'orderly' or 'structured heterogeneity' in a speech community. These variants often include non-standard usages, which are widespread; Britain (2007: 262), for example, suggests that there is a 'common core' of them used by 'the majority of people' in England. As Kretzschmar (2009: 262) says, the variants promoted by institutionalized Standard English 'may not in fact be top-ranked across large populations.' *All* language features vary within and across speech communities—there is 'extensive (really massive) variation in all features at all times' (p. 3), and 'language is ever so much more variable than any individual could predict from personal experience' (p. 100). Even without what Widdowson calls the virtual language, the actual language is bigger than most people realize.

The prime difference between someone who has grown up speaking a given language in a particular speech community, and a non-native speaker who has come to that language at a later age, is quite simply *quantitative*. An adolescent or adult L2 English learner will not have received all the input a native English speaker had as a child, which Cameron-Faulkner et al. (2003: 866) estimate at around 7,000 utterances a day in communicative contexts. This works out at roughly 25 million meaningful utterances by the age of 10, which in turn leads to a lot of constructions, and a lot of linguistic variables, becoming entrenched in the brain.[19] Native speakers will know an immense number of common collocations as well as a huge number of formulaic sequences (fixed and semi-fixed expressions) and idioms, many of which are used extremely infrequently (appearing, e.g., only once in a 10 million-word corpus).[20] They will have perceptions about the appropriateness of spoken utterances and the style of written texts that are not necessarily shared by non-native speakers. As Ellis (2012a: 203) puts it, unlike native speakers,

> Learners have to enter into communication from experience of a very limited number of tokens. Their limited exposure poses them the task of *estimating* how linguistic constructions work from an input sample that is incomplete, uncertain, and noisy. Native-like fluency, idiomaticity, and selection are another level of difficulty again. For a good fit, every utterance has to be chosen, from a wide range of possible expressions, to be appropriate for that idea, for that speaker, for that place, and for that time. And again, learners can only *estimate* this from their finite experience.

The same applies to written language. Parks (2007: 5) suggests that it is 'extremely difficult to judge, in one's second language, the appropriateness or otherwise of a departure from ordinary forms of discourse.' The non-native lacks 'a finely developed sense of all the other texts which stand in relation to [any given text] and which give it, for the native reader, its full significance.' Most native English speakers will laugh, for example, at clunkily translated, overly lyrical tourist brochures, written in an obviously inappropriate style, whereas the non-native speaker 'does not laugh, or laughs less, because, although aware that there is much that is unusual and even "wrong" with this English, his sensibility to the language is not such that he is acutely sensitive to its inappropriateness.'

None of this *disparages* the non-native speaker and reader in any way; it merely makes the obvious point that a speaker without the experience of many millions of utterances cannot have the same insider's knowledge of a linguaculture as someone who grew up in it. Jenkins (2000: 9) insists that it is 'entirely inappropriate, indeed offensive, to label as "non-native" those who have learnt English as a second or foreign language and achieved bilingual status as fluent, proficient users,' but most non-native speakers, however fluent and bilingual, are aware of the differences between their linguistic intuitions and language use and those of native speakers. (Conversely, Seidlhofer [2001: 149] makes the excellent point that native English speakers cannot have *intuitions* about ELF but only impressions.) As Mauranen (2012: 217) puts it, L2 learners are likely to have 'shaky entrenchment' as a result of restricted input.

As well as having had limited input in an L2, non-native speakers are also likely to differ from native speakers, certainly monolingual ones, because of crosslinguistic interaction (or to use a more common term, *transfer*)—the borrowing, codeswitching, calquing, and so on that inevitably ensue from having another language firmly entrenched in the mind. Indeed the chief cause of non-native-like performance in an L2 may not be maturational at all: Ellis (2006b: 185), who takes a usage-based approach to language acquisition, states that 'the difficulties of adult L2 acquisition are a result of prior L1 learning, entrenchment, and transfer, rather than of a fixed neurologically-given critical period.' In many cases the combined effects of restricted input and crosslinguistic interaction will lead to major differences between native and non-native uses. In other cases, with near-native speakers, these differences are, as Hyltenstam and Abrahamsson (2003: 580) put it, 'probably highly insignificant in all aspects of the second language speaker's life and endeavours.' But the differences exist nonetheless, which is why it is legitimate to investigate the differences between non-native and native uses of English and the possible effect of the former on the latter.

Given this focus on the differences between L1 and L2 acquisition and usage, I necessarily resist attempts to define away these distinctions. Canagarajah (2005: xxiii), for example, rightly stresses today's 'general fluidity and mixing in languages, cultures and identities' and 'the need to shuttle between communities in postmodern society.' He argues that *all* English speakers, in all three Kachruvian circles, now have to 'be proficient in negotiating multiple dialects, registers, discourses and, if possible, languages, to function effectively in a context of postmodern globalization' (p. xxv). Another way of putting this is that 'we have to relate to Global English as a plural system with heterogeneous grammatical and discourse conventions' (p. xxvii). But I think it is a rhetorical sleight of hand that 'all speakers are "native speakers" of this pluralized Global English' and that we can consequently 'abandon the distinction native or non-native speaker' (p. xxvii).

The following chapter elaborates on some of the mechanisms of second language acquisition and the effects of bi- or multilingualism, after which I consider arguments *against* the concept of native and non-native speakers, or what is now often called 'the native speaker construct,' and its corollary 'native speakerism,' with all its deleterious consequences. Chapters 3 and 4 are about language change and whether any of the changes seen in ELF are likely to spread to native varieties of English.

Notes

1 This witticism is said to have been first uttered in the Danish parliament and later appropriated by the Danish humorist Robert Storm Petersen in the 1940s, and thereafter spuriously attributed to Niels Bohr, Mark Twain, Yogi Berra, and many others; see http://quoteinvestigator.com/2013/10/20/no-predict/.

2 See, for example, Vennemann's (2003, 2010) fascinating work on the Vasconic substrate of many European languages and the Afroasiatic or 'Semitidic' superstrate of Germanic and substrate of Celtic.

3 For a history of the terms New, World, Global, International, etc. English(es), and of early work in these fields, see Bolton (2003, Ch. 1).

4 The 2010 Singapore census reported that more than 50% of Chinese and Indian Singaporean children between 5 and 14 years old had English as their primary home language (Kirkpatrick 2014: 434).

5 Schneider's model is not as monolithic as this brief summary makes it sound. He accepts that '[i]n some styles and for some social contexts, smaller, socially and ethnically defined speech communities coexist and allow for internal variability under a common roof' (2007: 32), but states that people keen on codifying the new variety will tend to downplay or ignore 'whatever linguistic heterogeneity remains' (p. 51). Richards (1972: 167–71) suggests that analogous processes to those operating in outer circle New Englishes are also operative in indigenous minority Englishes in inner circle countries, such as Cree Indian English in Canada and Maori English in New Zealand.

6 Countries for which the labels 'outer' and 'expanding circle' are problematic include Hong Kong, whose transition from an ESL to an EFL country is discussed in Görlach (2002, Ch. 6), and Cyprus and Namibia, both discussed in Buschfeld (2013). McArthur (1998: 54) divides the 'EFL territories' into two, with a group of 17 countries in which English is 'a virtual second language,' while Graddol (1997: 11) lists 19 countries that he claims are shifting from an EFL to an L2 status for English. In some cases—such as the Netherlands, Denmark, Norway, and Sweden—this is indisputably true; in others—such as Argentina, the Honduras, and Nicaragua—it is surely false, as Hamel (2007: 69, note 2) rightly insists.

7 Park and Wee (2012: 45–6) point out that collections of ELF data, and characterizations of ELF speakers (of which mine are scarcely an exception), often give the impression that they are all educated people from privileged class backgrounds, which is clearly not the case.

8 The profession I joined in the late 1970s was commonly known as TEFL—teaching English as a foreign language, at least in Britain, and by the many

British and Australian teachers working around the world. In North America the term TESOL—Teaching English to speakers of other languages—was preferred. The standard British qualification in this field used to be a Diploma in the Teaching of English as a Foreign Language to Adults. In 1996 this morphed into a Diploma of English Language Teaching to Adults (Delta), with the 'Foreign' disappearing.

9 The European Council for Cultural Co-operation's *Common European Framework of Reference for Languages* (2001: 4) uses 'multilingualism' to refer to societies, or simply to 'the knowledge of a number of languages,' and 'plurilingualism' to refer to 'a communicative competence to which all knowledge and experience of language contributes and in which languages interrelate and interact.' However I use the term 'multilingual' according to its common dictionary definition to refer to individuals who speak more than two languages, however interrelated or separate they are.

10 Three separate million-word ELF corpora are available to researchers: VOICE, the Vienna-Oxford International Corpus of English, version 2.0 (2013), directed by Barbara Seidlhofer, consisting of interviews, press conferences, service encounters, seminars, working group and workshop discussions, meetings, panels, question/answer sessions, and conversations (www.univie.ac.at/voice); ELFA, the Corpus of English as a Lingua Franca in Academic Settings (2009), directed by Anna Mauranen, made up of 131 hours of recorded lectures, presentations, seminars, thesis defences, and conference discussions at the universities of Helsinki and Tampere in Finland (www.helsinki.fi/elfa/elfacorpus); and ACE, the Asian Corpus of English (2014), directed by Andy Kirkpatrick (http://corpus.ied.edu.hk/ace/), made up of the same kind of interactions as VOICE. Unless otherwise stated, all the italicized examples in the succeeding paragraphs are from ELFA and VOICE.

11 This is a reason not to use the term 'Learner Englishes,' as, for example, Mukherjee and Hundt (2011) do.

12 All conceivable jokes involving elves have already been made.

13 A recent addition to this shelf is Proshina and Eddy, *Russian English* (2016).

14 These common ELF usages are described in James (2000); Erling (2002); Cogo and Dewey (2006, 2012); Ranta (2006); Breiteneder (2009); Nesselhauf (2009); Seidlhofer (2011); Mauranen (2012); MacKenzie (2014b, Ch. 4). They are discussed at greater length in Chapter 3.

15 See Platt et al. (1984); Schmied (1991); Kortmann et al. (2004); MacKenzie (2014b, Ch. 4).

16 Unfortunately, being 'alive and present in normal human societies' no longer seems to count for much in linguistics. Like scientists and economists, linguists are increasingly prone to saying that 'data is not the plural of anecdote.' 'Anecdotal' personal experience—not to mention armchair analyses of language contact and change—are, to put it mildly, distrusted. Rather than simply stating what is evident and moving on, one is expected to produce extensive *numerical* evidence from corpora and longitudinal case studies. To borrow a term often attributed to Lewis Thomas (1983: 145)—even though he said it already existed—and often levelled at the social sciences in general, I feel that this as a form of 'physics envy,' as after a certain point, personal experience and informal observations (or 'anecdata') clearly *do* count for something, even if you are not a paid-up phenomenologist. Things are different in philosophy. Many articles about epistemology, ontology, philosophy of mind, and so on are centred on their author's perceptions and observations, often with sentences that never leave the study ('Consider the desk in front

of me')—although admittedly, if what is at issue is the sceptic's or solipsist's 'problem of other minds,' there is no other option!

17 Edmund Wilson unwisely accused Nabokov of making 'errors in English,' but Nabokov knew better; see Remnick (2005).

18 The opposite are *Abstand* languages, or languages identifiable by linguistic distance from any others, such as (famously) Basque. The notion of a focused *Ausbau* language nevertheless goes hand in hand with an awareness of massive variation in speech. The claim that languages are not separated from each other is also likely to ring hollow to monolinguals—for example, the 44% of Europeans who admit to 'not knowing any other language than their mother tongue' (European Commission 2006: 8)—most of whom presumably have a clear sense of the difference between their mother tongue and all other languages, which are incomprehensible to them.

19 Kretzschmar (2009: 147), implicitly referring to monolinguals, adds words encountered through reading, radio, television, and so on to speech and suggests 'in the roughest of terms' that 'a person may encounter (say, hear, see) at most about 100,000 words of their language in an average day,' which makes a little less than 3 billion words in a lifetime of 80 years.

20 In conformity with Zipf's Law (1935)—that in a corpus of natural language utterances, a word's frequency is inversely proportional to its rank in the frequency table (so that the most frequent word will occur approximately twice as often as the second-most frequent one, three times as often as the third-most frequent, etc.)—approximately 50% of the words (types rather than tokens) in any given corpus are hapaxes (or *hapax legomena*): words that only appear once. The law does not work for phrases, but many expressions known to native speakers will not appear in corpora of several million words. Zipf (1949) explained the distribution of word use by the human tendency to communicate efficiently with the least effort, a principle that is *also* regularly referred to by linguists as Zipf's Law, to explain things like phonetic reduction.

2 Imperfect Learning and Multicompetence

As already stressed in the previous chapter, sequential second language learning (as opposed to the simultaneous acquisition of more than one language in early childhood) clearly differs from first language acquisition in that there is already a language (or a large number of constructions) firmly entrenched in the brain. This ineluctably leads to features from the L1 being carried over or transferred to the L2, and a large part of SLA theory is devoted to explaining the ensuing deficiencies of L2 performance, using negative terms such as imperfect learning, interference, approximative systems, interlanguage, fossilization, and imposition. One introduction to SLA defines it as 'the study of what is learned of a second language and, importantly, what is not learned' (Gass et al. 2013: 1).

The usual underlying assumptions are that the learner's goal is to attain native-like competence and that errors and imperfections will gradually diminish as learning advances. Yet where English functions as a nativized postcolonial L2 or as an international lingua franca, it makes little sense to describe its users as deficient inner circle native speakers. The nature of ELF—a fluid assortment of varieties without any native speakers, by definition spoken by bilinguals and used throughout the world as a language of wider communication with speakers of different first languages—clearly does not require its speakers to perfectly acquire or conform to the norms of native English speakers. What Firth (2009: 150) calls '[t]he inherent interactional and linguistic variability that lingua franca interactions entail' and the 'lingua franca outlook' adopted by ELF speakers are better explained by more recent theories of multilingualism, translanguaging, and multicompetence offering a neutral or even a positive account of the effects of crosslinguistic interaction and showing how the language use of bi- and multilingual speakers always differs from that of monolinguals. It is also possible that some ELF speakers are aware that they are using English differently from its native speakers, consciously and purposefully disregarding or regularizing forms known to be part of the native language (which still constitutes the bulk of the input in formal English teaching in the expanding circle) to enhance clarity and communicative effectiveness with other L2 speakers.

2.1 Imperfect Learning and SLA Theory

The differences between native speaker usage and the performance of post-adolescent and adult second language learners and users are conventionally described as resulting from imperfect learning. Up to a certain age (usually somewhere between 8 and 16, depending on the person), children are able to acquire a new language or dialect perfectly; thereafter, what Trudgill (2001: 372) pithily calls 'the lousy language-learning abilities of the human adult' almost invariably ensure that L2s are imperfectly acquired—compared with standard (monolingual) native speaker usage. L2 learners generally speak a somewhat simplified version of the language used by native speakers. In early stages of L2 production, learners regularly transfer L1 phonemes, word meanings and word orders, all of which have become deeply entrenched in their minds through regular use. In perception and comprehension, they impose L1 categories on L2 input, attaching L2 sounds, words and constructions to already existing L1 representations that are assumed to be equivalents. To put this more strongly, at lower levels of learning, the L2 is hugely parasitic on the L1 until the learner succeeds in building up a separate system of L2 representations.

According to usage-based and emergentist models of language acquisition, constructions and expressions that are frequently encountered in everyday conversational interactions are stored in the mind (rather than being composed on the spur of the moment by way of generative grammatical 'rules') and become 'entrenched' (Langacker 1987) or 'sedimented' (Hopper 1988). Every repetition strengthens this entrenchment in the mind and leaves a neuronal trace that facilitates habit formation and the reuse of the construction. We store *all* consequential linguistic information about constructions—their meaning, register, phonology, and so on (Barlow and Kemmer 2000)—while also unconsciously registering their relative frequencies of use (Bybee and Hopper 2001; Ellis 2002; Bod et al. 2003; Bybee 2007). Thus our L1 competence is the outcome of implicit memories of all the utterances we have ever heard, read, and used. Moreover, most of those utterances will have been 'closely similar to previous utterances,' because 'anything that is said has been said in something like that form before' (Hopper 1998: 165), as '[o]ur speech is a vast collection of hand-me-downs that reaches back in time to the beginnings of language' (p. 159).[1]

The more frequently a construction is encountered—whether it is a word, a collocation, a fully substantive fixed expression, a partially fixed expression, or a fully generalizable schematic pattern—the more accurately and more rapidly it is processed. Furthermore, words are mentally primed for collocational use (Hoey 2005): when we hear any given word, our language processing systems activate the words (collocates and longer phrases) we are most likely to hear next, allowing us to prospect ahead on the basis of the preceding context rather than listening carefully to each word (Sinclair 2004; Sinclair and Mauranen 2006). There is also a recency effect: the more recently a construction has been used, the higher the probability of it being used again, and the more rapidly it will be processed. There is an immense literature on the way speakers reuse constructions they have recently used and imitate interlocutors' constructions: see Giles et al. (1991) on linguistic accommodation; Pickering and Garrod (2004) on subconscious interactive alignment; Niederhoffer and Pennebaker (2002) on linguistic style matching; Bock (1986) and Pickering and Branigan (1999) on syntactic priming; and Szmrecsanyi (2005) on 'persistence' and 'micro-entrenchment.'[2]

The huge degree of entrenchment (or 'neural commitment') of regularly used constructions in the L1 unavoidably results in L2 learners transferring L1 patterns; indeed 'it would be impossible to construct a model of L2 learning that did not take into account the structure of the first language' (MacWhinney 2008: 342). As mentioned in Chapter 1, Ellis (2006b) argues that this dual account of entrenchment or automatization and transfer is sufficient to explain *all* the difficulties of adult L2 acquisition without the need to invoke biological explanations such as a fixed neurologically given critical period. The problem is that '[t]he L2 learner's neocortex has already been tuned to the L1, incremental learning has slowly committed it to a particular configuration, and it has reached a point at which the network can no longer revert to its original plasticity' (p. 189).

In the learning of an L3, and so on, there is clearly even more scope for transfer from all the previously learned or acquired languages (Jarvis and Pavlenko 2009), and most models of multilingual language processing propose that words of more than one language can be activated at the same time in both production and reception (see, e.g., Schreuder and Weltens 1993; Kroll and De Groot 1997; Paradis 1997; Kecskes and Papp 2000; Pavlenko 2009; Grosjean 2010; De Groot 2011).[3] The speaker's L1 or dominant language, being the most highly entrenched, would seem to the most obvious candidate as a source of transfers in L3 acquisition, but various researchers have suggested that there is a 'foreign language effect' resulting in the L2 being more likely to be activated than the L1 (Meisel 1983; De Angelis and Selinker 2001). Other research suggests that learners intuitively rely on the language that most resembles the target language, regardless of whether this is an L1 or L2 (Chandrasekhar 1978 calls this the 'base language' hypothesis; see also Cenoz 2003; De Angelis 2007). Ringbom (2001) argues that transfer of *form* is more common across typologically close languages, whereas transfer of semantic patterns and word combinations is nearly always from the L1.

The influence of other languages is likely to persist, even at progressively higher levels of L2 proficiency, as learners continue to calque and replicate elements from the L1, while also simplifying the target language's grammatical system by underdifferentiating and overextending rules, eliminating irregularities and exceptions, and disregarding non-salient or redundant markers. L2 learners and users often focus on the meaning rather than the form of utterances, practicing a kind of selective attention, or what Ellis calls 'rational contingency learning' (2006a) or 'automatically learned inattention' (2006b: 178). They notice the features of linguistic input that are (subjectively) salient and meaningful but often disregard (or simply fail to notice) elements that lack perceptual salience or communicative value (Schmidt 1990, 1993; Robinson 1995).[4] The things they notice are the result of L1-tuned expectations, which obscure some aspects of the L2, leading to limited L2 attainment and non-naturalistic usage, according to native-speaker standards.

This is particularly the case where L2-like structures are absent in the learners' L1, leading them to look elsewhere for cues to interpretation. Moreover, many languages grammaticize (make grammatically obligatory) a great deal of essentially redundant information that does not affect the overall interpretation of the message and is overshadowed or even blocked by more salient cues that have already been perceived[5] (e.g., the verb inflection in *he goes* duplicates the information given by the personal pronoun, and the tense/aspect markers in *he went yesterday* and *he will go tomorrow* duplicate information given by the time adverbs). Bybee (2008: 231) suggests that 'forms such as agreement markers, tense, aspect, and case inflections, have such a reduced communicative value that they seem to remain in the language largely for convention's sake,' and indeed Weaver (1949) famously estimated that the English language is no less than 50% redundant.

For many learners of English, non-salient elements notoriously include the third-person singular inflectional morpheme, -*s*. Learners presumably *do* sporadically notice or perceive this feature (especially if they have a teacher who loudly says '*Sss*' or '*Zzz*' every time they fail to inflect a third-person singular, present simple verb), but they don't *process* them—make a connection between the form and a meaning or function. This is why, in Corder's (1967) terms, *input* (even if it recurs thousands of times) can fail to become *intake*—target language that the learner utilizes in some way. As Ellis (2006b: 185) puts it, 'A sad irony for an L2 speaker under such circumstances of transfer is that more input simply compounds their error; they dig themselves ever deeper into the hole created and subsequently entrenched by their L1.' Today the standard pedagogical response to this is that naturalistic input is not enough; 'input enhancement' (Sharwood Smith 1993) and an explicit 'focus on form' in the language classroom are necessary too (Doughty and Williams 1998; Norris and Ortega 2000).

Hulstijn (2015) incorporates imperfect L2 acquisition into a dichotomous account of language proficiency, which he says can be divided into basic language cognition (BLC) and higher language cognition (HLC).

All native speakers (or 'L1ers') not suffering from cognitive impairments, regardless of age, literacy, or educational level, have BLC in common. This consists of largely implicit, unconscious, and automatically processed knowledge of phonetics, prosody, phonology, morphology, and syntax, combined with largely explicit, conscious knowledge of lexis in speech reception and production. It is restricted to the frequent words, constructions and expressions that can occur in any communicative situation and does not include reading and writing.[6] HLC is the complement or extension of BLC and involves the production and comprehension of utterances and written sentences containing less frequent lexical items or uncommon morphosyntactic structures involving topics other than simple, everyday matters. There can be considerable differences in HLC among adult native speakers, depending on their cognitive abilities as well as environmental factors such as exposure to oral and written language, level of education (including literacy), type of occupation, leisure time activities, and so on.[7]

Hulstijn suggests, however, that native speakers' BLC is not shared by most L2 speakers. Given what we know about persistent L1 interference in post-adolescent L2 acquisition,

> BLC, while being attainable by late L2 learners in the domains of vocabulary and many or even most grammatical structures, will generally not be attainable in the domains of pronunciation or with respect to the production of some grammatical features in spontaneous, unmonitored speech.
>
> (p. 48)

Thus L2 learners and speakers can perform more poorly in BLC than native speakers with lower profiles but also 'become as proficient in HLC as L1ers of the same intellectual, educational, professional and cultural profile, despite some deficiencies in their L2 BLC,' and 'more proficient [in HLC] than many low-profile L1ers (i.e., native speakers of the L2er's L2)' (p. 48). According to this account there can be any number of 'multicompetent language users' (Cook 1999), but they will not share native speakers' BLC because they do not have the same 'bio-developmental' profile.

To put this more precisely, early bilinguals—either simultaneous bilinguals from early infancy or consecutive bilinguals with a young (preschool) age of L2 onset—can acquire BLC in two (or more) languages and attain native-speaker proficiency as long as they receive a sufficient quantity and quality of input in both languages. Children who speak a minority language at home and only acquire an L2 as the language of schooling are also likely to acquire BLC in both languages. On the contrary (as already argued), children who learn an L2 as a foreign language at school in the country where their L1 is the dominant language, and learners who begin to learn an L2 as adults, typically because they move to another country, are very unlikely to attain full mastery of all the grammatical and phonological features of the BLC. Hulstijn argues (p. 50) that this equally applies to learners in elementary school immersion programs (Cummins and Swain 1986) and secondary school students in Content and Language Integrated Learning (CLIL) programs (Dalton-Puffer et al. 2010). Hulstijn's account of BLC and HLC constitutes a strong counter-argument to claims that the notion of nativeness (related to early childhood acquisition) in language is simply a 'myth' (Ferguson 1982/1992: xiii; Davies 2003: *passim*).

Whereas usage-based linguists tend to explain the differences between first and second language acquisition matter-of-factly in terms of the entrenchment of the L1 and limited exposure to the L2, many applied linguists have employed negative terms to describe these effects. Weinreich (1953: 1) used the term *interference* to describe all 'instances of deviation from the norms of either language which occur in the speech of bilinguals as a result of their familiarity with more than one language, i.e. as a result of language contact,' including intentional borrowing and codeswitching. Nemser (1971: 116) wrote of learners having an *approximative system* at any given stage of learning—a 'deviant linguistic system actually employed by the learner attempting to utilize the target language,' with the assumption that the endpoint—the learner's final approximative system—will almost always fall short of 'perfect proficiency.' Selinker (1972) popularized the alternative term *interlanguage*, a learner's linguistic system that typically includes errors resulting from various factors, notably including transfers from the L1, overgeneralization, provisional 'rules,' and learning and communication strategies. It might also involve *fossilization*: permanent traces of one language on the other, such as the continued use of erroneous structures, semantic extensions, and pronunciations, no matter how much L2 instruction or input the learner receives. Van Coetsem (1988, 2000) introduced the terms *imposition* and *source language agentivity*, which involve the assigning of phonetic, semantic, or structural properties from the dominant L1 to L2 words by analogy. (The contrary is borrowing or *recipient language agentivity*, when bilingual speakers incorporate features of an L2 into their L1, which will be discussed in Chapter 7.)

However, all of these negative concepts (interference, transfer, approximative systems, interlanguage, fossilization, imposition, etc.) and the entire deficit model of SLA are predicated on the notion that the ultimate goal is to attain native-like competence. Focusing on immigrant learners, SLA theorists assume that successful L2 learning requires integrative motivation, involving respect for the language's native speakers and a desire to participate in their culture with native-like grammar and pronunciation, and competence in the full range of speech acts, styles, and registers of the target language. Yet this is demonstrably not the case with most speakers of the New Englishes and ELF. The former need to communicate primarily with other speakers of a local nativized variety, the latter with speakers of other first languages, as most interlocutors in lingua franca contexts are not native speakers of English. On the other hand there is no point pretending, as some ELF theorists do (see, e.g., Firth and Wagner 1997; Cogo and Dewey 2012), that *every single non-standard usage* in ELF is part of a deliberate, conscious, rational (and extremely rapidly formulated) communicative strategy artfully designed for specific addressees in specific circumstances, as if SLA theory didn't exist and the ELF theorists themselves had never even *begun* to learn an L2.

2.2 L2 Users Are Not Deficient Native Speakers

Although New Englishes originate as learner varieties, just like ELF 'similects,' they evolve into relatively stable nativized varieties characterized by specific lexical, phonological, and grammatical features. Some usages in the speech of early generations of learners during colonization could reasonably be described as fossilized errors (often resulting from L1 transfer, invalid analogies, or the overextension of existing patterns), although the 'emancipatory' stance of theorists of New Englishes (Kachru 1991; Sridhar and Sridhar 1992; Williams 1987) tends to downplay this. But the same usages can be adopted and transmitted by later generations of speakers with a high level of competence. As van Rooy (2011: 204) puts it, 'these errors, with other kinds of innovations, fill a linguistic feature pool with additional variants, from which some are (mostly non-deliberately) selected by the community to attain conventional status among the speakers.' In this way they develop into stable, systematic features: structural innovations of a new variety, forms that differ from those customarily used in inner circle varieties but which are acceptable in a given New English. Acceptability involves things such as being used in the media; endorsed by teachers, examination bodies, and publishing houses; codified in textbooks; and so on (Bamgboṣe 1998). Once new variants become established in the speech community, the expected effects of SLA are 'likely to be overridden by cultural conventions' (Schneider 2012: 77).

Here are some examples—features that have been described as 'pervasive or obligatory' in Indian English (Kortmann and Lunkenheimer 2013): using the present perfect for the Standard English simple past—*Some of us have been to New York years ago*; extending the progressive to stative verbs—*What are you wanting?*; using *it* where Standard English favours zero—*As I made it clear before* [. . .]; dropping object pronouns—*We have two tailors who can make for us*; dropping subject pronouns—*Rained yesterday only*; extending *-s* to Standard English irregular plurals—*childrens, oxens, sheeps*; using zero article where Standard English has the definite article—*I'm not working in kitchen.*[8] Further examples of frequent New English forms—which coincide to a large extent with widespread features in ELF—are given at the end of the following chapter.

The 'errors' at the basis of *structural* innovations—and the similarities to be found across New Englishes—are more often simplifications or 'corrections' of the more eccentric elements of English grammar than features transferred directly from a local language. This is because, as Gut (2011: 112) points out, no indigenous African languages, and few Asian languages (except the Indo-Aryan languages: Hindi, Bengali, Punjabi, Gujarati, Marathi, etc.) are typologically close to English. *Lexical and phonological* innovations, on the contrary, are much more likely to result from contact with indigenous languages.

As Sridhar and Sridhar (1992) argue, orthodox SLA theory does not have an adequate conception of the combined and complementary roles that multilingual speakers' various languages play in everyday communication, or an adequate understanding of the functions L2 English performs for learners and users of a New English variety. In a given multilingual context, in which English is used with speakers who share a linguistic repertoire, transferring particular elements from shared languages is a normal communicative practice, and one that draws attention to the speakers' indigenous culture and identity (p. 96). With New Englishes, motivation is primarily instrumental rather than integrative. Most learners do *not* use the language to serve all the functions it generally serves for native speakers (certainly for monolingual ones), so they don't display the same range of competence as speakers in inner circle countries. New Englishes are more often used in academic and bureaucratic contexts than everyday, informal, affective ones. SLA theory also tends to disregard the fact that the primary input for learners of New Englishes, both in and out of the classroom, is the local, nativized variety, even if an exonormative standard (such as British English) is maintained officially (Williams 1987: 164).

English used as a lingua franca is clearly different from the New Englishes. It is *not* related to any particular speech community or target culture, with speakers who share lexicogrammatical norms, a cultural background, and agreed-upon ways of speaking. On the contrary every ELF interaction potentially involves a disparate group of speakers with dissimilar ways of using English.

Although extensive SLA research has shown that L2 speakers tend to simplify, overgeneralize, and underdifferentiate target language patterns, Seidlhofer (2001: 144) argues that the ways in which *ELF* speakers simplify, overuse, underuse, or avoid certain expressions or structures of the native language should not be regarded as learning strategies—'a constructive way of making do with the limited resources available at a particular stage of interlanguage'—but rather as 'communication strategies: evidence not of a linguistic deficit, but, if intelligible, of successful communication.' Although ELF speakers are, of course, not shifting to

English, but merely using English as a language of wider communication, there are analogies with groups of speakers shifting languages in the past. There are manifold examples of shifting groups not wishing to speak the target language the same way as its original L1 speakers. Thomason and Kaufman (1988) discuss imperfect learning in language shift but stress that they 'do not mean to imply' that this 'has anything to do with a lack of ability to learn' (p. 39); attitudinal factors may be crucial, and 'the lack of acquisition may just as well be due to a refusal to learn' (p. 51), and a desire to replicate source language constructions.[9]

ELF researchers in general insist that post-school-age ELF speakers—like adult speakers of all other second and foreign languages—are *users* and not 'eternal "learners" on an interminable journey toward perfection in a target language' (Mauranen 2006a: 147). Cook (2002a: 4) points out that '[t]he term *L2 learner* implies that the task of acquisition is never finished' and argues that instead of comparing L2 users to native speakers, and concentrating on what they are unable to do, we should focus on what they *can* do with the language, valorizing their actual 'knowledge and use of the second language.' L2 users have a certain linguistic competence at any given time, as do children; it may be an 'approximative system' compared with L1-speaking adults, but it is what it is, like a child's language system, rather than a partial imitation of what it might one day become.

There is nothing wrong with comparing L2 usage with native speaker usage for descriptive purposes, as long as one does not go from there to treating the L2 user as a deficient native speaker (Cook 2002a: 21). It is absurd to set L2 speakers, who can never replicate native speakers' childhood acquisition, the impossible target of becoming native-like and then defining them—in terms of what they cannot possibly be—as failed native speakers. Yet this is implicit in the very concept of English as a foreign language (EFL, as opposed to ELF); as Graddol (2006: 83) says, in the traditional concept of EFL, 'there is an inbuilt ideological positioning of the student as outsider and failure—however proficient they become,' and calling someone a speaker of EFL might even be said to be 'designed to produce failure.'

In short the 'ELF position' is quite simply that many orthodox SLA and EFL concepts are not relevant to English used as a lingua franca. Concepts like 'interlanguage' and 'errors' simply do not apply: 'ELF research in general, unlike SLA, treats these non-standard forms not as errors but divergent forms or "features"' (Björkman 2008: 36). Because many ELF speakers speak a particular hybrid variant (or 'similect'), strongly influenced by their L1, there can be a great deal of variability in ELF interactions. For this reason, Seidlhofer (2011: 77) argues that ELF must be 'functionally not formally defined; it is not a variety of English but a variable way of using it.'

It should be mentioned in passing that there are also many linguists who do *not* share the 'ELF position.' For example, Mufwene (2012: 368) wonders, 'who learns another group's language not caring at all about being understood (and being accepted) by the native-speaking community?' He argues that ELF speakers will also find themselves 'in settings where they interact concurrently with nationals of other countries, who might give up on you if they are from the Inner (or Outer) Circle and you do not satisfy the standards that they find acceptable,' and that as a learner of L2 English one has a choice 'between approximating standards from the Inner Circle and ignoring them, and therefore narrowing one's range of competitiveness.' Meierkord (2012: 2) suggests, for similar reasons, that ELF should be subsumed into a broader category, 'Interactions across Englishes,' that does not exclude either inner or outer circle speakers. Other commentators on the international use of English, including Berns (2008), Kachru and Smith (2008), Mesthrie and Bhatt (2008), and Prodromou (2008), similarly give short shrift to the ELF position.

However, the argument about the extent to which speakers of New Englishes and ELF do or should care about being understood and accepted by L1 English speakers is secondary to Cook's overarching logic of treating all L2 users *as* L2 users rather than deficient native speakers. Cook (2002b: 331) applies to L2 speakers what Halliday (1968: 165) said of native dialects: 'A speaker who is made ashamed of his own language habits suffers a basic injury as a human being: to make anyone, especially a child, feel so ashamed is as indefensible as to make him feel ashamed of the colour of his skin.'

2.3 Multicompetence and the 'Ordinary State of Mankind'

As we have seen, there are many good reasons why L2 learning is often imperfect, according to monolingual L1 norms, most importantly the entrenchment of the L1, the inevitability of transferring L1 patterns to later learned languages, and the lack of the 'linguacultural' childhood experience of the target language's native speakers. But transfer can also work in the other direction, from the L2 to the L1. This bidirectionality is already implicit in Weinreich's (1953: 1) definition of 'interference' quoted earlier, and it seems likely that *all* bilinguals use their languages differently from monolingual speakers, and deviate from monolingual native-speaker norms, because of inexorable *crosslinguistic influence* or *crosslinguistic interaction*.

The former, essentially neutral, term was put forward by Kellerman and Sharwood Smith (1986) and is designed to include unconscious conceptual transfer, convergence, and interference as well as conscious borrowing and avoidance strategies. The latter, largely positive, term comes from Herdina and Jessner (2002) and is intended to take into account the cognitive advantages that result from a knowledge of several languages (at least after a reasonably high proficiency threshold is reached). Proponents of plurilingualism tend to claim that the use of more than one language gives greater cognitive flexibility and develops the potential for original or creative or divergent thinking—a more imaginative, elastic, open-ended thinking style that gives the ability to see alternative responses to a problem. It also permits different forms of argumentation and aids decision-making and problem-solving. Bi- or multilingualism is further said to enrich and fine-tune conceptual networks, giving an awareness of the arbitrariness of linguistic signs, defamiliarizing supposedly familiar meanings, revealing hidden or implicit meanings, and creating new relationships among concepts, thereby providing alternative ways of perceiving and manipulating processes and objects. Multilinguals are also said to have higher levels of metalingual awareness, as well as greater communicative sensitivity and empathy, and to be more fluent and more prone to linguistic playfulness and experimentation.[10] Herdina and Jessner, however, sound a cautionary note, pointing out that 'it is not quite clear whether parameters such as lateral or creative thinking, metalinguistic awareness or communicative sensibility represent preconditions or consequences of multilingualism' (p. 28).

Grosjean (2010: 75) proposes a strong version of crosslinguistic interaction, a 'bilingual or holistic view of bilingualism' such that the bilingual 'is an integrated whole who cannot easily be decomposed into two separate parts.' Rather than being 'the sum of two (or more) complete or incomplete monolinguals,' the bilingual has 'a unique and specific linguistic configuration' in which '[t]he coexistence and constant interaction of the languages' have produced 'a different but complete language system.' Importantly Grosjean (2008: 38) also describes bilinguals' 'language modes': different states of activation of languages and language processing mechanisms. There is a continuum going from 'the monolingual speech mode,' in which 'the bilingual deactivates one language (but never totally),' and 'the bilingual mode,' in which 'the bilingual speaker chooses a base language, activates the other language, and calls on it from time to time in the form of codeswitches and borrowings.' Grosjean argues that a bilingual's languages are never totally deactivated and that there is constant interaction between them: 'bilinguals make dynamic interferences (ephemeral deviations due to the influence of the other deactivated language) even in the most monolingual of situations' (p. 46), as opposed to any 'fossilized' errors, which could be described as static interferences. But bilinguals who are consciously in the bilingual mode—that is, communicating with interlocutors who share the same languages—are free to codeswitch.

Cook offers an even more radical account of crosslinguistic interaction that he labels 'multicompetence,' in which languages (grammars and mental lexicons) are seen as conjoined rather than coexisting. Multicompetence was originally defined as 'the compound state of a mind with two grammars' (1991: 112), and more recently (because grammar is often interpreted to mean just syntax) as 'the knowledge of more than one language in the same mind' (2002a: 2), or indeed 'the overall system of a mind or a community that uses more than one language' (2016: 2). As a result of the partial mental integration of languages, multicompetent L2 speakers' 'knowledge of the second language' (after a certain threshold has been reached) 'is typically not identical to that of a native speaker' (Cook 2002a: 6), whereas their 'knowledge of their first language is in some respects not the same as that of a monolingual' (p. 6). Cook (2002a: 7) insists, quite simply, that 'L2 users have different minds from monolinguals' and that a bilingual's languages can never be deactivated. He avoids the term 'transfer' as this requires discrete languages between which one could transfer things, rather than an integrated system or at least overlapping systems: 'language acquisition or use is not transferring something from one part of the mind to another, but two systems accommodating to each other' (2002a:18). The same stricture applies to the standard notion of codeswitching. Cook's logic entails that speakers of outer circle New Englishes and expanding circle ELF, who are all by definition bi- or multilingual, will necessarily use English differently from monolingual native speakers, and that their usages can be described without recourse to notions like imperfect learning, interlanguage, fossilization, and so on.

Cook's account of multicompetence does not have much space for Grosjean's 'monolingual speech mode.' The same applies to García and Wei's (2014) and Otheguy et al.'s (2015) concept of 'translanguaging,' in which conventionally understood languages cannot be separated from each other or from other human cognitive and semiotic systems or resources for thinking and communicating.[11] In this account, language users strategically employ multiple semiotic resources and modalities (speech, writing, sign, gesture, etc.) and move freely and dynamically between so-called languages, varieties, registers, and styles (and writing systems) in an inescapably multisensory and multimodal process to fulfil a variety of strategic and communicative functions. The mental grammars of bilinguals are described as structured but unitary collections of lexical and structural features, which speakers are said to select without regard for 'watchful adherence' to the socially and politically defined boundaries of named languages (as opposed to codeswitching between separate linguistic systems). For Otheguy et al., languages are social constructs rather than mental or psychological ones, groupings of idiolects of people with shared social, political, or ethnic identities.

Otheguy et al. are careful not to claim any superiority for bi- and multilingual speakers, arguing that the idiolects of monolinguals and bilinguals are only quantitatively but not qualitatively different. The idiolects of bilinguals simply contain more linguistic features and a more complex sociocultural marking of when and where to use them. They also argue that unlike bilinguals, monolinguals are 'almost always and everywhere allowed to translanguage' or to 'deploy all or most of their lexical and structural repertoire mostly freely' (p. 295), which bilinguals can do only in the translanguaging mode, when 'their entire repertoire is appreciated as a tool for rich and unfettered expression' (p. 297). But this is clearly untrue—if monolinguals have a large repertoire (or a number of different ways of speaking), it is precisely because they *cannot* use all of them all the time; as argued in the previous chapter, 'structured heterogeneity' is all about style shifting and choosing contextually appropriate variants for a given interlocutor, time, and place (or text). The same applies to bilinguals; 'rich and unfettered expression,' disregarding the social walls erected by named languages, always depends on interlocutors' repertoires and the need to be understood.

Rather than deliberately disregarding *all* the boundaries between different languages, it is perhaps more likely that—without necessarily being aware of it—multicompetent bilinguals draw on what Kecskes and Papp (2000) call a 'common underlying conceptual base,' a fused or undifferentiated conceptual system that stores mental representations of two (or more) languages, from which thoughts are mapped onto linguistic signs and utterances in a particular language (or sometimes a combination of languages). This means that bilingual speakers' combined mental concepts (or at least frequently accessed ones) contain all the information and connotations connected with the corresponding words in the different languages. In Weinreich's (1953: 9–10) well-known terms, they are thus *compound bilinguals* (whom Weinreich assumes learned both their languages in the same context). Weinreich opposes compound bilinguals to supposed *coordinative bilinguals*, who learned their languages in two distinct environments and are consequently said to have two conceptual systems—two sets of conceptual representations associated with two sets of words, one for each language. There are also *subordinative bilinguals*, largely lower-level language learners who (as mentioned above) assign to words in the weaker language the meanings of the closest corresponding words (and conceptual representations) in the dominant language.[12]

Thus independently of any *overt* bilingual behaviour such as borrowing or codeswitching, compound bilinguals with merged mental concepts tend to use words differently from monolingual speakers of *either* the L1 or the L2, often with unconscious semantic extensions. Supposed translation equivalents in different languages rarely convey exactly the same meanings; in addition to shared aspects of meaning, each word in a translation pair will generally also have aspects of meaning specific to the language to which it belongs. (Translation and equivalence are discussed in more detail in Chapter 6.) The conceptual representations of many words are asymmetrically 'distributed' or spread out over a range of more elementary conceptual units, only some of which are shared across languages (see De Groot's [1993] 'Distributed Conceptual Feature Model'), although concrete words and cognates (words with similar orthographical and phonological forms across languages), as well as many high-frequency words, share more representations across translation pairs or 'equivalents' than those of abstract and non-cognate words (Van Hell and De Groot 1998). Compound bilinguals who use words in either their L1 or an L2 intending to communicate nuances (connotations or parts of combined conceptual representations) that are not in fact part of the standard conceptual representation in the target language may either simply fail to communicate part of what is in their heads or just sound slightly odd to interlocutors who do not share their language combination.

This kind of transfer or semantic extension is why some translators (certainly some of my translation faculty colleagues) like to say that 'bilinguals make lousy translators.' By this they mean Weinreich's compound bilinguals, who simultaneously acquired two languages in the same childhood environment, and they clearly do not share Grosjean's (2010: 4) broad definition of bilinguals as all those 'who use two or more languages (or dialects) in their everyday lives.' Yet it is easy to find evidence—namely bad translations, unintentionally full of source language words or source language meanings—that many translators using languages that were learned sequentially, in different environments, have also become compound bilinguals with a partially conjoined conceptual system.[13] It may well be that Weinreich's coordinative bilinguals are in fact mythical creatures. In fact different linguistic levels (semantics, pragmatics, morphosyntax, or phonology) can have different degrees of integration or separation, and Grosjean (1995: 260) points out that 'no amount of experimentation has brought conclusive evidence that bilinguals can be classified as co-ordinate, compound or subordinate,' so Weinreich's tripartite division is almost certainly an oversimplification.

As well as having a partially integrated conceptual system, which leads them to use words differently from monolinguals, compound bilinguals often transfer L2 collocations to the L1 (something translators have to be constantly on guard against) and use calques (word-for-word loan translations) of fixed expressions. They may also replicate L2 syntactic patterns in the L1, and vice versa, and transfer pragmatic strategies, perhaps to the extent that they 'create an intercultural style of speaking that is both related to and distinct from the styles prevalent in the two substrata' (Kasper and Blum-Kulka 1993: 3). Notwithstanding all the foregoing descriptions of the influence of the L2 on the L1 in neutral terms, one might also evoke the notion of attrition. Herdina and Jessner

(2002), conceptualizing crosslinguistic interaction, suggest that multilingual speakers work with approximative systems of their native languages as well as their non-native ones, with the result that their 'competence in one or more languages is likely to be restricted [. . .] there is ample evidence that bilinguals do not generally achieve the same levels of competence as monolingual speakers' (p. 13). This is because 'maintaining and managing more than one language' takes a great deal of cognitive effort (p. 60), probably more than is available, so that '[i]n the case of multilinguals we are frequently confronted with the phenomenon of language loss, language deterioration and/or attrition' (p. 93). On the other hand, given the standard claim that 'half of the world's population, if not more, is bilingual' (Grosjean 2010: 13), Laufer (2003: 30) cheerfully suggests that some L1 attrition—such as producing syntactically deviant L1 sentences under the influence of the L2, importing L2 collocations into the L1, making L2-influenced semantic extensions, and so on—is 'a small price to pay for achieving the ordinary state of mankind.'

If slight L1 attrition is a small price to pay, a wholly merged linguistic system would probably be a higher one. Singleton (2016: 512), for example, contesting the logic of multicompetence, insists that 'a degree of cross-linguistic conceptual permeability, influence and transfer does not undermine' the 'essential differentiation' of conceptual systems, and that 'users of multiple languages need to make use of conceptual systems specific to each of their languages' if they want to 'function intelligibly and comprehendingly in the relevant language communities.'[14] On this account compound bilinguals are the exception—and are indeed lousy translators. In fact the practice of translation—one of the rare bilingual situations in which, as a rule, the usual consequences of bilingualism have to be strenuously resisted—shows that it is worth hanging onto the notion of separable and describable languages, at least as what Vaihinger (1924) called a useful 'fiction,' an idea whose theoretical untruth, incorrectness, or falsity is readily admitted but which nonetheless has practical utility.[15]

But although the notion of separable languages remains useful (or even essential) for translators and interpreters, language teachers and syllabus designers, people defending minority languages and worrying about language death, and so on, it seems likely that the more languages people speak, the more they are conscious of—and unperturbed by—the effects of interaction among them. It could be that the 'lingua franca outlook' is just a slightly more extreme version of what we might call a 'multilingual outlook.' Zobl (1992: 193) suggests that there is 'an inverse relationship between the conservatism of the learning procedure and the pool of linguistic knowledge available,' so people learning an L3 or an L4 are less likely to worry about ungrammaticality than people learning an L2. And although most other languages are learned primarily to communicate with their native speakers, English is often learned to be used with other L2 speakers, allowing multilingual ELF users to be even less conservative.

Once we move away from the logic of errors and imperfect learning, we must also consider the possibility that some ELF speakers may be *aware* that they are using English differently from its native speakers, consciously and purposefully disregarding or regularizing forms known to be part of the native language but which they consider incongruous or idiosyncratic or communicatively redundant. (In Hulstijn's terms this is not a matter of a deficient BLC, but of a resourceful HLC.) This could be done to enhance explicitness, maximize clarity and transparency, eliminate ambiguity, reduce complexity, and generally improve communicative effectiveness and also, perhaps, to symbolize non-native English-speaking identity. The possibility of speakers making intentional functional changes to a language is the subject of the next chapter. But first, an excursus is necessary.

2.4 The Spectre of 'Native Speakerism'

The account of post-puberty L2 learning and acquisition in section 2.1, in terms of frequency of use, lack of entrenchment, interference, selective attention, the mismatch of input and intake, and so forth, is based on robust experimental evidence of the kind that leads Abrahamsson and Hyltenstam (2009: 289) to state that 'the *probability* of a late learner developing a native-like command of all (or even a majority of) relevant linguistic aspects (and across all linguistic domains, too) is close to zero.' Many people could also adduce their own 'anecdotal' language learning experience, and language teachers their teaching experience. But even if one avoids the term 'native-like' and writes about 'L1ers' and 'L2ers,' explaining adult L2 learning in its own right inevitably draws comparisons with the acquisition of a native language. And everyone is a native speaker of at least one language.[16]

This is a cognitive or psycholinguistic argument, not a political one. But in English-language teaching circles, political arguments appear to be crowding out psycholinguistic ones, and the term 'native speaker' has almost become taboo and is now frequently followed by the word 'construct' or given the suffix '-ism.' For example, Riley (2015: 391) reminds us that 'native' is cognate with 'nationalism,' which is why the native speaker has become 'a symbol of oppression and neo-colonialism.' To use the term 'native speaker,' we are told, is to believe in 'monolingualism and standardisation' (p. 392) and 'resist (or ignore) any form of autonomy or variation' (p. 393), thereby rendering speakers of non-standard varieties 'invisible, subaltern, and powerless' (p. 393).[17] The opposing term is, necessarily, 'non-native,' and Firth and Wagner (1997: 291) insist that 'the negative connotation of the "non-" prefix is hardly coincidental.' Unless, perhaps, 'non' just means 'not,' without a negative connotation, as in non-carcinogen, non-dairy, non-fiction, non-governmental, non-linear, non-profit, non-sectarian, non-smoker, non-stop, and so on.

Aneja (2016a: 591) adds the accusation of racism: to have any use for the concepts of nativeness and non-nativeness is to be 'complicit in re-creating racialized, nationalized, or other monolithic conceptualizations of language or (non)native speakers,' and in 'the marginalization of colonial subjects and noncitizens' (2016b: 363). It also seems to involve 'asking a person of color how they learned English so well' (p. 364).

Applying the labels 'native' and 'non-native' to teachers as well as learners and users makes one guilty of 'native speakerism,' an ideology that is said to pervade the ELT profession. According to Holliday (2006: 385–6; see also Holliday 2005), this involves 'the "othering" of students and colleagues from outside the English-speaking West' and 'the belief that "native-speaker" teachers represent a "Western culture" from which spring the ideals both of the English language and of English-language teaching methodology.' 'Native-speaker' (in scare quotes) teachers are said to partake of the 'colonialist myth' or 'native-speakerist "moral mission" to bring a "superior" culture of teaching and learning to students and colleagues.' This is all a far cry from focusing on form in the classroom and retuning selective attention to counteract frequency and transfer effects, limited intake, the overshadowing and blocking of redundant and less salient features, and so on.

Many psycholinguists consider the bio-developmental account of linguistic nativeness, and of the differences between early L1 and late-onset L2 acquisition, to be a purely linguistic matter and potentially an aid to learners and teachers alike in understanding the usual difficulties of L2 acquisition. It is not designed to demean or disempower L2 users, and it says nothing about the supposed 'ownership' of language (Widdowson 1994, 2003: 35–44)—an inherently spurious concept—or the 'authority' of any given group of speakers, or the imagined 'superiority' of English speakers from inner circle countries: frequent childhood L1 input has the same effect in Malta, India, and Singapore as it does in Ireland, Canada, and Australia. But 'critical' applied linguists disagree. For example, Selvi (2014: 597–8) calls for the 'reconfiguration' of the 'native speaker construct,' 'beyond a pure linguistic phenomenon,' in a way that 'accounts for other factors such as accent, race, gender, religion, personal affiliation, self-positioning, country of origin, schooling, age, sexual orientation, physical appearance, or even the passport carried, or a combination of these constructs.'

Language is, of course, socially constructed, and used in social (and educational) interaction, and learning involves social as well as cognitive competences (Lantolf and Thorne 2006; Pavlenko and Lantolf 2000). Individual attributes—age, personality, motivation, attitude, aptitude, perseverance, intelligence, level of education, learning strategies, knowledge of the world, sense of identity and level of investment in the L2 as 'cultural capital' (Norton Peirce 1995), readiness to accommodate to interlocutors (Giles et al. 1991), and so on—all play a part in how languages are acquired and learned. So do sociocultural circumstances (social background, socialization, peer group, career, leisure-time activities, etc.), and the quality, range and quantity of the linguistic input (which is always constrained by the nature of the speakers, the topic, the setting, the context of interaction, etc.). As Ellis (2008: 17) concedes, 'good old-fashioned psycholinguistics' tends to oversimplify the learner 'as unembodied, unconscious, monologic, autistic, unsituated, asocial, uncultured, asocial, and untutored' and needs to combine this caricature with an account of 'meaning, embodiment, attention, consciousness, dialogue and dialectic, situated, cultured, social and tutored interaction.'

In a well-known article, Firth and Wagner (1997: 285) complain that SLA research has an 'individualistic and mechanistic' view of discourse and communication and neglects the 'interactional and sociolinguistic dimensions of language.' They call for enhanced awareness of the social (contextual and interactional) dimensions of language use and acquisition, as well as its cognitive dimensions, and criticize 'SLA's general preoccupation with the learner, at the expense of other potentially relevant social identities' (p. 288). For Firth and Wagner, 'NS or NNS is only one identity from a multitude of social identities, many of which can be relevant simultaneously, and all of which are motile' (p. 292). But as several responses to Firth and Wagner's article pointed out, they propose examples of L2 (or interlanguage) *use* in natural social contexts at a single point in time rather than the acquisition of new elements of the (inter)language, which is what the 'A' in SLA stands for (see Kasper 1997; Long 1997; Tarone 2000). And individual differences among learners and social contexts (and among countries of origin and passports carried) do not override the learning mechanisms, developmental sequences, processing constraints, and so on involved in post-adolescent language acquisition or the cognitive consequences of bi- or multilingualism.

Sociolinguists would expect L2 usage to vary according to the age, gender, status, and so on of the speaker, and L2 users to vary their speech in different social settings in which they encounter different registers and levels of formality, and monitor or pay attention to how they speak to differing degrees. And indeed advanced learners who use the L2 outside the classroom might well develop an interlanguage comprising social variation, which is to say contextually appropriate shifting among a range of styles, possibly involving fine-tuned frequencies of use of alternating formal and informal variants in accordance with the sociolinguistic norms of a particular speech community (Tarone 2000).[18] Yet less advanced learners (not sharing what Hulstijn calls a speech community's BLC) are more likely to display variation in some of the basic forms of the language, perhaps random variation between an (ungrammatical) non-target language form and a (grammatical) target language form (or even between two non-target forms).[19]

Thus although early accounts of approximative systems and interlanguage were wholly individualistic, more recent work *does* recognize the social dimensions of SLA, and both Canale and Swain (1980: 30) and Bachman (1990: 94–8) include 'sociolinguistic competence' as an element in their models of communicative competence.[20] This competence, however, is defined in terms of the acquisition of *native* speaker patterns of variability, which brings us back to denunciations of native speakerism.

Unfortunately, accounts of native speakerism (by Holliday, Riley, Selvi, Aneja, etc.) tend to deploy a whole detachment of straw men—the native-speaking English teachers who believe in the primacy of the idealized monolingual and monocultural native speaker-hearer, the standardization of the mother tongue, the moral mission of bringing a superior culture to those from outside the English-speaking West, the necessary whiteness of native speakers of English, and so on.[21] Furthermore, despite the claim that '[t]he idealization of mythical native speaker-hearers and the marginalization of their nonnative counterparts imbues almost every subfield of TESOL and applied linguistics' (Aneja 2016a: 59), there is nothing in the psycholinguistic account of transfer effects and selective attention in SLA that could be taken as an endorsement of native-speaking teachers of the target language, least of all unqualified, monolingual, inner circle gap-year backpackers. In fact such accounts of the difficulties of second language acquisition could easily be used as arguments in favour of employing local non-native speakers.

As Medgyes (1994) argued nearly a quarter of a century ago, for classes sharing an L1, local bi- or multilingual teachers who have also learnt the target language as an L2 can serve as imitable models of the successful learner of English, with an extensive declarative knowledge of the L2. They might be better at anticipating and empathizing with the learners' language difficulties and providing appropriate learning strategies, drawing on the shared L1 if necessary. Similar arguments have frequently been made ever since by both critical applied linguists and researchers into New Englishes and ELF (including Phillipson 1992: 193ff; Widdowson 1994; Cook 2002b: 337; Graddol 2006: 114; Jenkins 2007: 25; Kirkpatrick 2007: 184ff; and even MacKenzie 2014b: 133). And indeed there is a vigorous 'NNEST' movement, standing for either 'non-native English-speaking teachers' or 'non-native English speakers in TESOL,' which advocates for their rights, especially in the United States, and denounces discriminatory employment practices and proficiency assessments (see Braine 1999; Llurda 2005; Moussu and Llurda 2008; Braine 2010; Mahboob 2010; Selvi 2014).[22]

The problems faced by 'NNESTs' are often more to do with perceptions about 'foreigners' than with their language abilities. There is a whole subgenre of research articles (including Liu 1999; Brutt-Griffler and Samimy 2001; Faez 2011; Aneja 2016a) which attempt to demonstrate that the native (or non-native) speaker is a social construct. They do this by way of case studies of English teachers and trainee teachers in North America, whose own ascriptions of nativeness or otherwise do not always coincide with other people's—including their university instructors. These case studies do not disprove the psycholinguistic argument about a native-like BLC that necessitates childhood acquisition, but they *do* show that as long as there are Americans who are aghast at the idea that an Asian or African could even claim to be a native speaker of English, nativeness will remain 'a non-elective socially constructed identity rather than a linguistic category' (Brutt-Griffler and Samimy 2001: 100). There are evidently widespread preconceived notions of what a native speaker of English should look or sound like, involving nationality, ethnicity, and race, which are not part of the psycholinguist's notion of nativeness.[23]

Brutt-Griffler and Samimy's conclusion that nativeness is a 'non-elective' identity that needs to be validated by others (especially when it comes to getting a job as a native-speaking English teacher) contradicts more upbeat accounts of identity in terms of performativity, self-creation, and self-ascription. Faez (2011: 378), for example, insists that 'linguistic identities are multiple, dynamic, dialogic, and situated rather than unitary and fixed' and do not have to 'fall under the native/nonnative categories,' irrespective of how they are considered by others, which allows us to 'reconceptualize' and 'move beyond' this 'simplistic dichotomy' to a continuum. Similarly Aneja (2016b: 364) draws on Judith Butler, and argues that '[l]ike gender, (non)native speaker status is performative,' and what is performed is a repeated series of acts that, in Butler's (1990: 33) words, 'congeal over time to produce the appearance of substance.' Thus '(non)native speakered subjects are defined by what they *do* and how others perceive and define their behavior rather than defined with regard to any sort of inherent or innate quality' (p. 365).

Also drawing heavily on Butler's account of performativity—or as they modestly put it, 'reinvigorating' it—Harissi et al. (2012) argue that language and identity are constantly being remade in performance. We are as we are because of what we do while 'performing' linguistically and trying out, resisting, and changing identity categorizations. As Butler (1990: 25) puts it, 'identity is performatively constituted by the very "expressions" that are said to be its results.' Such a poststructuralist conception of performativity denies the existence of fixed, stable categories of identity or of subjects who pre-exist deeds: 'there need not be a "doer" behind the deed' because 'the "doer" is variably constructed in and through the deed' (p. 142).

A psycholinguist, however, might still object that the factors affecting adult L2 acquisition described above will pertain regardless so that the subject that is performatively realized—or created or born in discourse (is this 'perfor-nativity'?)—is necessarily the expression of a prior identity, either as a (perfor-)native speaker with a shared BLC or as a (perfor-)

non-native speaker, perhaps with an extremely developed HLC but without the native speakers' BLC. I insist on this distinction for the purposes of this book because my main focus will be on the possible influence of non-native uses of English on native ones (which are often different). This has almost certainly occurred in the past (see section 4.1) and could equally happen in the future.

Notes

1 Until recently Google Translate was entirely based on a similar premise: any phrase that is written has probably been written before, and translated, and the original and any paired translations are likely to be somewhere on the Internet, which serves Google as a translation memory database (Bellos 2011: 253–4). See Chapter 5, note 3.

2 There is also a countervailing tendency, particularly in writing, which involves deliberately *not* repeating constructions one has just used. Rohdenburg (2003: 236) describes this as a 'widespread (and presumably universal) tendency' and calls it the '*horror aequi* principle.' 'Universal' is probably overstated, but attested examples in English include the semantically unmotivated avoidance of adjacent infinitival and gerundial complements (Vosberg 2003) and consecutive *s*-genitives and *of*-genitives (Hinrichs and Szmrecsanyi 2007). Formal writing in Romance languages tends to take this to the extreme: here avoidance of repetition even extends to *proper names*, which are replaced by elegant variations.

3 Priming can sometimes be seen to occur crosslinguistically: in bilingual interactions (involving receptive multilingualism, codeswitching, etc.) speakers who have processed a structure in one language sometimes replicate it in the other language, which can safely be described as interference if the structure is not part of the language in question (Hartsuiker et al. 2004; Schoonbaert et al. 2007).

4 Focusing on meaning often involves concentrating on (and perhaps learning and storing) the most important words. Unfortunately, as Wray (2002: 206) says, this often involves ignoring 'all the really important information,' which is what other words they occur with. This form of analytic, lexical processing (as opposed to the holistic processing of children acquiring an L1) tends to blind L2 learners to standard collocations and common formulaic sequences.

5 See MacWhinney's (1987a, 1987b) 'competition model,' according to which utterances provide cues, largely based on previous exposure (i.e., frequency), that adjudicate between competing interpretations of lexical items, phonological forms, and syntactic patterns. In L2 learning, however, transfer and interference intervene.

6 Given that BLC does not include literacy, it only covers a small portion of standard scales of language proficiency. Hulstijn (2015: 153–4) suggests that for adult native speakers, it only coincides with the Common European Framework of Reference for Languages (CEFR) A2 level, or perhaps B1, and that many adult native speakers with modest or low intellectual abilities clearly never attain the C1 or C2 levels, which require higher levels of education and/or functioning in higher professions. This is to say that the CEFR authors fail to distinguish between L2 development and intellectual development and functioning.

7 Hulstijn's account of basic and higher language cognition has similarities with earlier dichotomous models, such as Bernstein's (1964) restricted and

elaborated codes, and Cummins's (1984) 'basic interpersonal communication skills' (BICS) and 'cognitive academic language proficiency' (CALP), or put more simply, conversational language and academic language. Yet unlike Bernstein, Hulstijn makes no mention of social class as such, suggesting that the degree to which L1ers acquire HLC is related to 'their psychological, educational and social profiles (intelligence, level of education, leisure-time activities' (2015: 30). Unlike Cummins, Hulstijn doubts that 'all people (not affected by cognitive impairment) acquire BICS irrespective of differences in intelligence or academic aptitude' (p. 32).

8 See http://ewave-atlas.org/languages/52.

9 Irish English provides instances of this, for example, the '*after* perfect' (or 'hot news perfect' or 'immediate perfective') with the preposition *after* (*be* + *after* + verb with *-ing*, as in *He's after running up the stairs [He's just run up the stairs]*), which indicates that something occurred in the recent or immediate past relative to the time of speaking and is clearly a transfer or a calque from an Irish construction, which Irish speakers shifting to English must have found more expressive than the standard English equivalent. See Hickey (2013) and Thomason (2013).

10 See, for example, Hamers and Blanc (1989), Romaine (1995: 107ff), and Jessner (2006), who draws on Vygotsky (1934) and Peal and Lambert (1962), and Berthoud et al. (2011, 2013). See Kharkhurin (2016) for a more sober account of multilingualism and creativity. It is worth mentioning that this valorization of bilingualism is relatively recent; it was previously believed to cause intellectual deterioration, mental conflict, conceptual poverty, moral deprivation, emotional difficulties, superficiality, laziness, and so on; see Weinreich (1953: 119–29) and Pavlenko (2011: 10–15).

11 García et al.'s 'translanguaging' has unexamined similarities with Harris's integrational linguistics (which he opposes to what he calls mainstream 'segregational' linguistics). Harris (1990: 45) denies that 'the concept of "a language," as defined by orthodox modern linguistics, corresponds to any determinate or determinable object of analysis at all, whether social or individual, whether institutional or psychological.' He sees language as integrated with everything else in our lives, which means that language is not an autonomous object; experience is not divided into linguistic and non-linguistic domains; words exist only by virtue of their integration into many and varied forms of human activity; and all signs are intrinsically indeterminate. One could accept most of these arguments, however, while still holding onto the concept of languages as *non*-autonomous objects integrated with everything else in our lives.

12 From his multicompetence perspective, Cook (2013: 35) objects to the term 'English as an additional language' as it implies that 'becoming plurilingual is adding another language to your first [. . .] maintaining in perpetuity Weinreich's notion of coordinate bilingualism.' Weinreich's account of subordinate bilinguals, and indeed his whole tripartite model, is essentially bilingual rather than multilingual and does not take into account the additional possibilities of transfer if L3 (etc.) learning involves a subordinative relation between languages.

13 For example, Gardner (2016) complains about the European Union's French-English translators (at the top end of their profession), whose English regularly includes words such as *actual* (meaning current), *adequate* (meaning appropriate), *assist at* (meaning attend), *controls* (meaning checks), *delay* (meaning time limit), *dispose of* (meaning have or possess), *elaborate* (meaning draw up or prepare), *eventual* (meaning possible), *evolution* (meaning development or trend), *externalise* (meaning outsource or contract out),

formulate (meaning draft or draw up), *hierarchical superior* (meaning line manager), *homogenize* (meaning standardize), *important* (meaning large), *normally* (meaning supposed to or expected to), *opportunity* (meaning advisability), *to precise* (meaning to specify), *precision* (meaning detail or clarification), *planification* (meaning planning), *punctual* (meaning occasional or ad hoc), and so on. It is very unlikely that *all* the people in question are simultaneous early bilinguals and thus part of the supposedly de facto 'lousy translators' category.

14 Singleton (2016: 506) also points out that the selective recovery of languages and dialects by multilingual stroke patients (see, e.g., Schwyter 2011) provides evidence of the boundedness of languages.

15 Vaihinger's (1924: 15–84) examples of expedient 'as if' fictions include philosophical ones, such as Platonic Ideas and Kantian ethics, as well as the subject/object distinction and the Kantian *noumenon* or *Ding-an-sich*; mathematical ones, such as negative, irrational and imaginary numbers, infinity, differential calculus, and most of Euclidian geometry (lines made up of points, curves regarded as straight lines, points without extension, lines without breadth or depth, surfaces without depth, and spaces without content); scientific ones such as matter, force, motion and space, electromagnetic waves, the 'plum pudding' and 'planetary' models of the atom, and nearly all (artificial) analogical categories and classifications, including geological periods and the Linnaean taxonomy of organisms; economic ones, such as Adam Smith's assumption that all human actions are dictated by egoism; and legal ones, such as laws that are deemed to cater for individual cases. Vaihinger's concept clearly applies in studies of language too; indeed translation theory all but *consists of* useful fictions (MacKenzie 2014a).

16 At least one language: the existence of simultaneous early childhood bi- and multilinguals renders the term 'L1' imprecise. So nothing much is gained by substituting the terms 'L1,' 'L1s' and 'L1 users' for 'native language,' 'native languages' and 'native speakers.'

17 Riley apparently can't conceive of someone who uses the term 'native speaker' but also discusses variation and multicompetence, and (exaggeratedly) declares bilingualism to be the ordinary state of humankind. 'Native' is also cognate with 'nativist,' but an account of native (and non-native) speakers based on usage-based and emergentist models of language acquisition is equally incompatible with the 'nativist' theories of generative grammarians, involving an 'innate' universal grammar, a 'language instinct' or 'language acquisition device,' 'the poverty of the stimulus' (and similar not very useful fictions).

18 This might require living in a country in which the learner's L2 is the L1; see, for example, Regan (1996) on Anglophone learners of French developing their sociolinguistic competence in France and increasing their contextually appropriate rate of *ne* deletion in negatives.

19 Berdan (1996: 208), however, complains that '[m]any of the published examples of non-systematic variation are the introspection of linguists themselves' and insists that 'no one has ever established the systematic nature of variation on the basis of introspection'; what is required is a lot of longitudinal data and computerized multivariate variable rules analysis.

20 See, however, Widdowson's (2003: 166–70) critique of such multi-component models of competence. In a position akin to (and prior to) that of most ELF theorists, Widdowson also argues that what is important in language learning (especially *English*-language learning) is a twofold 'capability' involving 'the ability to exploit the virtual language' as well as 'the readiness to adjust to the conventions of actual encoding as and when required' (p. 173).

21 Quite simply, critics of native speakerism and defenders of 'NNESTs' (non-native English-speaking teachers) tend not to engage with the psycholinguistic side of SLA research, whereas researchers into bilingualism and SLA tend not to engage with the concept of native speakerism, critically oriented applied linguistics, or 'epistemologies and paradigms' that are *not* 'well represented in research in language learning and teaching [. . .] e.g., indigenous, feminist, critical, Queer, postcolonial, postmodern, Green, and more' (Talmy 2014: 388).

22 The NNEST movement persists with the term 'non-native' with its negative prefix for reasons discussed in Selvi (2014: 595–7). Unlike the TESOL NNEST activists, Medgyes has always been happy to say things like 'I am a NNEST whose language instinct (in English) is wont to lead me astray' (2012: 122)—the kind of thing that Selvi denounces as a 'deficit model'—and 'I find it hard to empathize with NNS teachers seeking employment in a foreign country. Rather, my sympathy lies with NNS colleagues in the outer and expanding circles when they find themselves at a disadvantage compared to unqualified NS backpackers' (2011: 191).

23 Brutt-Griffler and Samimy's article also shows that some people believe their own bi- or multilingualism to be incompatible with nativeness in any language.

3 Purposeful Language Change

As outlined in the preceding chapters, English spoken as a lingua franca generally differs from English used as a native language. In some cases this may simply be a consequence of incomplete learning. In others, ELF users may be *deliberately* altering various native usages with which they are familiar to make them more communicatively effective—clearer, simpler, more explicit, more economical, more regular, less redundant, less ambiguous, and so on—with other L2 speakers. This would be a case of speakers intentionally changing the language they use, a notion that does not, on the whole, seem to appeal to linguists. In this chapter I discuss conflicting accounts of language change, including those that attribute it to languages themselves (internal or endogenous change) and those that attribute changes to active human agency and, often, the effects of language contact (external or exogenous change). I will argue that speakers can indeed make conscious and deliberate changes to the way they use a language in pursuit of enhanced expressivity, in an attempt to use optimally comprehensible constructions to avoid misunderstanding, and sometimes (although clearly not in the case of ELF) to follow the dictates of prescriptivists. Speakers' individual choices are often intentional and purposeful, and although they are not setting out to 'change the language,' the aggregate result of their multiple choices can indeed be language change. This process is rather more apparent in ELF than in native English.

3.1 Language Change as a Random Process

The idea that speakers might deliberately attempt to alter the language they speak for the sake of clarity and communicative effectiveness is not a particularly popular one among linguists. For example, Keller (1994: 13) states apodictically that 'speakers change their language neither intentionally, nor to a plan, nor consciously. This is generally true, and there is nothing more to it,' while Lass (1997: xviii) insists that language users 'simply have to make do with what's historically presented to them, and cope with it when it changes.' But most of the linguists who make statements like these are concerned with L1 speakers (and, at least implicitly, monolingual ones at that) rather than users of a widespread lingua franca.

The kind of argument I am going to contest is typified by Lass, for whom language change is neither rational nor meaningful. According to Lass, who tends to write about languages rather than their speakers, languages do not *seek* to evolve any more than biological organisms do; they just evolve (1997: 303) as change 'is a built-in property of the kind of system that a human language [. . .] happens to be' (p. 386). Languages undergo internal or endogenous change—things like 'word-order changes, inflectional simplification, analogical extension or levelling, grammaticalization, and vowel shifts'; this is simply 'part of the nature of the beast' (p. 208). They do not progress or become more natural, simple, or efficient as a result of change; neither do they decline or decay. They just change, and indeed '[a]ny possible language-state [. . .] can become any other' (p. 302). Speakers are the end users of historically evolved systems that are massively contingent rather than rational or optimal, so teleological arguments are superfluous.

Lass rejects the notion that speakers are 'rational agents' who have intuitions about the supposed communicative 'efficiency' or 'optimality' of their language and are able to compare its present state with an imagined improved one. For ordinary speakers—unlike 'those special speakers for whom making language focal is a professional concern'—language is 'a non-focal historical given' (p. 361). Furthermore, Lass denies that speakers could possibly rectify disequilibriated or non-optimal states because there's never anything to rectify: 'any existing language state is by definition "adequate," or it wouldn't exist' (p. 350), and no language state 'can be more or less well-suited to its speakers' needs than any other' (p. 358), as it will 'have by definition a sufficient set of structures and categories available for doing anything that a speaker "needs" to do' (p. 367). This also entails that 'borrowing is never necessary' (p. 209).

For Lass, functional explanations of language change, whether prophylactic or therapeutic, are 'always irreducibly *post hoc*' and 'totally non-predictive' (1980: 69). He invites us to imagine Middle English speakers worrying, 'If we lose our case endings and don't stabilize our word order, we won't be able to tell subjects from objects,' or thinking, 'We've lost the subject/object distinction; better fix the word order and get it back' (p. 85)! Hence 'function' is just 'an *a posteriori* fudge, conferring a spurious "motivation" on what might as far as we know be a random process' (1997: 358). Nevertheless, after dropping case endings, Middle English speakers *did* largely stabilize their word order, consciously or unconsciously, which clearly had a functional effect.

Lass argues that as well as having all the structures and categories speakers might need, languages can be full of 'junk,' 'detritus' and 'garbage' (p. 12), 'linguistic male nipples' (p. 15), 'disarticulated fragments of once-coherent systems' (p. 309), and 'non-functional, non-semiotic debris' (p. 310), all of which continue to be used for centuries or even millennia. Speakers will use non-functional forms if they are not actively *dysfunctional* because there's no particular motivation to make the effort required to change them. Consequently languages contain 'a lot of material that simply makes speakers do things, whether or not there is any (functional, discourse, pragmatic) "need" to do them' (pp. 367–8). This is a strong argument against linguistic relativity or the so-called Sapir-Whorf hypothesis, the idea that the structures and categories available in a language influence thought (an idea we will return to in Chapter 6). Different languages grammatically encode—or perhaps 'overspecify' (McWhorter 2007, 2011)—different things, for example, different types of aspect—habitual, continuous, completive, anterior, resultative, perfective, and imperfective—and different deontic and epistemic modalities. But for Lass these may be the contingent and unintended outcomes of historical processes rather than the results of purposive functional change, and they do not determine anyone's worldview or perception capacity (cf. McWhorter 2014). Like other human cultural products—painting, music, literature, clothing, and fashion—language undergoes stylistic change in which the amount of 'functional' motivation is minimal. Lass sees functional explanations as stemming from a misguided urge to make purposeless language change intelligible and to impose order on chaos.

Lass further argues that if linguistic changes *were* functional, they should be adopted by all members of a speech community at once. But this does not happen: changes start somewhere, and then either die out or are propagated through communities, via different social networks or according to variables such as age, gender, class, ethnicity, and so on. Milroy (1992: 38) reverses this argument, stating that 'variation and change must be functional for speakers of languages,' otherwise 'languages would be uniform and they would not change.' He counters Lass's claim that endogenous change constitutes 'part of the nature of the beast' with the objection that 'it is in the nature of the beast to resist satisfactory explanations of how it can change within itself' (Milroy 2003: 145). But Lass and Milroy use the term 'functional' differently. As mentioned in Chapter 1, sociolinguists assume that variability in a native language is a form of what Weinreich et al. (1968: 101) describe as 'orderly' or 'structured heterogeneity,' in which linguistic variables—two or more ways of saying 'the same thing'—are conventionally associated with social values that determine their appropriate use. Social values include the roles and status of the interlocutors, and speakers can attempt to accommodate to each other, to establish or reinforce group identity, or to signal social difference or exclusion (Giles et al. 1991). People perceive particular forms as having social as well as semantic meaning, perhaps indexing a speaker's age, sex, regional origin, and so on. Milroy (2003: 83) insists that 'people are normally aware of differences of this kind, and they often attach utmost importance to them.' Thus even though, objectively, one linguistic variant 'is just as "good" or "efficient" as the other' (1992: 83), and no variant is more *functionally adapted* to communication, speakers' choices among variants have a clear *social* function.

Most of the time speakers select from already existing variants, depending on the situation, but occasionally novel variants are produced. In fact all variants must begin as innovations, which are then adopted (and maintained) by different groups who 'assign strong social values to what are essentially arbitrary differences' (p. 43). As social values in a speech community slowly change, speakers might make different choices in their acts of identity (Le Page and Tabouret-Keller 1985) and accommodation, leading to changing frequencies of variants of a structure and shifts in their relative meanings. All such choices are *socially* functional, but they are not teleological—speakers are not setting out to change the language for the better. They might, nevertheless, be changing the language. Hence unlike Lass (1997: 370), who insists that change is not 'something that speakers "do"' but rather 'something that happens to their languages,' one might well argue, as Croft (2000: 4) does, that 'languages don't change; people change languages through their actions.'

Lass, however, denies that choices among variants are necessarily motivated or meaningful. He prefers to see linguistic variation as the result of historical inertia and local contingency, having 'no significance whatever for the individuals manifesting the behaviour' (1997: 372). Moreover, 'it'd be more parsimonious to suppose lack of significance unless there's strong evidence the other way' (p. 372). Parsimony, however, is an arbitrary methodological principle or heuristic technique, and it is not sufficient to adjudicate between rival interpretations. The most economic explanation is not necessarily the right one (Filppula 2003: 170), and most phenomena (not just language change) can have multiple causes. The most parsimonious explanation of why the sun moves across the sky every day is that the sun moves across the sky every day while going round the Earth. The most parsimonious explanation of why the next defendant is up before the court might be that he's irrational, violent, and unpredictable—which, incidentally, is also precisely how Labov (1994: 10) describes linguistic change! But this neglects the possibility—as the Jets inform Officer Krupke—that the defendant's bringing-upke is to blame: he's misunderstood and psychologically distoibed and needs a kindly social woika and an analyst's care. Moreover, this attempted orthographic representation of a caricature of a 1950s working-class New York accent, adapted from a song in the musical *West Side Story*, is a rather corny example of the way in which the choice of linguistic variables clearly *can* have social significance and index speakers' regional and class origins.

3.2 Language Contact

Lass is equally dismissive of external explanations of language change as resulting from language contact. Despite the extensive historical record of population movements, speech communities shifting to different languages, neighbouring languages converging, and so on (see Chapter 7), Lass describes language contact as a 'rather gross' contingency (1980: 139) and insists that languages would change in just the same ways if speakers were totally isolated from any contact with speakers of other languages (with—*ex hypothesi*—the exception of borrowing).[1] Given the inherent adequacy of all language at all times, Lass believes in 'transubstantiation' or 'transindividuation' (1997: 281)—one thing turning into or 'becoming' another—rather than one thing being replaced by an element borrowed from another language or created anew: languages 'innovate preferentially by utilizing (including transforming) existing material; as a second recourse they borrow; as a third they just might (in certain domains anyway) invent' (p. 305). Morphosyntactic inventions are now rare (and have been for a long time), although of course new lexis is regularly invented, but Lass points out that even here new words 'use available material, and could be taken as simple deployments of combinatorial possibilities that (contingently) happen not yet to have been utilized' (p. 307; cf. MacKenzie 2014c). This is analogous to Widdowson's (2003: 48–9) concept of the virtual language, already outlined in relation to ELF in Chapter 1—the exploitation of latent possibilities immanent in the language—but here it is the *language* rather than language users that is exploiting its virtual possibilities.

Lass does not refute the argument that 'given enough time and intensive contact, virtually anything can (ultimately) be borrowed' (Campbell 1993: 104) but simply states that even if anything *can* be borrowed, 'in a given case it's always both simpler and safer to assume that it isn't, unless the evidence is clear and overwhelming' (Lass 1997: 201). Lass will only accept arguments for extensive contact influence if there are examples of phenomena 'that could not have happened any other way' (p. 207). He argues that endogenous explanations must be preferred to exogenous ones on—once again—'considerations of parsimony' (p. 207). But parsimony remains an arbitrary methodological principle, and we should always bear in mind 'the possibility of multiple causation' (Thomason and Kaufman 1988: 57) and the fact that equivalent changes can have internal motivation in one language and external causes in another (p. 59).

One can also take another tack and object that the very notion of internal and external factors is predicated on an essentially monolingual model and the assumption that the majority of speakers have only a single language, albeit one that might conceivably be affected by the linguistic behaviour of a minority of bilinguals. But as argued in the previous chapters, for bilinguals language contact is not so much a rather gross contingency as a constant mental reality (Weinreich 1953; Cook 2002a; Grosjean 2010). As Matras (2009: 5) puts it, contact is not 'an "external" factor that triggers change' so much as a factor that is 'internal to the processing and use of language itself in the multilingual speaker's repertoire of linguistic structures.' Unless we abandon the very notion of separable languages, as discussed in Chapter 2, we can conceive of bilingual speakers as selecting materials from more than one linguistic system. Heine and Kuteva (2005: 92) argue that in cases of intensive, long-term contact, bilingual speakers often 'notice' that there is a particular grammatical category in an L2 ('the model language') and 'to this end' develop an equivalent category in their L1 (the 'replica language'), if this appears to be useful or beneficial, by manipulating existing grammatical forms. This form of grammatical replication 'reduces the cognitive load that the simultaneous handling of two or more languages entails' (p. 264), and the cumulative uses of individual speakers under the influence of the model language can lead to change in the replica language. Importantly Heine and Kuteva's wording—bilingual speakers *notice* a grammatical category and *to this end* replicate it in their L1—suggests that this is a *conscious* process of language change. This is very much a minority position—for example, Ross (2007: 135) rewrites Heine and Kuteva's account of grammatical replication in a way that removes conscious intention—but it is one that I share, at least in the other direction in relation to L1 > L2 replication in ELF, as I will argue.

Another way to downplay the significance of language contact and bilingualism in language change is to claim, as Jakobson (1938/1962: 241) does, that a language only accepts foreign structural elements when they correspond to its own '*tendances de développement*.'[2] Thus, as Weinreich (1953: 25) puts it, 'language contact and the resulting interference could be considered to have, at best, a trigger effect,' releasing or accelerating latent internal tendencies. This claim is wholly unfalsifiable as it means that any posited contact-induced change must, de facto, be described as having corresponded to the target language's tendencies of development, but it does have a certain plausibility. Indeed Thomason and Kaufman (1988: 54) make the 'tentative hypothesis' that 'in cases of light to moderate structural interference, the transferred features are more likely to be those that fit in well typologically with corresponding features in the recipient language.'

The idea that speakers can *only* innovate in ways or directions that a language already allows leads Coseriu (1988) to state that '[l]inguistic change does not exist.' He redescribes change as 'the construction, the making of language [. . .] the ordinary phenomenon through which a language arises, comes into being' (p. 150), and 'the application of procedures of production given in the language itself' (p. 157), so that linguistic change should really be seen 'as "non-change" (as the mere application of previously given rules or procedures [. . .])' (p. 155). Because language is an inherently creative activity directed towards other people, linguistic change is merely 'the immediate manifestation, the primary emergence of the creativity and alterity of language' (p. 151). Coseriu suggests that from a diachronic point of view, it is not a matter of A being replaced by B, or changing into B; rather, 'the elements A and B are equivalent products at different stages of the produced language' (p. 150).

Importantly, however, Coseriu concedes that the material for linguistic change (now redefined as creation) can also come from *another language*, which is more difficult to describe as 'the application of the system' (p. 157). But to argue that a syntactic pattern 'borrowed' from another language, or replicated using host language lexis, *necessarily* corresponds to the language's latent internal tendencies (like Jakobson's phonological tendencies of development), and consequently its 'system' is to stretch the definition of 'system' past the breaking point. This is especially the case if the borrowed pattern triggers a chain reaction of reanalysis or reinterpretation of other elements of the host language.

In short it would seem more logical to describe contact-induced grammatical change as precisely that—language change. Describing *all* change as the continuation of latent tendencies of development is as useful as Zeno's paradox that shows motion to be an illusion because an arrow must first cover half the intended distance, and then half again, and then half of that, and so on, in an unending, infinite number of steps without ever reaching its target. Motion nonetheless exists, and so does linguistic change (and indeed, in Aristotle's physics, motion and change were essentially interchangeable; see Kuhn 1977).

Yet the fact remains that the contact origin of a linguistic feature that has been diffused and adopted by monolingual speakers can rarely be *proved*; it is more a matter of possibility or probability. As Lass (1997: 334ff) points out, contact explanations have to rely on what Peirce called abduction. Rather than making a deductive inference (which is necessarily true), one infers an antecedent condition (in this case, contact with speakers—or possibly writers—of another language) by heuristic guessing from a given fact (the appearance of a new linguistic feature in one language that resembles an equivalent feature in another language). But even if the premise (language contact has taken place) is true, the conclusion need not be, as one may match the wrong result (or linguistic feature) with the premise (Hopper and Traugott 2003: 43). Lass (1997: 335) objects to the irreducibly personal element in abduction and hermeneutic approaches in general: 'other people's abductions (unlike their correct deductions) may fail to convince, since the nature of a particular abduction depends on contingent attributes of the abducer.' But all one can do is marshal the evidence and look for the best possible explanation.

Sometimes the evidence for language contact seems convincing. A recent case is the use of V2 (in place of V-final) word order in subordinate clauses beginning with *weil* (because) in spoken and informal written

German (e.g., *weil das Wetter war so schön*—'because the weather was so nice'—instead of *weil das Wetter so schön war*). Farrar (1999) argues that this trend results from an increasing amount of indirect contact with English through the media. Her data show that this pattern is much less prevalent in the former East Germany, which had much less exposure to English.[3] But in other cases what looks very much like L2 influence turns out to have a perfectly plausible internal explanation, as Poplack et al. (2010, 2012a, 2012b) show with preposition stranding in Quebecois French. *Le mec que je t'ai vu avec* and *C'est ça je travaille dessus* look for all the world like calques of *The guy I saw you with* and *That's what I'm working on*, but Poplack et al. explain them as the extension to relative clauses of 'orphaning'—the use of phrase-final prepositions with no overt complement, as in *Oui mais, il [ne] veut pas payer pour* ('Yes, but he doesn't want to pay for,' without 'it' at the end), which is perfectly acceptable in standard (colloquial) French.[4] This example leads Poplack and Levey (2010: 412) to the rather overstated conclusion that 'contact-induced change is a good deal less common than the literature suggests' and that it 'is *not* an inevitable, nor possibly even a common, outcome of language contact.'

Yet even if one chooses to reject language contact explanations for changes in L1s, they are often plausible for explaining L2 uses. For example, English speakers learning German will find putting the verb in second position in a subordinate clause beginning with *weil* much more natural than putting it at the end, and Anglophone learners of French will find a phrase like *la fille que je sors avec*—'the girl I'm going out with'—easier to construct than *la fille avec qui je sors*—'the girl with whom I'm going out.'

In the case of ELF, where everyone is speaking an L2, contact explanations for innovations and variants are a lot more plausible. Where there is an indifference to native norms, speakers are even more likely to transfer patterns from the L1 to the L2 (which is, in Heine and Kuteva's terms, the replica language). For example, speakers of many European languages will find it easier to transfer L1 patterns to English and pluralize 'uncountable' nouns—*the informations you want to transmit*; use the present perfect with past time reference—*I've been there yesterday*; and use the present simple to express duration—*he's here since a couple of years* (examples from VOICE)—than to follow native English norms. This argument will be developed below, but first it is necessary to show that linguists who describe *all* linguistic changes as random are overlooking several well-documented domains of language in which people *can* be seen to intentionally change (or should that be 'seen intentionally to change'?) the way they speak or write.

3.3 Purposeful Language Change

As we have seen, Lass (1980: 168) claims that he 'can think [. . .] of no linguistic change that can legitimately be taken as involving purpose';

disregards the role of individuals or communities in language change; and downplays the role of language contact. But other linguists grant speakers rather more agency and have put forward various reasons why they might deliberately alter the way they speak. Common suggestions include enhancing expressivity; acceding to other people's prescriptive recommendations; avoiding misunderstandings; and reorganizing utterances to optimize their information structure. I will consider these factors in turn before returning specifically to the uses and motivations of speakers of ELF.

3.3.1 Expressivity

Sociolinguists tend to play down the significance of the individual language user. (Perhaps the clue lies in the combining form *socio-*.) As Labov (1989: 52) puts it, 'individual behaviour can be understood only as a reflection of the grammar of a speech community. Language is not a property of the individual, but of the community.' So 'to do justice to the elegance and regularity of linguistic structure,' description 'must take the speech community as its object.' But most people also believe, to differing degrees, in the existence of idiolects—individual ways of speaking—which can often be demonstrated with the aid of large spoken corpora. Barlow (2013) illustrates this, and opposes the Labovian focus on the community, stating that 'there are differences in the speech of individual speakers across a wide range of lexicogrammatical patterns' (pp. 474–5)—differences that can be found in 'the central components of lexicogrammar, and not only in some idiosyncratic peripheral phraseology' (p. 445).

Yet as well as computing and analyzing speakers' regular choices, we must also do justice to *irregularity*, and most people *do* occasionally play with language and innovate deliberately. Notwithstanding all the evidence of accommodation, alignment, style matching, and the rest of it, Johnstone (1996: 187) insists, mustfully,

> All talk displays its speaker's individual voice. This is necessary because self-expression is necessary [. . .] individuals must on some level express individuated selves. In order to do this, speakers must do things with language that other speakers do not do. Each speaker must, quite literally, be idiosyncratic.

This may be somewhat overstating the case, but I share Thomason's (2007: 45) 'quite radical' position that the question of the *possibility* of deliberate linguistic change

> is settled as soon as a single speaker produces a single instance of the change at a single time. Whether a deliberate change will become a

> permanent part of that one speaker's idiolect or of the speech community as a whole is then a matter of social and linguistic probability, not possibility.[5]

The most commonly evoked reason for changing normal ways of saying things is enhanced expressivity. As well as a static maxim—'Talk like the others talk' or 'Talk like the people around you' (Keller 1994: 100)—Keller posits dynamic maxims like 'Talk in such a way that you are noticed' and 'Talk in an amusing, funny, etc. way' (p. 101). Harris and Campbell (1995: 54) discuss what they call 'exploratory expressions': constructions that 'may be judged ungrammatical, stylistically odd, or foreign, but will nevertheless be understood.' Lightfoot (1991), who does not accept that adults can continue to change their 'grammar' throughout the life span, nevertheless acknowledges that new constructions are introduced for their expressiveness, novelty value, and stylistic effect. He describes constructions taking on an expressive function as 'a greatly under-estimated source of linguistic change' (p. 160) and indeed states that if it was not for constructions being used for stylistic effect, 'linguistic change would be [. . .] nonexistent; languages would be stable' (p. 171).

Novel expressions can be variously used for persuasion, emphasis, reinforcement, clarity, and avoidance of ambiguity. They can also be used for social reasons, such as prestige or self-image; for aesthetic reasons—exploiting the poetic function of language to introduce some stylistic weirdness into a conversation or a text (e.g., *a rose is a rose is a rose*; *curiouser and curiouser*); for economic reasons—to save articulatory energy or memory capacity (*long time no see*; *no can do*; *been there, done that*); or just for fun. An example of a structure used for expressive purposes is 'left dislocation,' as in *Universal grammar, I don't believe in* (Lightfoot 1991: 170—although not this example sentence!). Alongside the various intentional acts just listed, odd or ungrammatical expressions can also be uttered by mistake: just as bilinguals experience interference, Croft (2000: 148) suggests that there can easily be *intraference* between words or constructions from the same language that share linguistic substance. Lexical intraference is the most fragrant (*sic*): I've had native-speaking graduate students of English who confuse *flaunt* and *flout*, *militate* and *mitigate*, *principal* and *principle*, and *regretfully* and *regrettably*. Fixed expressions can also be altered for fun, for example: *a baffle of wits*, *wrecked my brains*, *a clowning achievement*, *chickens coming home to roast*, *monotonize the conversation*, *witticisms too humorous to mention*.[6]

The pervasive process of grammaticalization, in which words are used in new, sometimes metaphorical senses, to achieve special effects, with the long-term result that content words turn into function words, has also long been described in terms of expressivity. Meillet (1912), who coined the term *grammaticalisation*, wrote of *expressivité*, and the use of more elaborate, periphrastic constructions to obtain *une expression intense*. Examples include Romance grammatical prepositions (which replaced the Latin cases), the Romance definite and indefinite articles (grammaticalized from a demonstrative pronoun and the numeral *one*); futures with *will* and *go* and equivalents; periphrastic progressive and perfect constructions with *be* and *have* and equivalents; and so on (Bybee et al. 1994; Lehmann 2002; Hopper and Traugott 2003).

Haspelmath (1999b) objects that expressiveness just means saying very clearly what you think, which is not very different from another of Keller's maxims (which Haspelmath labels the maxim of clarity): 'Talk in such a way that you are understood.' He suggests that there is rather a maxim of extravagance, or better still, because the intention is to be noticed and to impress the hearer, a maxim of impressiveness. Speakers occasionally deviate from convention and use elaborate, vivid expressions to be noticed (or to show off). Thus for Haspelmath, grammaticalization is 'a side effect of the maxim of extravagance' (p. 1043) rather than expressiveness. But whichever way we choose to describe it (expressiveness, impressiveness, or extravagance), grammaticalization provides manifold examples of individual creative usages developing into standardized forms for entire speech communities.

3.3.2 *Obeying Prescriptivists*

A second reason why some people change the way they say things is the influence of teachers, prescriptive grammarians, and individuals and institutions that try to change language use for political motives. Most linguists are contemptuous of self-appointed prescriptivists, with their idiosyncratic, and often Latin-based, aesthetic sensibilities, for whom Pinker (1994) popularized the term 'language mavens': see, for example, Bauer and Trudgill's *Language Myths* (1998) and Pullum's (2009) anniversary review of Strunk and White's *Elements of Style*, called '50 Years of Stupid Grammar Advice.' Yet the 'rules' and recommendations put forward by prescriptivists, stupid or otherwise, do sometimes seem to have an effect.

Curzan (2014) distinguishes among four types of prescriptivism, concerned with standards, style, restoration, and political intervention. The first and third of these (imposing standards and restoring a language to a glorious earlier state) clearly run counter to the actual patterns of use of a language and its general historical drift and consequently tend to fail, but stylistic recommendations concerning choices among variants—different ways of saying 'the same thing'—are less likely to be ignored or meet strong resistance. This is particularly the case where the rules recommend the more informal and colloquial of two options (e.g., avoid passives) rather than a bookish, formal, 'rationalizing' one (e.g., avoid double negations, don't split infinitives, and don't strand prepositions at the end of clauses).

Prescriptivists almost unanimously criticize the use of the passive voice rather than active lexical verbs, and both Mair and Leech (2006) and Leech and Smith (2006) chart a decline in the use of the passive in written English through the 20th century, which they attribute to the influence of prescriptivism. Another change that follows prescriptivist recommendations is what Hinrichs et al. (2015) call a 'substantive shift,' between the 1960s and the 1990s, in restrictive relative clauses in written Standard English from *which* to *that*, revealed by the Brown Corpora.

The so-called *that*-rule (use *that* in restrictive relative clauses) has a certain symmetry because non-restrictive relative clauses can take only *which* as a relativizer, and it is recommended in the best-known style guides, including Fowler and Crystal (1926/2009: 635) and Strunk and White (1999: 59). According to Biber et al. (1999: 609–11), *that* is the most frequently used relativizer in both conversational English and fiction, whereas *which* is the most frequently used in academic English and news writing (with zero relative coming in third position).[7] But the proportion of *which* clauses in academic prose and journalism—the genres most subject to editing—declined sharply between the 1960s and 1990s. Hinrichs et al. find that writers with a formal style who use a lot of passives (thus ignoring the prescriptive rule 'avoid passives') also use *which* a lot in non-restrictive relative clauses (ignoring the '*that*-rule') and tend to follow the 'avoid preposition stranding' rule too (p. 826). But by the 1990s use of *that* had spread to more formal writing, in which it increasingly co-occurs with lower frequencies of preposition stranding. They conclude that

> the staggering rate at which *that* has been taking over the [restrictive relative clause], along with the observed increase over time in writers' compliance with other prescriptive rules, suggests that the ideas of prescriptive grammarians, handed down through usage guides and the educational systems of the English-speaking world, had the effect of massively reinforcing and accelerating an existing trend in the direction of colloquialisation.
>
> (pp. 830–1)

Seeking to circumvent my copy editor, I changed a number of *which* clauses to *that* clauses while revising this book, which is a further example of how people can and do consciously change the way they use language.

Like many people, I am also not immune to what Cameron (1995) called 'verbal hygiene,' and Curzan (2014) calls politically or socially responsive prescriptivism, in particular non-sexist language reform. In English there have been so-far unsuccessful attempts to introduce a gender-neutral, third-person singular pronoun and more successful campaigns to introduce gender-neutral job descriptions (no more *air hostesses*, *maids*, or *midwives*) and non-sexist words (*of human origin* rather than *manmade*, *valiantly* instead of *manfully*). In my own oppressive household, I can rarely use the word *actress* without it being disapproved of, and my resistance to change is crumbling. I have also registered, over the decades, shifting perceptions of acceptable vocabulary, such as the transformations from *Indian* to *Native American*, from *illegal alien* to *undocumented worker*, from *gay* to *LGBT* to *LGBTQ*, and so on. Examples such as these show that the linguistic orthodoxy expressed, for example, by Haspelmath (1999a: 192) as 'clearly languages don't change because speakers want to change them' is not entirely true.

3.3.3 Avoiding Misunderstandings

A third commonly evoked reason for changing one's way of saying things is to avoid being misunderstood. As Keller (1994) argues, this allows for conscious human purposes being a factor in language change but without the need to describe changes as being *intended* as such; instead they merely result from the aggregation of speakers' selections of alternative ways of saying things. Keller gives the example of German speakers in the 19th century no longer using the adjective *englisch* to mean 'angelic' (using alternative forms such as *engelhaft* instead) because with the advent of industrialization, they found themselves talking about England more often than about angels. It is not always the case that one of a pair of homonyms eventually gets replaced—German still has a lot of them—but not wishing to run the risk of being misunderstood, speakers stopped using *englisch* in the angelic sense because, in most sentences in which it was used this way, it could plausibly have been interpreted as meaning English (e.g., a choir of *englisch* girls, an *englisch* greeting, *englisch* customs), which was not the case the other way round (there is nothing angelic about an *englisch* lawn or *englisch* cloth).

So there was a *reason* for the progressive change in the meaning of this word as used by German speakers, but the change was not so much intentional as the epiphenomenon or by-product or non-intended consequence of people's aggregated linguistic choices.[8] Keller applies a theory that is as old as Adam, in this case Adam Ferguson and Adam Smith during the Scottish Enlightenment, to explain 'social phenomena which result from individuals' actions without being intended by them' (p. 35), namely the theory that Smith called 'the invisible hand.' This theory explains spontaneous order or outcomes that result from the uncoordinated actions of many individuals. Ferguson (1767/1995: 205) described how 'nations stumble upon establishments, which are indeed the result of human action, but not the execution of any human design,' and 'arrive at ends which even their imagination could not anticipate,' while Smith (1776/1909: 351) showed how a private investor intending only his or her own gain, and without intending to promote the public interest, is 'as in many other cases, led by an invisible hand to promote an end which was no part of his intention.' Similarly 'speakers of a language generally do not intend to produce change in their language,' and 'they are generally not aware of language change taking place' (Keller 1994: 80), but the unplanned change is nevertheless functional. In the present example it allows people to be understood better, and Keller posits a maxim, 'Talk in such a way that you are not misunderstood' (p. 94).

Croft (2010: 41) points out that one cannot follow Keller's different maxims at the same time, and that if everyone was expressive most of the time, no one would be likely to be noticed, unless being expressive involved being incomprehensible. Instead he argues that 'an individual utterance by a speaker is a mixture of expressive and nonexpressive linguistic forms' and that neither expressiveness nor avoiding misunderstanding is 'a special type of speaker behaviour' but rather 'the normal way of speaking' (p. 41). Croft argues that people construe events differently, that any given situation can be verbalized in multiple different ways, and that '[t]he speaker's choice of words and constructions are (*sic*) based on her prior exposure to and use of those words and constructions in other communicative acts' (p. 11), which will be different from the hearer's knowledge and experience. Moreover, no two experiences or situations being communicated are identical. Consequently linguistic variation is *not* a matter of 'saying the same thing' in different ways. What's more, no choice of words and constructions will 'precisely characterize the construal of the experience being communicated anyway' (p. 12). Speakers may attempt to express finer-grained construals of events, resulting in constructions that appear to be more elaborate or periphrastic but without intending to be especially 'expressive.' Thus linguistic change arises naturally as a consequence of the indeterminacy of construals of experience and of language. This argument may well be true, but it does not preclude the possibility that people might *also* attempt to be expressive and/or avoid being understood.

3.3.4 Optimizing Grammar

The logic that changes in a language can be the unintended, cumulative outcomes of numerous intentional individual actions extends far beyond changing word meanings and eliminating homophony. A strong argument can be made for speakers' choices leading to grammatical structures becoming adapted to the needs of language users. Languages show structural variation in most areas of grammar, and language change results from differential variation, or shifts in the relative frequencies of use of variant structures, which in turn is primarily a function of their usefulness, or 'user optimality' (Haspelmath 1999a). Speakers tend to choose those variants that suit them best, with the result that high-frequency structures become entrenched in speakers' minds, and may even become obligatory, whereas dis-preferred, low-frequency variants fall out of use.

Thus without speakers intending to change their language, over the long term their aggregated choices can lead to a 'more adapted' grammar. The evolution of linguistic structures is 'Lamarckian' as acquired features (preferred structures) are passed on to (and 'inherited' by) the next generation as part of a 'population' of utterances (Haspelmath 1999a: 193).

Hawkins (2012: 623) argues that '[g]rammars have conventionalized syntactic structures in proportion to their degree of preference in performance, as evidenced by patterns of selection in corpora and by ease and efficiency of processing in psycholinguistic experiments.' Efficiency involves delivering an intended message rapidly, with minimal processing effort required on the part of the hearer. Moreover, acts of communication between speaker and hearer 'are generally optimally efficient; those that are not occur in proportion to their degree of efficiency' (2014: 35), and 'the preferred word orders that are selected by users in languages with freedom appear to be those that are grammaticalized in languages with less freedom and with more fixed and basic orderings' (2012: 623).

Hawkins argues that speakers' grammatical preferences are based on principles of efficiency (or least effort) and the avoidance of complexity. Complexity is a function of the amount of structure associated with the terminal elements or words of a sentence, and efficiency is increased by minimizing the number of words that must be processed and parsed before a syntactic and semantic representation can be assigned. In short the principles are 'Express the most with the least' (or 'Minimize forms' and 'Minimize domains'), and 'Express it earliest' (or 'Maximize On-line Processing') (Hawkins 2004: 25). For example, the sentence *The man looked for his son in the dark and derelict building* is easier to process than *The man looked in the dark and derelict building for his son* (Hawkins 2014: 12) because the verb and the two prepositional phrases can be recognized in fewer words in the former, thus making fewer demands on working memory. Similarly it is easier to process *It would be a good thing for ELF researchers to engage with criticisms of their views rather than just ignoring them* than *Rather than just ignoring them, for ELF researchers to engage with criticisms of their views would be a good thing*.

Hawkins argues that speakers generally try to avoid temporarily ambiguous 'garden path' structures, even though, contrary to verb-final languages, the SVO syntax of English gives rise to temporary ambiguities, as in '*While Mary was reading the book* fell down' and '*The candidate expected to win* lost' (2014: 139).[9] In fact Hawkins (2012: 625–6) shows that many of the changes that English has undergone over the centuries have actually produced *greater* lexical and syntactic ambiguity, with the result that '[c]ommon forms or structures can now be mapped onto a wider range of meanings and meaning types than was possible in Old English, and than is possible in Modern German.' The range of possible interpretations is greater because the surface forms of the language are less explicit and less constrained than they used to be, necessitating appeals to context and more processing effort. But this is compensated for by the fact that there are fewer components to process, which reduces processing effort, so there is a trade-off between ease of form processing and form-to-meaning mapping.

For poetic purposes, the logic of processing efficiency can obviously flouted be,[10] but in everyday language there is, as Hawkins (2014: 48) puts it, 'a preference for selecting and arranging linguistic forms so as to provide the earliest possible access to as much of the ultimate syntactic and semantic representation as possible.'[11] At some point in the history of English, for example, the Old English Object—Verb word order must have coexisted with the newer Verb—Object order, with the latter eventually being chosen for pragmatic (or processing) reasons (cf. Faarlund 1989).

In *The Descent of Man*, Darwin (1871: 60) argued that language evolved by the same kind of natural selection as biological evolution and endorsed the German philologist Max Müller's claim:

> A struggle for life is constantly going on among the words and grammatical forms in each language. The better, the shorter, the easier forms are constantly gaining the upper hand, and they owe their success to their own inherent virtue.

Labov (2001: 9) quotes this, but only to argue (p. 10) that '[t]here is general agreement among 20th-century linguists that language does not show an evolutionary pattern in the sense of progressive adaptation to communicative needs. He then quotes a number of 19th-century philologists (including Müller) who argued that language change, or at least sound change, is destructive, maladaptive, dysfunctional, barbarous, and so on.[12] Yet Haspelmath's and Hawkins's accounts of the selection of forms according to usefulness, and ease and efficiency of processing, *do* seem to show an adaptation to needs (and hence 'inherent virtue').

In short, *pace* Lass, it can be shown that in many instances speakers' selections from a 'population' of utterances *do* seem to involve purpose. Speakers make deliberate choices, and sometimes the cumulative result is language change.

3.4 ELF as Purposeful Language Change

Having established that there are many reasons why people might change the way they speak, or speak differently from some other speakers of the same language, it is time to return to speakers of ELF. As outlined in Chapter 1, ELF is a language with no native speakers and hence no native-speaking community whose ways of speaking have to be adhered to. This gives speakers greater leeway than in most other language varieties and communicative contexts. Of the purposeful acts described above, trying to be expressive, using what seem to be optimally comprehensible constructions, and seeking to avoid misunderstanding, can obviously all be part of an ELF speaker's armoury, while equally obviously, obeying prescriptivist injunctions does not apply.

It appears that in the attempt to be optimally intelligible to other L2 speakers, some ELF users have effected conscious, deliberate, functionally motivated lexicogrammatical changes from L1 English usages to which they are almost certainly also exposed (in education, in the media, etc.). As outlined in Chapter 1, Mauranen (2012: 29) describes ELF as a site of 'second-order language contact'—a contact between hybrids, that is, contact varieties or similects resulting from crosslinguistic transfer from particular L1s. The special features of these similects come together in ELF rather like dialects in contact.[13] As one would expect the innovative or hybrid forms that have diffused into common ELF usage are those that are found in many similects. These are essentially simplifications or 'corrections' of the more incongruous and idiosyncratic elements of English grammar which differ from the majority of natural languages and thus appear odd or afunctional to most L2 speakers. Some examples include the following:

1) the sporadic non-use of the communicatively redundant *third-person singular -s* inflection in an otherwise unmarked verb tense
2) the use of regularized past and participle forms of verbs (*bringed, feeled, fighted, losed, teached*, etc.)
3) the use of stative verbs as well as dynamic ones in the progressive form (*I'm understanding, are belonging to*, etc.)
4) the use of uncountable nouns as pluralizable count nouns (*advices, feedbacks, furnitures, informations, luggages*, etc.)
5) the use of past-time adverbials (*yesterday, last year*, etc.) with the present perfect
6) the use of the present simple instead of the present perfect to express duration (*I am here for/since three years*)
7) the use of new explicit prepositional verbs (*to answer to* [a question], *contact with, criticize about, demand for, discuss about, emphasize on, enter into* [a place], *explain about, mention about, phone to, reject against, request for, return back*, etc.)[14]

These usages can easily be explained in terms of L1 transfer or grammatical replication as well as by various psycholinguistic processes that are generally active in L2 acquisition: simplification, regularization, overgeneralization, underdifferentiation, analogical extension or levelling, reconceptualization, the minimization of redundancy, and its opposite—increased clarity and explicitness by the exploitation of redundancy,[15] and so on. More than one of these factors or causes could be at play in each instance: as already argued, linguistic change generally involves multiple causation. All of these usages are also found in many nativized New English varieties.[16]

In expanding circle countries, it is evident that learners are *not* presented with models that abandon the third-person singular *-s* inflection and do away with non-count nouns, the restriction of the progressive to dynamic verbs, the distinctions between the present, the past, and the perfect, and so on. Speakers who use these constructions have certainly been exposed to the standard forms as well, both in and outside the classroom. Teachers all know that learners appropriate language selectively so that their 'intake' or 'uptake' never corresponds with teacher input (otherwise EFL learners would all be speaking native-like English). As Seidlhofer (2011: 186) puts it, 'What is achieved, and put to use in ELF, is clearly not the English that has been taught, but the English that has been learnt.' Even if learners' attention is not drawn to what in EFL terms are common errors of countability and aspect in elementary classes, it certainly is in advanced classes, particularly those preparing learners for international English examinations. The fluent and formerly self-confident university students who complain 'I thought I was good at English until I took this course' (Erling 2002: 11) *have* been exposed to standard forms but often continue to use their non-standard version of the tense and aspect system, certainly outside the classroom.

As mentioned in the last chapter, this could be because learners simply do not *notice* some of the standard forms as a result of what Ellis calls rational contingency learning or automatically learned inattention. Or it could be because learners most readily learn what they 'intuitively recognize as having the greatest inherent valency, the most potential for exploitation' and 'what is most conceptually salient or communicatively usable' (Seidlhofer 2011: 187) while disregarding elements that appear 'surplus to communicative requirement' (p. 188). This would make the use of non-standard forms a matter of overgeneralization, underdifferentiation, and imperfect learning, as discussed in the previous chapter. But it could also be a matter of *choice*, of speakers being perfectly aware of the standard forms, but electing not to use them, to make themselves more readily comprehensible to non-native interlocutors. As Lass (1997: 368) says, '[A] great deal of linguistic structure does not respond to "speakers' needs" in any intelligible way; it's simply there.' Except that in ELF it often isn't; speakers purposefully use non-standard forms instead, thereby removing what appear to be unnecessary redundancies, irregularities, complications, and structural distinctions found in native English grammar. These forms spread as people unconsciously accommodate to each others' uses or imitate other speakers in conscious acts of identity. This goes far beyond the usual L2 inability to acquire what Hulstijn calls the Basic Language Cognition of L1 speakers.

Importantly the innovations attested in the New Englishes and various ELF similects circumvent what Weinreich et al. (1968: 102) call the *actuation problem* inherent in functional accounts of language change: if a change in a structural feature that takes place in a particular language at a given time has a functional motivation, why doesn't it occur simultaneously in other languages with the same feature, or indeed why wasn't it actuated sooner? Clearly the changes outlined here are not necessary per se—native English speakers have not made them—and as Lass (1980: 131) puts it, if any language change *were* necessary, 'it would have happened everywhere, and we wouldn't know about it.' But they equally obviously have functional utility for L2 English speakers. It can safely be assumed that speakers of ELF similects are speaking English in much the same way that speakers of their L1 did in the past, even though there used to be fewer L2 English speakers. The difference is that in the days when ELF was known as EFL, these speakers would probably not have had the insouciance and self-confidence that come with what Firth (2009) calls the 'lingua franca outlook.'

Analysis of attested, innovative (or at least non-native) usages of speakers of New Englishes and ELF also sidesteps the problem that explanations of language change often account for dissemination rather than innovation. It is often taken for granted that novel variants already exist *somewhere*, perhaps in 'a restricted subgroup of the speech community' (Labov 1972: 178), or in another social network with which a speaker has weak ties (Milroy and Milroy 1985), so that as Croft (2000: 55, 185) points out, the Milroys' 'innovator' is in fact merely a transmitter or an introducer of an innovative form to a new network.

Thus contrary to the argument that most linguistic changes are essentially unmotivated, generally diffuse below the level of conscious awareness, and do not necessarily have any social significance,[17] it seems that many 'ELF innovations' may indeed be intentional. It seems plausible that a certain proportion of ELF speakers *are* aware that their usages differ from those of native English speakers and that they purposely use their 'ELF variants' because they believe them to have functional (communicative, discursive) advantages, including explicitness, clarity, and the avoidance of misunderstanding. Although most innovation and accommodation in ELF is online, pragmatic, local, and contingent, and certainly not carried out with the teleological aim of improving the language, intentional usages employed by many individuals *can* be diffused and adopted by wider speech communities. Whether such changes are likely to spread to native English is the subject of the next chapter.

Notes

1 This wholly neglects all the evidence that languages spoken by isolated speech communities tend to become more and more complex, whereas those that are used for 'exoteric' or inter-group communication, and consequently learned by post-adolescents and adults, tend to become simplified (Trudgill 1989, 2011; Wray and Grace 2007); see Chapter 4.

2 Jakobson was specifically writing about phonological change.
3 Rejected alternative explanations, in a very thorough analysis, include *weil* taking on new pragmatic functions, contact with Sorbian or Yiddish or with *Gastarbeiter* with imperfectly learned German, and the spread of a particular regional dialect.
4 Poplack et al. discuss Quebecois French, but there is more extensive use of preposition stranding in the French spoken on Prince Edward Island on Canada's Atlantic coast, with more prepositions involved than the four identified by Poplack et al. For example, King (2000:139) reports *Je cherche une fille à avoir confiance en* (I'm looking for a girl to have confidence in [trust]) and *Marie a été parlé à* (Marie has been spoken to), and Corrigan (2010: 117–8) quotes *Le gars que je te parle de* (the guy I am talking to you about) and *Le gars que j'ai donné la job à* (the guy I've given the job to). Here the influence of English seems rather harder to deny. King argues that the huge number of lexical borrowings into Prince Edward Island French 'have triggered particular language-internal changes, resulting in the emergence of a number of structural changes' (p. 173). See also Mougeon and Beniak (1991, Chs. 9–11).
5 In a less radical mood, Thomason (2008: 52) adds a caveat: 'it is still the case that the great majority of linguistic changes seem to be unconscious, not deliberate.' Yet like the authors of most books on language contact (e.g., Thomason and Kaufman 1988; Croft 2000; Thomason 2001; Myers-Scotton 2002; Winford 2003; Matras 2009; etc.), she has also described purposefully developed mixed languages, defying most of the principles of typological and historical-linguistic theory, that clearly demonstrate the possibility of deliberately changing a language, such as Michif (a mixture of Métis Canadian French and the Algonquin language Cree), the Ecuadorian Media Lengua (a mixture of Spanish and Quecha), and Mednyj Aleut on Bering Island (a mixture of Aleut and Russian), not to mention pidgins, creoles, and koinés.
6 This is Mark Singer (1977/2002), quoted in Davidson (1986/2005: 89), imitating the radio comedy writer Ace Goodman.
7 That is, the three options are, for example, *the book that I'm reading*, *the book which I'm reading*, and *the book I'm reading*.
8 Croft (2000: 62) disputes Keller's analysis and argues that a 'social selection process' (imitation of other speakers) is a much more likely reason for the propagation of the new form than a desire not to be misunderstood. But imitation could also involve a desire not to be misunderstood.
9 Speakers also tend to avoid sentences with very complex syntactic structures. Dąbrowska (1997) shows that the type of sentences often used as examples in articles about generative grammar (e.g., *It was King Louis who the general convinced that this slave might speak to*) are both hard to find outside articles about generative grammar and incomprehensible to quite a lot of (less educated) speakers.
10 For example, Milton was not thinking about maximizing online processing at the beginning of *Paradise Lost* ('Of Man's first disobedience'), where the main verb 'sing, Heavenly Muse' comes in the sixth line. In the 1970s, the American literary theorist Stanley Fish argued that readers of literature read and interpret one word at a time and therefore make many fleeting (mis)interpretations, all of which are a crucial part of the literary or poetic reading experience. His first example, from Thomas Browne's *Religio Medici* (1643) is '[t]hat Judas perished by hanging himself, there is no certainty in scripture' (Fish 1981: 23). Fish suggests that after reading the first six words, the reader is prepared—'less than consciously'—for constructions like '*is* (an example to us all),' '*shows* (how conscious he was of the enormity of his sin),'

and '*should* (give us pause),' and so on. The range of possibilities narrows considerably after the next three words are read, and Fish states that 'the reader' (at least if the reader is Stanley Fish) is expecting 'there is no [. . .] doubt' but instead finds 'certainty,' and so on.

11 See also Haiman (1985), who suggests that grammatical form often involves iconicity, reflecting the structures of experience, with syntactic structures that are simple one-to-one mappings of conceptual structure, although there are also contrary tendencies that pull languages away from this; and Givón, who proposes an 'iconicity meta-principle' that 'a coded experience is easier to *store*, *retrieve* and *communicate* if the code is maximally isomorphic to the experience' (1985: 189), and a 'proximity principle' (1994: 51) according to which elements that are closer together functionally, conceptually, or cognitively are normally placed closer together in the sentence.

12 Darwin slightly altered his quotation from Müller; see Müller (1870: 257).

13 Trudgill (2004) outlines a similar process in the formation of new colonial dialects (in Australia, New Zealand, South Africa, etc.) by way of dialect mixing. Children were faced with a hugely variable set of models, with no single peer-group model to accommodate to. Eventually a new dialect appeared, largely consisting of those variants that were most widely shared in the mixture.

14 See Erling (2002); Cogo and Dewey (2006, 2012); Ranta (2006); Breiteneder (2009); Nesselhauf (2009); Seidlhofer (2011); Mauranen (2012). See also MacKenzie (2014b, Ch. 4) and the references therein. Other 'unfocused' aspects of 'ELF grammar,' not always attributable to specific similects, include the very varied use of prepositions, articles, plurals, and verb complementation patterns (the varied use of infinitives and gerunds without what in native English are governed or grammaticalized prepositions, etc.). Another common 'ELF usage' is 'fronting' or 'left dislocation' (Mauranen 2012: 191–2), which is one of Lightfoot's examples of a structure used for expressive purposes. It could also be described in terms of Hawkins's account of ease and efficiency of processing.

15 There is no contradiction here: reduced redundancy involves the omission of inflections and distinctions that are not salient to non-native speakers; increased explicitness (such as adding prepositions by analogy with other verbs) is only redundant from a native speaker viewpoint.

16 See Platt et al. (1984); Williams (1987); Schmied (1991); Brutt-Griffler (2002); Kortmann et al. (2004); Trudgill and Hannah (2008); Kachru and Smith (2008); Szmrecsanyi and Kortmann (2009); Kortmann and Lunkenheimer (2013).

17 This is more likely to be true of *phonological* changes than structural ones. For example, there is an ongoing trend in British English to pronounce words such as *collect*, *connect*, *select*, and *police* as one syllable, completely dropping the unstressed schwa vowel (resulting in /klekt/, /knekt/, /slekt/ and /plis/), a phonetic reduction that goes unnoticed by most speakers and certainly does not involve conscious decisions or considerations of social meaning.

4 Will English as a Lingua Franca Impact on Native English?

Given that L2 speakers of English now hugely outnumber the language's native speakers, many researchers expect the kinds of English used as a lingua franca to influence native English. For example, Seidlhofer (2003: 7) has asserted that 'it is the non-native speakers of English who will be the main agents in the ways English is used, is maintained, and changes,' while Mauranen (2012: 33) argues that 'it is reasonable to expect the sheer scale of ELF use to have an effect on the English language.' Mauranen describes current ELF speakers as the 'first generation' following the 'explosive expansion' of English use that coincided with the rise of the Internet in the mid-1990s and suggests that 'by the time the third generation learns English, we may expect English already to show clear traces of lingua franca influence' (p. 33). All in all, she says, 'it would be surprising' if ELF did not 'have a significant impact on ENL communities' (p. 57).

In this chapter I will consider the psycholinguistic and sociolinguistic mechanisms that might lead to—or prevent—ELF usages being disseminated among native English speakers. It certainly appears that non-native acquisition significantly changed English in the past: English in Britain has a long history of language contact and language shift, with Celts, Scandinavians, and Normans adding to and subtracting from the language, as a result of transfer and imperfect learning, with the Anglo-Saxon population imitating their usages. It is also generally assumed that, other things being equal, processes that produced language change in the past are likely to be occurring in the present and to continue to occur in the future. In this instance, however, I will argue that circumstances have changed and that, *pace* Seidlhofer, the main agents in the ways *native* English 'is used, is maintained, and changes,' are likely to be its native speakers.

4.1 English as a Contact Language

As outlined in Chapter 2, post-puberty and adult language learners generally prefer regularity and transparency to irregularity and opacity. They find things like inflections and grammatical gender and agreement hard to learn, so they tend to simplify or indeed pidginize (Trudgill 2011: 35) the language they're learning by regularizing irregularities, increasing morphological transparency, and reducing redundancy. In particular they have a tendency to replace synthetic structures involving declensions and conjugations with periphrastic analytic ones. A fully analytic construction has a transparent, one-to-one mapping of meaning units and forms, using separate words to express different concepts and a fixed word order. For example, *let's go* is more analytic than the Spanish *vámonos*; *more healthy* is more analytic than *healthier*; and 'To those who were never defeated—we who have been conquered shall one day conquer for them'[1] is rather more analytic than the Latin *invictus victi victuri*. If sufficiently large numbers of adults learn a language in a country in which it is spoken, their simplified analytic constructions can end up being disseminated among native speakers. This process has demonstrably occurred in English, as well as in 'most of the major standard language varieties in Europe today' (Trudgill 2011: 67), as a consequence of language contact.

The first person to describe this consequence of language learning may have been Adam Smith, in *Considerations Concerning the First Formation of Languages and the Different Genius of Original and Compounded Languages*, which appeared as an addendum to *The Theory of Moral Sentiments* in 1759 (see Coseriu 1983). Although Smith is famous among economists (and notorious among anti-free-marketeers), and his concept of the 'invisible hand' has been used in explanations of language change (notably by Keller—see Chapter 3), his essay on language is very rarely quoted.

Smith distinguishes between primitive, simple, original, or uncompounded languages, which use inflection (declension and conjugation), and compounded languages, which use 'composition,' today usually called periphrasis (separate words to express grammatical relationships). As examples of composition he cites the use of prepositions instead of inflections to express case, and the use of auxiliary verbs. Nearly 60 years later, in the much better-known *Observations sur la langue et littérature provençales* (1818), A. W. Schlegel proposed the alternative terms synthetic and analytic for Smith's uncompounded and compounded languages, and gave further examples of periphrastic analytic grammatical forms, including articles, personal pronouns with verbal forms, and the use of adverbs for the comparatives of adjectives.

Smith (1759/1853: 535) wrote (from an understandably Eurocentric perspective) that

> every case of every noun, and every tense of every verb, was originally expressed by a particular distinct word, which served for this purpose and for no other. But succeeding observation discovered, that one set of words was capable of supplying the place of all that

> infinite number, and that four or five prepositions, and half a dozen auxiliary verbs, were capable of answering the end of all the declensions and of all the conjugations in the ancient languages.

This discovery was made by adults obliged to learn foreign languages, following 'the mixture of different nations [. . .] by conquest or migration' (p. 530).[2] As Smith says, in what is a linguistic commonplace today, 'As long as any language was spoken by those only who learned it in their infancy, the intricacy of its declensions and conjugations could occasion no great embarrassment.' Whereas people who slowly acquire a native language are 'scarce ever sensible of the difficulty,' this is not the case with adults, who generally learn foreign languages imperfectly. As Smith puts it, adults learning a new language 'by rote, and by what they commonly heard in conversation, would be extremely perplexed by the intricacy of its declensions and conjugations' and would endeavour to avoid them 'by whatever shift the language could afford them,' notably prepositions (p. 530), which 'in this manner seem to have been introduced in the room of the ancient declensions (p. 531). Smith gives the example of a Lombard trying to say in Latin that someone was a citizen of Rome without knowing the genitive and dative cases of the word *Roma*, and hence using the prepositions *ad* and *de* with the nominative instead (as indeed Italians do today), and saying *ad Roma* and *de Roma* rather than *Romæ*. Smith also gives examples of the introduction of periphrastic verbal forms, for instance, a Lombard who wanted to say *I had loved*, but couldn't recollect the word (or verb form) *amaveram*, and so used the verb *habere* (have) instead, and said either *ego habebam amatum* or *ego habui amatum* (p. 531).[3]

Smith doesn't just describe the progress of analyticity, but disparages it, arguing that the simplification of inflection renders languages 'more and more imperfect, and less proper for many of the purposes of language,' making them more prolix and more monotonous because of the more constrained word order and the smaller variety of word endings (p. 535). So it goes. Rather than the Lombards, Schlegel (1818: 24–5) suggests that it was the later Barbaric conquerors of the Roman lands who misused case endings and that the local populations, hearing the badly spoken Latin of their new rulers, imitated it. He also argues that languages have a natural tendency to become analytic even without migration or conquest, citing the differences between Homeric and classical Greek, and Gothic and German (p. 18).[4]

Notwithstanding any 'natural tendencies' in language change, there is a long history of contact-based change in English (and in all the other languages spoken natively in the British Isles for the past 2,000 years). Although Smith stated that '[t]he English is compounded of the French and the ancient Saxon languages' (p. 534), this is not the whole story. (In fact the Norman French influence on English is almost entirely lexical and orthographical, not structural.) Leaving aside the question of what proportion of the British population shifted from a Celtic language (Brittonic or Brythonic) to Latin (Late Spoken Latin) during four centuries of Roman occupation,[5] there are many reasons to believe that speakers of later Celtic languages (Cornish and Welsh), who gradually assimilated to Anglo-Saxon culture, transferred Celtic syntactic constructions to Old English. This would have happened over several generations, sometime after the sixth century, especially in the western and northern regions furthest from the Anglo-Saxon heartlands. Examples of probable substratum influence notably include periphrastic *do* or *do*-support and the progressive form.

Cornish, Welsh, and Gaelic have a construction with the equivalent of *do*, used as a semantically empty syntactic place filler indicating tense, and a verbal noun. Evidence of periphrastic *do* first appears in English in 13th-century texts, beginning in the South-west (the region closest to the neighbouring Celtic languages), but it may have existed in vernacular registers for several centuries, originating as a transfer from Cornish that was considered too colloquial or inelegant to be suitable for the written language. From the 14th century onwards, periphrastic *do* was used in affirmative declaratives, negative declaratives, and questions (Filppula et al. 2008: 57ff). Although it is still used in negatives and interrogatives, since the 18th century it has been used only in affirmative sentences as an intensifier. It is argued that the use of *do* in negatives and interrogatives, which displaces the main verb after the subject (*why do you use this word order?* rather than *why use you this word order?*) aided the change from Old English's SOV order in subordinate clauses (and frequent VS order elsewhere) to the SVO order that became standard in Middle English (McWhorter 2011: 279). Using *do* (even though it had more inflections then than now) removes the need to conjugate the main verb, which would have simplified English for Celtic speakers learning the language. It is similarly suggested that the (periphrastic) English progressive with *be* + the *ing* verb form derives from the Brythonic construction of copula verb + preposition *yn* + verbal noun (Filppula et al. 2008: 27, 60).

In cases of language shift, children learn their parents' imperfectly acquired L2 as their L1 and subsequently transmit this simplified grammar to the next generation. If there is a large enough number of non-native speakers shifting to a new language, native speakers are likely to accommodate to simplified aspects of the non-native variety, which are thereby transferred to the native variety. As Thomason and Kaufman (1988: 43) put it, the target language 'is not so much accepting the changes as giving in to them.' Of course attitudinal factors can come into play, 'but such attitudes do not seem to protect a [target language] from interference if the shifting group is numerically strong.'

In England the Germanic immigrants, who were heavily outnumbered by the Celts or Romano-Britons,[6] would appear to have ended up imitating a number of their usages. Tristram (1999) points out that early language contact and the shift from Brythonic to English has been supplemented by continuous contact with Welsh speakers ever since, with geographical mobility and loose-knit, open-network ties along the Welsh-English border. She argues that speakers of Celtic languages triggered what must be seen as a typological change in English from a predominantly synthetic language to a predominantly analytic one. Thus present-day English can be described as 'a "Celticised" West-Germanic language' (Tristram (1999: 30), a regularized and simplified high-contact koiné (Trudgill 2011: 67), or a semi-creole (McWhorter 2011: 295). Filppula et al. (2008: 24) point out that the pattern of extensive societal bilingualism with considerable L2 transfer before the Celts in England shifted to English sometime before the 10th century or so was repeated more recently when there was a shift from Celtic languages to English in most of Wales, Scotland, and Ireland. As well as periphrastic constructions like *do*-support and the progressive, today both English and the Celtic languages have a preference for a nominal style with light verbs (*have a think*, *take a walk*), analytically formed prepositional and phrasal verbs, relative clauses with stranded prepositions, and the internal possessor construction (the use of possessive pronouns rather than the definite article for body parts, etc.—e.g., *she's washing her hair*, rather than *the* hair).

There are many other differences between Old and Modern English (or between Modern English and all the other Germanic languages) that can also be described as simplifications. These include the *absence* of grammatical gender marking on articles, pronouns, nouns, and adjectives; of inflectional case marking; of inherent reflexivity marking (e.g., English *to remember* vs. German *sich erinnern*, 'to remember yourself'); of directionally marked adverbs (such as the former *hither* and *thither*); of the second-person singular *thou* pronoun; and of V2 word order, that is, placing finite verbs in second position of a declarative main clause (McWhorter 2007, Ch. 4). It has been widely suggested that these simplifications are also the result of non-native acquisition (see McWhorter 2007, Filppula et al. 2008, and the references therein).

So far, so good—where disagreement arises concerns the respective roles of the Celts and Scandinavians. Trudgill (2011: 34) argues that the simplification of Old English into Middle English must have resulted from contact with the Brittonic Celtic language (or languages), because later Anglo-Saxon/Norse bilingualism would logically have complexified English rather than simplified it, as this was a case of long-term contact involving territorial co-habitation, intermarriage, and child bilingualism. Because children are capable of acquiring languages perfectly however complex they are, in cases of bilingualism resulting from language contact, they can make them more complex still. As Trudgill puts it,

> simplification is actually not normal. If it were normal, all languages in the world would by now have been maximally regular and

> maximally transparent. [. . .] [I]t is actually complexification that is, in an important sense, more normal. If languages are 'left alone,' the natural tendency is for them to accrue more and more complexity [. . .] not to simplify.
>
> (p. 152)[7]

McWhorter (2011), on the contrary, argues that the Celts maintained their languages for generations and acquired English gradually, infusing it with Celtic features along the way, whereas the Scandinavian Vikings—largely males who practiced exogamy—needed to function in Old English almost as soon as they invaded. However, they only acquired (and passed on to their children) a functional but approximate and incomplete version of the language. Old English and Old Norse had similar phonetic and morphological patterns, many parallel grammatical structures, and many cognate words. But specific forms (such as verb conjugations and gender attributions in the noun phrase) often conflicted. It may have been the case that omitting certain grammatical features did not impede communication. Hence mutual accommodation between speakers of two languages with an adstratal rather than a superstratal or substratal relation led to convergence and koinéization and a linguacultural fusion of Angles and Danes in the north of England, in which English lost various grammatical features, including some that it shared with Old Norse.

For present purposes it doesn't matter whether the contact-induced simplifications in English during this period were the work of the Celts, or the Vikings, or both; the point is that they seem to have occurred,[8] making present-day spoken English the result of many centuries of contact-based simplification.[9] Indeed, given the multiplication of high-contact situations in recent centuries, *most* major contemporary languages bear the mark of post-childhood second language acquisition; as Trudgill (2011: 169) puts it (notwithstanding the uniformitarian principle), '[T]he dominant standard modern languages in the world today are likely to be seriously atypical of how languages have been for nearly all of human history.' Elsewhere Trudgill (2005: 87) has written, wryly, that 'even if native speakers do not "own" English, there is an important sense in which it stems from them, especially historically' (!), although to the consternation of ELF theorists, he continued 'and resides in them.' But it appears that English as we have it today also partly stems, historically, from the Celts, the Vikings, and other L2 learners too.

4.2 The Propagation of Innovations

Thus it seems likely that English in Britain was long ago modified quite significantly by extensive non-native acquisition. And there is no reason to suppose that the well-documented cognitive factors at play in L2 acquisition will cease to have their effects on L2 speakers of English. But one obvious difference between the current situation and the language contact of the Middle Ages is that the vast majority of today's English learners are not living in Britain. The non-native speakers of English and speakers of nativized New English varieties who greatly outnumber native English speakers in the world today are (logically, if not by definition) mostly *not* living in inner circle English-speaking countries.

Moreover, most ELF usage most likely takes place in the absence of native English speakers. Thomason (2001: 21) states that most users of ELF 'have no opportunity (and often no desire) to practice by talking to native speakers of English,' while Jenkins (2006: 161) describes native English speakers as a 'small minority' in intercultural communication, so presumably most of them must be spending most of their time at home in the inner circle countries. When she still used the term 'English as an International Language' (EIL) rather than ELF, Jenkins even suggested that this variety would need to be incorporated into the secondary school curriculum in inner circle countries, whereas '[f]or those who have already reached adulthood, it will be necessary to attend adult EIL classes in the same way that "NNS" [non-native speaker, in scare quotes] adults do.' But if international English is different enough to require native English speakers to *study* it, and if they rarely encounter 'international' or ELF variants, how or why will they imitate them? Language change via accommodation and diffusion is generally held to require wide-scale, protracted, intensive, naturalistic, face-to-face interaction, and there is a critical threshold for the *awareness*—or perhaps just the unconscious perception—of new features.

I will first discuss the principle of density in language change, as well as the possible role of the media in diffusing innovations, and then consider expressivity and prestige as motives for adopting new ways of speaking, and lastly the language acquisition patterns of children exposed to different 'lects.'

4.2.1 Density

Both Bloomfield (1933: 476) and Labov (2001: 19) posit a principle of density, such that the diffusion of change can be explained mechanically by the amount and frequency of communication. The more frequently people interact with each other, the more similar their speech will be. It's all about who talks most often to whom, with social evaluations and attitudes towards innovations playing a minor role.[10] It seems unlikely that inner circle speakers of English today experience a sufficient amount of ELF/ESL-ENL communication to reach that density. (There are, e.g., more than 800,000 Polish-born people living in Britain today, which is probably about 10 times the number of Vikings in England in the ninth and 10th centuries, but being quite widely dispersed among a population of more than 65 million, they will *not* influence the English language the way the Norse settlers did.)

Furthermore, although it's possible to identify a number of widely diffused innovative ELF forms, shared by speakers of many L1s (and hence common to many ELF 'similects'), they exist alongside a huge amount of fairly random variation, which diminishes the probability of specific forms being diffused. As already mentioned, variability in a native language is now generally assumed to be a form of 'orderly' or 'structured heterogeneity' (Weinreich et al. 1968), in which variants are conventionally associated with social values that determine their appropriate use in different situations and discourse types. Hearers perceive or recognize particular variants as encoding social as well as semantic information. Particular forms can index a speaker's age, gender, ethnicity, socioeconomic class, level of education, regional origin, and so on. Native-like command is taken to include the evaluation and use of heterogeneous structures and sensitivity to contexts of use. However, this is often *not* the case in ELF, in which speakers generally do not replicate native users' contextually determined style shifting (although competent users *do* use forms appropriate to specific ELF speech interactions). Whereas some ELF speakers systematically use the widely diffused forms described at the end of the previous chapter, others are much less consistent in their linguistic choices. They use a seemingly random range of variants, with different degrees of conformity to the preferred expressions of the native language, and to those of their supposed L2 contact variety or similect, as a result of what Mauranen (2012: 41, 217) calls the fuzzy processing and shaky entrenchment to be expected in a second language. Consequently, given the wide range of L1-influenced similects, as well as speakers whose usages are less consistent than the logic of similects would suggest, native English speakers often experience ENL-ELF interactions as a form of multiple dialect contact rather than the coming together of a standard native variety and a potentially imitable non-native one.

Another reason to doubt that ELF-ENL communication will reach a density that might lead to the diffusion of ELF innovations is that most ELF (or ESL) users who spend any length of time in an ENL environment are more likely to try to adhere to Keller's maxim of talking like the people around them than to try to 'express both their L1 identity and membership of the international ELF community' (Jenkins 2007: 25). The same applies to migrating speakers of nativized New English varieties, but *not* to tourists, short-term exchange students, and so on. ('Any length of time' doesn't literally mean *any* length of time!) Cogo and Dewey (2012: 43) have based a number of conclusions on a corpus recorded in a 'community of practice' of foreign language teachers living and working in London.[11] Although this community does indeed appear to constitute an ELF setting in an inner circle country in which native speakers are 'no longer the norm providers' (Cogo and Jenkins 2010: 275), Cogo and Dewey (2006: 78) also suggest that L2 speakers tend to accommodate much more to native uses when (perhaps due to some 'unplanned and unavoidable occurrence') an L1 English speaker is present. Many other professionals in inner circle countries *do* feel the need to conform to native English norms (and ask their native English-speaking colleagues to proofread their written communications). As Ferguson (2012: 179) suggests, '[W]hat counts as an effective use of linguistic resources in an ELF context in Bratislava, say, may [. . .] attract different, less favourable evaluations, when used, say, in a formal presentation to a mixed American/international audience in New York.'

4.2.2 *The Media*

All in all, although most native English speakers probably *are* exposed to L2 usages, the average Briton or American or Australian today probably hears far less non-native English than, say, the Anglo-Saxons in the seventh to 10th centuries who were exposed to the L2 English of speakers of Cornish, Welsh, or Old Norse. Moreover—and crucially—the conditions that led to the simplification of English in the seventh to 10th centuries no longer exist. As McWhorter (2011: 17) stresses, languages that were simplified when their transmission was 'interrupted' by incomplete non-native acquisition were largely used orally at a time when reading and writing were 'elite activities.'[12] The epoch of simplification stemming from extensive L2 acquisition preceded 'widespread literacy, education, and language standardization.' Today, on the contrary, the standard native version of the English language 'is always available and influential in print, the media, and schools.' Native English speakers in the inner circle countries are very unlikely to be exposed to more non-standard ELF and ESL usage than to spoken, written, or broadcast manifestations of the standard language. Consequently, as McWhorter says, today 'a highly complex language can survive endless waves of second-language acquisition intact' (p. 17).

To be sure L2 English is also to be found in the media, but linguists who believe that the diffusion of innovations requires face-to-face interaction and accommodation logically downplay the potential role of electronic media in language change (see Trudgill 1986: 40; Chambers 1998; Labov 2001: 228). One might occasionally shout abuse at people on the television (referees, politicians, or people on reality shows), but no real interaction and certainly no accommodation are taking place. To adapt St Paul, it's the difference between seeing through a glass, darkly, and speaking face-to-face. *Lexical* diffusion does not require interaction (one can learn words from both print and electronic media), but Trudgill insists that phonological and structural change do. He states that television may, at most, play a role in a 'softening-up' process leading to the more rapid adoption of dialect features (1986: 55).

Today native speakers might also encounter varying amounts of *written* L2 English on various websites and communicate with non-native

English-speaking acquaintances via texts, emails, and so on. But Trudgill (2014b: 221) downplays this kind of interaction too, evoking the uniformitarian principle: written media have existed for around 5 percent of language history, at most, and electronic media for perhaps 0.1 percent, so they don't have much explanatory value for language change and the spread of innovations, which have been taking place for as long as there have been languages.

Other linguists grant the media a bigger role. Eckert (2003: 395) suggests that there are innovations that 'can be taken right off the shelf' from exposure to media rather than social interaction. Sayers (2014: 187) argues that emotionally invested engagement with the media can lead to 'parasocial interaction' (p. 187), and the spread of socially attractive innovations, and that we need to add this as 'a codicil to a model based principally on face-to-face contact and network ties' (p. 191). Gunter (2014: 264), drawing on communications and media research, goes further, stating that 'there is every reason to believe that media texts such as movies and television programs can influence the speech behaviours of people in the audience.' But again native English speakers in the inner circle countries are primarily exposed to their own and other native varieties in the media rather than non-native ones.

Although the innovations and variants of L2 speakers are easily explicable—either as the accidental outcome of imperfect learning or as the deliberate disregard of structural features deemed to be communicatively redundant—their replication and dissemination by native speakers would have to involve different reasons. There *would* have to be reasons (if speakers didn't perceive *some* kind of advantage in new forms, they wouldn't use them), and the most plausible candidates are the perception of heightened expressiveness or expressivity and considerations of prestige.

4.2.3 Expressivity

The use of what Harris and Campbell call 'exploratory expressions,' in the quest for increased expressivity or in the attempt to impress interlocutors, was discussed in the previous chapter. Harris and Campbell (1995: 49) insist that '[t]he grammar of an adult can change' and is 'best viewed, not as an inflexible completed object, but as an adaptable, constantly growing set of generalizations.' Similarly Kerswill (1996: 178) states that 'people of all ages can (and do) modify and restructure their language' and continue to acquire additional social and stylistic registers.[13] Linguists who take an adaptive, usage-based view of grammar tend to argue that languages are creatively stretched with use and change, even when they are *not* being widely learned and used as L2s. For example, Hopper (1988: 120) states that grammatical regularities 'are always provisional and are continually subject to negotiation, renovation and abandonment' so that grammar is forever *emergent*, while Hilpert (2013: 2) argues that 'with every new text genre and every additional speaker, more variation enters the picture, and less of an invariant core system remains.' Certainly ELF and the New Englishes have led to an expansion of the feature pool, bringing about what Meyerhoff and Niedzielski (2003: 547) call 'a broadening of the set of forms available to English speakers.'[14]

Kretzschmar (2015) argues that language in use obeys what he calls 'the 80/20 rule,' a hallmark of a complex system. For any linguistic feature one chooses to study—'every imaginable element of the language' (p. 168)—it will be found that one or a few constructions account for the great majority of the instances for the feature—approximately 80%—whereas a large number of lesser-used variant constructions account for the other 20%.[15] Thus the different possible ways of putting words together have a non-linear distribution, and 80% of what can be said is only said rarely. But the rare forms are still part of the language, accounting for about 20% of usage, but about 80% of possible constructions. This gives what Kretzschmar calls an 'A-curve' (for asymptotic hyperbolic curve) for every linguistic feature, which slopes sharply downwards and then tapers off into a long, almost flat tail. Speakers generally perceive the most commonly used forms or top-ranked variants, which make up 80% of usage and are reinforced in linguistic interaction by positive feedback, as normal, expected, grammatical, and acceptable. People tend to belong to various networks, social groups, and communities of practice and use different variants in different settings and situations, which 'is what allows the simultaneous existence of many regional and social patterns in language use, and also many discourse types, all distinguishable on the basis of differential frequency' (p. 152). Because speakers interact in temporary, contingent, and occasionally unpredictable settings, the complex system of speech changes by way of alterations in the frequency of use of different features (so that synchronic A-curves can be mapped onto the standard diachronic S-curve showing successive frequencies of use of a given variant).

Because of the huge amount of variation in language, Kretzschmar describes the idealized and reified 'grammars' proposed by linguists as perceptual or observational artefacts based on the non-linear distributional patterns. So-called grammar rules, arranged in hierarchies, are just generalizations after the fact of usage, arising from people's perceptions of their own language and that of those around them. He thus reinforces Hopper's (1988, 1998) argument that grammar is emergent, in a continual process of becoming, or movement towards a structure that is always deferred, provisional, and epiphenomenal—a secondary effect of the complex system of speech rather than a set of rules that precedes discourse.[16] Because of their rarity, people may perceive some of the low-frequency variants in the long tail—which can be both residual historical forms as well as novel features entering the language—as different, exceptions, ungrammatical, or unacceptable. But they might also perceive any given rare or non-standard usage—including those of ELF speakers—as an attractive novelty and choose to use it 'as a poetic expression, as a periphrasis motivated by the desperation of not finding a more appropriate means of expression, as a way of deliberately producing stylistic oddity or foreign flavour, or for other stylistic reasons or communicative needs' (Harris and Campbell 1995: 54). An expression deriving from ELF speakers picked up in this way by native speakers and widely adopted would come to be reanalyzed as an acceptable part of the grammar (although probably not part of the top-ranked variants making up 80% of usage). In short, although native speakers are very unlikely to see any functional advantage to abandoning, say, delicate nuances of meaning provided by an aspectual system that was many centuries in the making, they might easily pick up on particular non-native variants—different ways of saying 'the same thing'—or particular tokens of particular constructions if they sound more expressive (or impressive) or appear to have a certain stylistic or poetic effect or discourse function.

4.2.4 Prestige

The other main reason to replicate other people's usages is usually described as prestige. This could be what Labov (1966) called *overt prestige*, or imitating the speech of a culturally dominant group, but also the contrary, *covert* or *negative prestige*, or imitating the speech of a non-dominant but socially attractive group. As Milroy (1992: 129) points out, although many people seeking socioeconomic advancement consider it to be in their interests to use standard forms, prestige can also 'be subjectively attached by speakers to forms or varieties which are very distant from, and in conflict with, the codified norms of the standard.'[17] Thus some native speakers could identify with particular groups of ELF speakers and imitate or accommodate to some of their usages in what might be called acts of identity. For example, people who regularly interact with ELF speakers with the same type of job, background, and educational qualifications as themselves could form relatively strong ties with them and imitate some of their ways of speaking English.

Yet the diffusion of linguistic innovations among native speakers does not *necessarily* require large-scale identification with the innovators. According to the Milroys' (1985) account of language change, it is only necessary that a suitably respected or admired member of a social network also has ties (probably weak ones) with another group or network, begins to imitate one of their usages in interactions with his or her own primary network, and is imitated in turn. (This would still require sufficient density of ELF-ENL communication for the influential member of an ENL social network to register ELF usages elsewhere.) As James Milroy (1992: 180–1) puts it, '[M]obile individuals who have contracted many weak ties [. . .] are in a particularly strong position to carry information across social boundaries and to diffuse innovations of all kinds.' If a few members of a (largely or wholly native-speaking) social network take up an innovation (in this instance originating with ELF speakers), it can then diffuse to the group as a whole. The innovation would thereby assume a certain social significance, symbolizing or indexing some sort of social value associated with the group but without any conscious aspiration to sound like or identify with its originators. As long as there are a few early adopters, the standard S-curve is likely to appear (or, rather, as Aitchison [2013: 95] suggests, lots of little overlapping S-curves, each corresponding to a different register or genre or linguistic environment). The change, which started slowly, will pick up speed and proceed rapidly before slowing down again when most speakers have adopted the change in question.

If enough people adopt new variants (probably individual expressions—particular tokens of certain constructions), they will progressively become more automatized or routinized or more deeply entrenched in most hearers' minds (Langacker 1987: 58–9). They will thereby become primed and more likely to be activated merely as a function of exposure to use and independently of any intentional goals (Croft 2000: 32). As Bolinger (1976: 2) put it, memorably, '[T]he human mind is far less remarkable for its creativity than for the fact that it remembers everything,' and according to usage-based and emergentist models of language, and indeed according to common sense, the more frequently we experience something, the stronger our memory for it (Ellis 2012b). Thus the diffusion of innovations—leading to differential variation (Croft 2000: 4) or a shift in the relative frequencies of variants—can proceed by way of what Thomason (2001, Ch. 6) calls 'passive familiarity' rather than 'deliberate decision.'

On the other hand, many native English speakers are likely to encounter a wide range of ELF speakers who use the language very differently and for very different purposes. For example, professional people might well have ELF-speaking colleagues while also interacting with ELF-speaking service industry employees, and service industry employees might have ELF-speaking colleagues while also interacting with professional ELF-speaking people as customers. These speakers cannot *all* be perceived as belonging to a prestigious group with a social status to identify with. Consequently ELF variants are just as likely to be perceived as usages lacking any sociolinguistic value or stylistic salience as to be reanalyzed as indicators of social prestige that should perhaps be imitated. Extensive weak ties in loose networks are *necessary* conditions for change, but they clearly aren't *sufficient* ones.

4.2.5 Children

Most ENL-ELF interactions, in professional contexts, social life, and tourism, tend to involve adults. Children are fairly marginal in the social networks that could conceivably lead to the propagation of linguistic changes from non-native to native speakers. There are, nevertheless, plenty of children of L2 English speakers who have relocated to Anglophone countries. But just like children whose parents speak a markedly different native dialect from the local one, such children will almost invariably acquire the variety of the wider local community rather than their parents' ESL or ELF (Weinreich et al. 1968: 145, note 36; Labov 1982: 47). Children who acquire their particular dialect pattern from a relatively homogeneous peer group are likely to perceive occasional ESL or ELF usages by their parents as irrelevant ungrammatical oddities. Chambers (2002: 123) even argues that the children of immigrants seem to be wholly *unaware* that their parents speak differently from the wider community until they reach the critical period around puberty. They have an 'innate accent filter' that leads them to pick up native patterns of phonology and speak like their peers; it is as if they had

> a device which allows individuals to disengage themselves from certain eccentric or at least diversionary communities of practice that fall within their worlds, presumably in order to allow them to participate fully in the communities that will play more integral roles in forming their identity.

This disengagement seems to apply to lexicogrammar as well as phonology so that community norms are perpetuated by the offspring of immigrants. Cheshire et al. (2011: 167–8) suggest instead, perhaps more plausibly, that such children *are* aware of their parents' variants as part of the feature pool, but choose to orient to community norms.

All in all, immigration most often results in linguistic assimilation by the second generation. As Sankoff (2002: 643) puts it, phonological change is 'almost universally characteristic of adult L2 speakers, but for social reasons, the "substratum potential" such speakers have is usually very limited.' Yet things are different for second-generation immigrants where there is an absence of established community norms, for example, in multilingual urban immigrant communities. In such circumstances children may largely acquire the target language by way of unguided, informal, group second language acquisition in multi-ethnic friendship groups rather than from their caregivers. This can result in 'a new "multi-ethnolect" containing some features of minority origin' (Kerswill et al. 2013: 267) or, if not a 'lect' as such, at least a smallish repertoire of shared innovations. One example of this is 'Multicultural London English' (Cheshire et al. 2011), an emergent dialect containing a number of transfer-based phonological features from various African, Asian, and Caribbean L2 Englishes, which may in time become focused and turn into a fully fledged native speaker dialect. Whether it will extend from the city neighbourhoods in which it is currently spoken remains to be seen.

Several linguists have also described the way in which teenagers in multi-ethnic 'late-modern urban youth groups' (Jørgensen (2008: 161) in cities in north-west Europe, including native speakers of the majority language, often choose to mix forms from languages spoken by their friends, probably as a way of negotiating individual and group identities. Rampton (2005) describes this as 'crossing' and Jørgensen as 'polylingual languaging.' Many of these usages, however (certainly morphosyntactic ones as opposed to phonological ones), are likely to recede in adulthood, and the majority of native English speakers in Britain and the United States are no more likely to accommodate to such innovations, or to similarly innovative hybrid forms from ELF, than they have accommodated, over the past two centuries, to major immigrant varieties (e.g., Irish, Italian, Yiddish, Hispanic, or indeed African American).[18]

As already mentioned, changes or simplifications arising from SLA today have to compete with prescriptivism (see Chapter 3) and a highly standardized language used in schools, in the media, and in print. Native-like command of heterogeneous (and socially marked) structures also implies an awareness of what is *not* native-like. All non-native usages run up against a community's linguistic regularities or conventions, and as Croft (2000: 98) says, the nature of conventions is that almost everyone in a speech community conforms to them, expects almost everyone else to conform to them, and would prefer any additional member of the community to conform to them. Thus, although there are various established mechanisms by which innovations can be diffused, there are also many sociolinguistic factors that might hold back this diffusion.

4.3 So Will ELF Impact on Native English?

I have suggested that grammar is inherently variable, probabilistic, usage based, and forever emergent, and that adolescents and adults might accommodate to new usages if they consider them to be more expressive or impressive than conventional usages or see them as somehow carrying social prestige. So will native English speakers accommodate to the lexicogrammatical variation of ELF and depart from the entrenched constructions of their native speech community? For the moment corpora show no evidence of *any* of the widely diffused ELF usages listed at the end of the previous chapter spreading into native English.

The present simple third-person singular *-s* inflection is indeed a 'systemic excrescence' (Lass 1990: 99) and a 'typological oddity' (Trudgill 2002: 98), given that most English verb inflections disappeared hundreds of years ago, perhaps partly as a result of non-native acquisition by the Vikings. It is just the type of 'afunctional grammatical category' (p. 92) likely to be simplified as a result of language contact, but native speakers continue to use it.[19]

Regularization of verb morphology (such as past-tense forms) has been happening for hundreds of years, and Mair (2006: 194) suggests that this has advanced further in American English because the regular forms were boosted during colonial dialect levelling and the later acquisition of

English by generations of non-English-speaking immigrants.[20] Extensive ELF usage might be expected to boost this further, and indeed Cogo and Jenkins (2010: 277) argue that 'ELF is simply quickening the pace of regularisation processes towards which the English language is predisposed, and which are already underway more slowly in native English.' Yet of the regularized simple past and past participle forms found in the ELFA corpus listed in the previous chapter, the British National Corpus (BNC)[21] gives just three hits for *feeled*, three for *bringed* (but all from a book about children's language), and zero hits for *fighted*, *heared*, *losed*, and *teached*. Even if the regularization of past-tense forms would seem to be a prime candidate for ELF-ENL propagation, it hasn't taked place yet.

Leech et al. (2012: 130) state that native English corpora (of written language) between the 1960s and 1990s show no sign of a growing acceptability of the (Celtic-derived) present progressive form with stative verbs, and Mair (2006: 93) finds a mere 12 (statistically insignificant) instances of progressive *understand* in the BNC. Mair suggests that using progressives with stative verbs is 'an instance of contextually/pragmatically licenced rule-breaking for specific rhetorical or expressive effect' that has been available as an option 'ever since the present system of rules emerged in the eighteenth century' (p. 92) and that it only appears to be more frequent today because there are more informal written genres than in the past.[22] This means that if native English speakers *were* to begin to use the present progressive with stative verbs, it *would* be a change, and Poplack and Levey's (2010: 391) objection that 'the inherent variability characteristic of spoken language' often gets 'mistaken for change' would not be applicable.

In airports outside the inner circle countries one is almost invariably offered *informations*, and *advices* about *baggages*. So it is conceivable that these particular tokens of uncountable nouns being used countably could become entrenched in native English speakers' minds and create an 'island' from which a new pattern or construction could grow (Croft and Cruse 2004: 326). However, even though the related countable/uncountable *fewer/less* and *amount/quantity* distinctions *are* certainly receding,[23] there are no signs of this happening yet. For example, the BNC gives just six hits for *advices*, 16 for *feedbacks*, one for *furnitures*, 15 for *informations*, and zero for *luggages*.

Trudgill (1984: 42) described the use of past-time adverbials (*yesterday*, *last year*, etc.) with the present perfect as spreading in Standard English English. Given that the use of such adverbials with a *have*-perfect is grammatically correct in many other European languages, and that this form of grammatical replication or convergence (Weinreich 1953; Heine and Kuteva 2005) or reanalysis (Harris and Campbell 1995) of the present perfect as the past tense is frequently carried out by ELF speakers, this is perhaps a prime candidate for ELF influence on native English, although corpora do not suggest that it is becoming standard.

The use of the present simple to express duration can lead to 'cross-dialectal miscomprehension' with speakers of Standard British or American English. Milroy (1992: 33) gives an example: two speakers (let us call them James and Lesley) reply to a question in colloquial Irish English, 'How long are yous here?' (rather than 'How long have you been here?') with 'Oh, we're staying till next week,' corrected after a two-second pause to 'We've been here since Tuesday,' which was the answer the Irish English question required. An ELF speaker might well have understood the question and replied with the present tense—'We are here since Tuesday' (instead of 'have been') or 'We are here for/since x days' (again instead of 'have been'). Probably because of this potential for misunderstanding, there seems to be no sign of the present simple replacing the present perfect in Britain (despite the long-standing presence of many speakers of Irish English).[24]

Thus, overall, it would appear that few of these widespread ELF features offer particular expressive gains to native speakers of English, and they seem unlikely to appeal to speakers who want to be noticed and to impress by finding new ways to say old things. And these features *are* certainly salient to native speakers: just as much as the third-person singular *-s* inflection, the logic of uncountable nouns, and the constraints on using stative verbs in the progressive form have low salience and communicative value for L2 speakers, the absence of the *-s* inflection, the use of the plural with uncountable nouns, and the use of the progressive with stative verbs tend to be noticed by native speakers. The last of these features in particular is frequently used by comedians and scriptwriters to imitate non-native English.

Few linguists would expect the 'koinéized' grammatical forms common to many ELF similects to influence native English; as Sankoff (2002: 658) says, 'Morphology and syntax are clearly the domains of linguistic structure least susceptible to the influence of contact.' Lexical borrowing is much more common, and it can potentially 'lead to structural changes at every level of linguistic structure' (p. 658). If loanwords aren't totally adapted to the phonology of the receiving language, foreign pronunciations can potentially spread to other words, leading to adjustments in the phonology of the recipient language. In an inflectional language—although probably not in a simplified language like English—loanwords can also bring morphological and syntactic changes in their wake.[25] However, ELF being a form of English rather than a foreign language, the only scope for lexical borrowing would be of different uses of existing English words, and there is little sign of this happening.

Ferguson (1982/1992: xvii) mentioned the 'continental meanings of *eventual* and *actual*,' as well as 'continental uses of tenses' and 'dozens of other features' of an emerging European English, and suggested that 'native speakers of English' attending international conferences in Europe 'may find themselves using some of these features as the verbal interaction take place.' The continental meanings of *eventual* (possible) and *actual* (present or current) are widespread because these originally Latin words have equivalents in all Romance languages and have also been borrowed in most Germanic and Slavic languages. They are semantic extensions in L2 English because native English has long used these words with changed meanings (real, existing in fact; and at a later time or at the end). But the semantic extensions show no sign of spreading to L1 English usage. In the same foreword, Ferguson argued that 'the whole mystique of native speaker and mother tongue should probably be quietly dropped from the linguists' set of professional myths about language' (p. xiii), but this example shows that differences between native and non-native usage exist and that these concepts might just have explanatory value. All that needs to be dropped is the *mystique*, the idea that the native speaker is 'the only truly valid and reliable source of language data': there are also non-native speakers and non-native language data.

The last item on the list of forms that have diffused into common ELF usage, explicit prepositional verbs, seems a credible candidate for diffusion to native speakers, who could start using them by a process of unselfconscious or subliminal convergence with ELF speakers rather than by conscious adoption (see Hundt 2013: 190). But once again, so far native corpora record very few, or sometimes zero, instances of the prepositional verbs found in ELF corpora (and the New Englishes). For example, of the verbs from VOICE cited in Seidlhofer (2011: 145–6), the half-billion-word Corpus of Contemporary American (CoCA)[26] gives nine hits for *discuss about* (compared with 12 in the million-word VOICE), zero for *reject against*, and 64 for *return back*.

Many native speakers *do* modify their speech when talking to non-native speakers with limited proficiency, usually by syntactic simplifications, recasts, and repetition; this is often called 'foreigner talk' (Ferguson 1971) and parallels the way parents modify their speech for young children (caretaker talk). In fact interactional adjustments by native speakers and more competent language learners are at the heart of the 'interactionist approach' to foreign language teaching (Mackey et al. 2012). But of course such dynamic modifications tend not to diffuse into everyday native English usage.

On the other hand, as already mentioned, usage-based theory holds that speakers are intuitive statisticians who keep an unconscious mental record of the relative frequency of use of all the constructions they hear (Ellis 2002; Bybee 2007). Thus the more native speakers are exposed to L2 usages, the more they will become entrenched (in a kind of positive feedback loop) and potentially primed for use by way of passive familiarity.

Like the ELF researchers (Seidlhofer and Mauranen) quoted at the beginning of this chapter, Crystal (2003: 172) suggests that 'the course of the English language' will be influenced by L2 users. But rather than arguing from the sheer mass of numbers, he suggests that a linguistic fashion 'started by a group of second- or foreign-language learners, or by those who speak a creole or pidgin variety' could catch on among other speakers (p. 173), if the originators were sufficiently fashionable and famous. One of his examples is variations in countability (*furnitures, kitchenwares*), which I have already mentioned. Another is the African American verb form *he be running*. Crystal also suggests that 'the appointment to high office in first-language countries of people with strong Hispanic or African-American Creole accents' could lead to syllable-based (as opposed to stress-based) speech becoming part of most people's phonological repertoires (p. 171). I find this unlikely, but Peter Schrijver (personal communication), who believes that given time, native English is likely to be 'changed beyond recognition,' suggests that my position resembles that of 'a first-century AD upper-class Roman from Rome' stating that 'New Latin' would not succeed in taking over 'because in the 200 years or so that Rome had been a world power nothing of the sort had happened yet'!

There may be many *other* frequent ELF usages that are less salient (and less likely to be stigmatized by English-language teachers), as well as individual speakers' 'exploratory expressions,' that are slowly finding their way into native English (into the inherent variability of some individual speakers' heterogeneous repertoires) through ELF-ENL contact. Language contact is inherently unpredictable: given intense and/or long-lasting contact, almost anything can (theoretically) happen, and to quote Thomason and Kaufman (1988: 14) again, '[A]s far as the strictly linguistic possibilities go, any linguistic feature can be transferred from any language to any other language.' Moreover, as Heine and Kuteva (2005: 5) point out, 'Contact-induced language change is a complex process that not infrequently extends over centuries, or even millennia,' as with some of the Celtic examples cited. Even though ELF-ENL contact is *second-order* language contact, with native speakers being exposed to other varieties of English rather than another language, as in canonical contact situations, it could still potentially lead to the transfer of features from other languages to ELF and thence to native English. Consequently, any predictions we make should be suitably modest or cautious.

Hundt and Vogel (2011: 159) report finding in New Zealand 'the co-occurrence of the present progressive with a temporal adverbial that would require a present perfect in British English' in a warning sign on a camping ground that included '*We are experiencing too many accidents of late*,' which speakers of New Zealand English (NZE) did not find unusual. They compare this with sentences in New Englishes such as '*the economy is fast rising ever since the Ramos Administration started*' in the Philippine segment of the International Corpus of English (ICE)[27] and surmise that 'this particular extension of the progressive to contexts of perfective marking might be relatively unobtrusive to some speakers in the inner circle' because the past progressive is used in a similar way, as in '*Tom, you were just telling me that.*' But they also suggest that the 'similarities between NZE and some ESL varieties' might show that 'NZE has been influenced by ESL varieties to the extent that the ENL-ESL distinction in this country is beginning to get blurred (at least with respect to the usage of the progressive).'[28] This leads to the more radical conclusion that 'the somewhat simple categorization into inner-, outer- and expanding-circle varieties is in need of revision' and that 'increasing globalization might eventually blur distinctions between ENL, ESL, and EFL varieties' (p. 161).

This is indeed possible, but the kind of blurring of the ENL-ESL distinction that Hundt and Vogel describe has *not* (yet) been reported in large cities with larger proportions of ESL speakers than in New Zealand (e.g., London, New York, Los Angeles, Toronto, Vancouver, etc.). And by way of comparison, the syntactic variants involving presents and perfects used in British and America for many decades by a far greater number of Irish immigrants than there are ESL speakers in New Zealand do not appear to have influenced the local speech communities.

In short I believe that we *can* safely predict the following: adults acquiring L2s will continue to simplify, reduce, and regularize them and transfer elements from their L1s, but many expanding circle speakers who relocate to inner circle countries will strive for something resembling native-like usage; many people will continue to innovate linguistically, trying either to express themselves better or just to impress other people; and most people will continue intermittently to imitate the speech of culturally dominant or socially attractive groups. What we cannot state with any degree of certainty is that native English speakers will find non-native English speakers either culturally dominant or sufficiently socially attractive to imitate. We can also predict that whereas most younger and second-generation immigrants will acquire or adopt the local community's ways of speaking, parts of larger cities with multicultural communities and ongoing immigration could see the development of multi-ethnolects containing various L2-derived features. However, such forms are unlikely to be widely diffused beyond these communities. As McWhorter (2011: 17, quoted earlier) points out, unlike in the seventh to 10th centuries, when it appears highly probable that native English speakers *were* influenced by the imperfect L2 English of Celts and Scandinavians, today there is widespread literacy, and standardized native varieties of English remain dominant in education and the media and will probably resist the effects of non-native acquisition. At present there is little evidence that L1 English speakers are accommodating to usages deriving from nativized New Englishes or from ELF or that this is going to happen in the future. But of course, as always, time alone will tell.

Notes

1 This is an English translation of Gadamer's paraphrase of the Latin inscription on some German memorials to the dead of World War I in Misgeld and Nicholson (1992: 135–6).

2 It will be seen that this 1759 account of L2 learning and migration predates the supposed 'invention' of languages and ethnolinguistically pure European nation-states in the 19th century (Makoni and Pennycook 2007).

3 See also Clackson and Horrocks (2007, Ch. 8). Histories of grammaticalization (e.g., Lehmann 2002) tend to mention Condillac, Horne Tooke, A. W. Schlegel and W. Humboldt as precursors of Antoine Meillet (1912), who coined the term, but no-one seems to mention Smith's earlier account of the grammaticalization of *habere* or *have*.

4 In fact the Koiné Greek of Hellenistic and Roman Antiquity and Late Antiquity (and consequently the Greek spoken as a native language in the medieval and modern periods too) was almost certainly simplified by bilingualism and contact with other languages of the Hellenistic empires; see Adrados (2005); Horrocks (2010); Trudgill (2014a).

5 Schrijver (2014: 31–3, 48, 82) argues that Latin-speaking Britons (or possibly Latin-Celtic bilinguals) from the higher social classes fled west and north from the Anglo-Saxon warrior-settlers. As they greatly outnumbered the speakers of Highland British Celtic, they Latinized its sound system and consequently that of its present-day survivors Welsh and Breton.

6 Estimates of the number of invading Germanic warriors in the fifth and sixth centuries go from 10,000 to 200,000, compared with about a million Romano-Britons, giving a ratio of Anglo-Saxons to Britons of anywhere between 1:5 to 1:50 (Filppula et al. 2008: 15).

7 Wright (2013: 73) calls the argument that child bilingualism generally leads to complexification whereas adult acquisition tends to result in simplification 'the Trudgill insight,' making it sound like the title of a Robert Ludlum novel. Given his insight Trudgill (1983: 103–5) uses the terms 'natural' and 'non-natural' language change rather than the more common 'internal' and 'external' or 'contact-induced.'

8 There are also rival theories. Thomason and Kaufman (1988: 264) deny that 'the degree of change exhibited in English' in this period was 'anything other than normal' and insist that the simplifications seen in Middle English 'probably were taking place in OE before Norse influence became relevant' (p. 303). They see the 'Norsification' of English as less a case of accommodation to imperfect learning than 'a fad whereby an English speaker would parade his knowledge of Norse while speaking English' (p. 298), a kind of prestige borrowing because Norse added 'a few subtleties of meaning and a large number of new ways of saying old things' (p. 303). Thomason and Kaufman disregard the possible influence of Celtic speakers. Meanwhile, as outlined in the previous chapter, Lass rejects external or language contact explanations of language change on principle, describing language contact as a 'rather gross' contingency (1980: 139) and bemoaning those 'contact romantics' who seek to derive 'the maximal number of characters in a given language from contact sources' (1997: 201). It will be apparent that the present author is an unreconstructed contact romantic.

9 The history of English is in fact slightly more complex than this: Szmrecsanyi (2012) shows that there was a huge increase in analyticity in the 13th and 14th centuries, and stasis between the 14th and 17th centuries, with a steady drift toward more syntheticity and less analyticity since then. Szmrecsanyi (2009) shows that speech always tends to be more analytic and less synthetic

than writing and that written English has become more synthetic over the past half century.

10 See also Trudgill (2004, 2008) on the primacy of mechanical factors (such as density and accommodation) over social evaluations and 'identification.'

11 Cogo and Dewey (2012: 55, 57, 100) make what appear to me to be very exaggerated claims about emerging developments, distinct and innovative patterns of use, and shifts away from existing patterns in this community, based on a relatively small corpus, which I have discussed elsewhere (MacKenzie 2014b, Chs. 4 and 8).

12 McWhorter (2007, 2011) also places Persian, Mandarin, Malay, and Riau Indonesian, among others, in this category.

13 This is all in contrast to the Chomskyan theory that language change results only from children internalizing new grammars by setting the parameters of a supposedly innate Universal Grammar differently from their caregivers (or the previous generation as a whole) as a result of changes, possibly minute ones, in the primary linguistic data, which can trigger a new system that generates a very different set of sentences and structures (Lightfoot 1991, 2006).

14 It could be argued—and quite possibly demonstrated—that this *is not* in fact a broadening of the set of available forms because every conceivable variant used by an ELF speaker has at some point been attested in a traditional, rural dialect in the inner circle and/or somewhere in outer circle varieties (see, e.g., Kortmann and Lunkenheimer 2013), but many usages may *appear* to be new to inner circle speakers not conversant with traditional dialects or New Englishes.

15 Kretzschmar gives lexical, collocational, and phonological examples of the 80/20 rule (but not structural ones), largely drawn from elicited data recorded in the American Linguistic Atlas Project. For lexis, the 80/20 rule complements Zipf's Law; see Chapter 1. Testing the 80/20 rule against a large corpus of non-native English has yet to be done.

16 Kretzschmar (2015: 59–60), in combat mode, reproaches Hopper for backsliding in his book on *Grammaticalization*, co-written with Traugott (Hopper and Traugott 1993/2003), in which grammar is objectified and reified. He makes similar criticisms of Beckner et al. (2009), also known as the 'Five Graces Group,' including Bybee, Croft, Ellis, and Larsen-Freeman, the last of whom has long used complex systems as a metaphor to describe language and language acquisition (see Larsen-Freeman 1997; Larsen-Freeman and Cameron 2008). Yet Hopper's original position may be somewhat exaggerated; as Lass (1997: 354–5) puts it, 'the notion that linguistic structure in some way "grows" out of discourse [. . .] is roughly equivalent to saying that hammers grow directly out of people's attempts to nail things'; syntax may have grown out of discourse 'in the beginning,' but today it 'grows almost exclusively out of the syntax bequeathed by previous generations, although a certain amount of tinkering gets done in discourse itself.'

17 Lass (1997: 186), however, complains that 'prestige' is invoked as a catch-all explanation for 'non-cultural' lexical borrowing—that is, of words that do *not* fill a gap in the recipient language—for motivations that are 'probably random and contingent' (p. 188). The same could well be true for the imitation of non-native usages.

18 Trudgill (2010, Ch. 5) gives some examples from American English of what seem to be the results of contact with German, Yiddish, and other European languages, including the grammatical constructions *I like to skate* (as opposed to *I like skating*) and *Are you coming with?* (as opposed to *Are you coming?*), and restricted collocations of verbs like *have* and *take* compared with British English. However, these constitute only a few very minor features.

19 Except in traditional (but shrinking) East Anglian dialects in England—Trudgill (2002: 97–9) gives a speculative but convincing explanation of the origin of this feature involving the high proportion of non-native speakers in the area in the 16th century, alongside competition between the northern English *-s* form and the southern English *-eth* form (see also Trudgill 2010, Ch. 2). This critical mass of non-native speakers is not found in inner circle countries today.

20 With or without the influence of L2 learners, the regularization of irregular past-tense forms is a function of frequency (or infrequency). Lieberman et al. (2007) chart the progress of 177 Old English irregular verbs, of which 145 remained irregular in Middle English and 98 are still irregular today, and show that the rate of regularization depends on the frequency of usage. To be precise the half-life of irregular verbs is proportional to (approximately) the square root of their frequency, which is to say that a verb used 100 times less often than another one regularizes 10 times as fast. (The good news for L2 learners of English is that if current trends continue, only 83 of the 98 currently irregular verbs will still be irregular in the year 2500!)

21 See http://corpus.byu.edu/bnc.

22 British English (recorded in the BNC) is, however, just one of several inner circle varieties, and Hundt and Vogel (2011: 146) argue that 'some varieties in the inner circle are more advanced in the spreading use of the progressive than others.' Hundt (1998: 75–6) illustrates more frequent use of progressives with stative verbs in New Zealand and Australian English than in the British and American varieties.

23 I have had a number of native English-speaking graduate translation students (i.e., people with a certain interest in and feel for languages) who claimed to be wholly unaware of these distinctions.

24 Moreover, such a change would go against the standard path of grammaticalization. Bybee et al. (1994) describe a common path in which resultative constructions in a language (expressing a past action with a resulting current state) develop into perfects (expressing the current relevance of a past action), which then evolve into pasts or perfectives (expressing temporarily bounded situations); there are no cases of perfects giving way to the present.

25 In Russian, for example, many borrowed nouns, mostly from English, are used unchanged, in non-inflected forms, whereas others are combined in new noun + noun phrases (replacing existing adjective + noun collocations) in which the first noun is not declined for case or gender, 'which can gradually lead to typological changes in the language' (Proshina et al. 2016: 50).

26 See http://corpus.byu.edu/coca/.

27 See http://ice-corpora.net/ice/.

28 As mentioned in note 22, Hundt (1998) found a higher overall frequency of progressives in New Zealand English than in British and American English but largely attributed this to its use with stative verbs (*thinking*, *hearing*, *feeling*, etc.). Although Hundt and Vogel (2011) draw on a 42,000-word corpus of student essays and exam scripts from the New Zealand component of the International Corpus of English, the only New Zealand example they give of the present progressive being used in place of a present perfect is the campsite notice—a 'corpus' at the anecdotal end of the scale. But I have already defended the use of anecdotal evidence (in Chapter 1, note 16).

5 ELF and the Alternatives

The subsequent chapters of this book concern the potential consequences of the fact that scientists and academics writing for an international audience are more or less obliged to write in English, and the effects of widespread contact with English on other languages. Neither of these topics would be especially significant if the dominance of English was a temporary state of affairs, but in this chapter I will argue (somewhat uncontroversially) that it is likely to be long-lived.

5.1 The Dominance of English

English, in its assorted native, nativized, and non-native varieties, is probably in contact with more languages today than any other language in history. It is also used in a far wider range of functions than previous lingua francas. For example, whereas Latin had a scholastic and religious function for many centuries, and Arabic and Sanskrit have long had a religious function, English today has what Kachru (1994: 135) rightly describes as 'an unprecedented functional range.' It is used worldwide in international politics, diplomacy, law, business, the media, popular culture, tertiary education, scientific research, and many other fields.

Some people view this as an irreversible phenomenon, and a positive one, that potentially permits everyone to communicate effectively across borders. For example, van Parijs (2011) argues that 'the powerful dynamics that currently drives the spreading of competence in English should not be resisted or reversed, but on the contrary welcomed and accelerated' (p. 50) for democratic reasons: it is emphatically a good thing if everybody can communicate directly with each other. Indeed 'people committed to egalitarian global justice should [. . .] see it as their duty to contribute to this spread in Europe and throughout the world' (p. 31). The use of English as a lingua franca creates and expands a transnational demos 'without the cumbersome and expensive mediation of interpretation and translation,' and thereby 'enables not only the rich and the powerful, but also the poor and the powerless to communicate, debate, network, cooperate, lobby, demonstrate effectively across borders.' For

Van Parijs the historical causes of the spread of English—essentially British industrial dominance and imperialism, followed by the economic dominance and international influence of the United States (Phillipson 1992; Crystal 2003)—are irrelevant to its current utility.

When extolling English, Van Parijs echoes many of the arguments of ELF researchers outlined in Chapter 1: for example, 'there are as many legitimate ways of using it as there are people who bother to use it' (p. 33), and non-native English speakers should use English with their own distinctive accents and styles and not allow native English speakers to hog speaking time. He further states that L2 speakers have many advantages over native ones in terms of cultural sensitivity and linguistic accommodation in transnational and intercultural communication.

There are, of course, other people who oppose the dominance of English as the world's lingua franca because they favour linguistic diversity, because they see English as the vehicle of American imperialism and neoliberalism (Phillipson 1992; Hagège 2012), or because the exclusive use of English clearly entails 'a considerable transfer of material and symbolic advantages to [its] native speakers' (Gazzola and Grin 2013: 94). Phillipson (2008: 263) insists that '*lingua franca* is a pernicious, invidious term if the language in question is a first language for some people but for others a foreign language, such communication typically being asymmetrical,' and that 'it is a misleading term if the language is supposed to be neutral and disconnected from culture.' Phillipson may very well be right here, but however misleading and pernicious it is, the term ELF has become established.

Paradoxically, however, as de Swaan points out, the maintenance of linguistic diversity in local or national contexts tends to go hand in hand with the dominance of English rather than work against it. Where local languages take pride of place (and their speakers' linguistic 'rights' are upheld), people who interact with a wider community need to learn one or more languages of wider communication—either a regional lingua franca or, in de Swaan's (2001: 4–6) terms, a 'central' language, a 'supercentral' language, or the world's 'hypercentral' language, English. De Swaan (2004: 574) argues that the recognition of multiple official languages—for example, 24 in the European Union (so far), and 11 in South Africa—actually consolidates the hegemony of English: 'The more languages, the more English. [. . .] Thus works the ruse of history: the opponents of English linguistic imperialism, at the height of their influence, have accomplished precisely the opposite of what they hoped to bring about.'

Even so, proponents of linguistic diversity propose alternatives to the use of 'hypercentral' English, including multilingualism, with everyone using the language or languages of their choice (which consequently requires interpreting and translation); receptive multilingualism, in which speakers use a language different from their hearers but still understand each other without the help of an additional lingua franca or the need for translation; and codeswitching or language mixing in which speakers use two or more languages (if you adhere to the conventional, but increasingly contested, notion of languages as essentially separate entities between which speakers can switch).[1] Another possibility, which would not do much for diversity, would be the replacement of English by another dominant language, the general consensus being that the most plausible candidate is Mandarin Chinese.

In this chapter I will consider the potential scope of these possible alternatives to the use of (spoken) English (whether conceived of as EFL or ELF) and suggest that they are far more likely to complement English than to displace it to any great extent.

5.2 Translation

A lingua franca would obviously be unnecessary if everybody used their dominant language and relied on interpreting or translation, and indeed in many circumstances using an L1 is preferable, as most people are more at ease communicating in their mother tongue and find speaking, writing, and understanding an L2 much more effortful. Most people can probably think and comprehend better, write more quickly and express nuances more easily, and be better understood and more effortlessly persuasive and impressive in their L1. Although high-quality interpreting and translating can be prohibitively expensive, there are clearly compelling reasons for having multilingual regimes in public and democratic bodies representing speech communities of different languages, whatever the cost (Gazzola and Grin 2013). Most bi- or multilingual countries (with societal rather than individual bilingualism) have policies requiring the translation of all kinds of official documents, and all countries need myriad translations from foreign languages of technological, cultural, and other materials, unless they are to live in isolation and ignorance (Grin 2017).

Most private sector organizations offering goods and services internationally translate (or localize) their documentation, advertising, websites, and so on (and, in domains such as software, the products themselves) into the languages of the territories in which they are sold. Yet at the same time, many commercial organizations and public and private institutions expect their staff to be able to speak and write English. Today scientists writing for an international audience almost invariably write in English (see Chapter 6), and the stock of articles in English is currently growing by more than 1.5 million a year, or 4,100 a day, or nearly three a minute (Montgomery 2013: 170), and no-one (and no machine) has translated, or is likely to translate, most of this work into any other language. Given translation and the widespread use of English, many Anglophones are able to function monolingually, and indeed with a sufficient range of translations, speakers of most major languages might feel it unnecessary to learn other languages.

Ostler (2010), however, does not expect the current dominance of English as an international language to last. He places great faith in the future growth of low-cost machine translation, hence his book title *The Last Lingua Franca: English Until the Return of Babel*. He believes that English will go the way of all the widespread lingua francas that preceded it—including Arabic, Aramaic, Greek, Latin, Persian, Sanskrit, French (in diplomacy), German (in science), Portuguese, Russian, and Spanish—all of which were overthrown, but in this instance Babel will return because machine translation will make the use of many languages in international communication possible: 'Recorded speeches and printed texts will become virtual media, accessible through whatever language the listener or speaker prefers. In such a world, English might have—and might need—no successor as the single language of the future mass-connected world' (Ostler 2010: xix). Yet although Ostler might be right about the fate of all dominant languages, he seems to have inordinate faith in the necessary colossal advances in speech recognition and automatic translation. Most people involved in machine translation believe that instant, accurate translation of idiomatic language is a chimera, about as likely as the arrival on Earth of Douglas Adams's (1979) convenient ear-hole-sized translating Babel Fish (see, e.g., Wilks 2009; Pool 2010; Bellos 2011, Ch. 23; Montgomery 2013: 162).[2] Computer-assisted translation (CAT) tools are steadily improving, and most (non-literary) translators now use translation memory (TM) software, terminology databases, corpora, and so on, but pure machine translation (MT) almost invariably needs 'post-editing' by a human translator.[3]

Leaving aside speeches and texts, Ostler disregards the fact that many people might well prefer to have a real conversation, whenever possible, to speaking and then reading or listening to a reply produced by a translation device—necessarily a device with no real-world contextual knowledge, no information about the purpose of the words to translate, and no sense of style, which often leads to quite jarring sentences entering a would-be friendly exchange.

5.3 Receptive Multilingualism

Backus et al. (2011) are developing a 'toolkit' for multilingual communication in Europe, in which they consider the use of ELF as well as other regional lingua francas, codeswitching, and receptive multilingualism, a partial alternative to both translation and lingua francas in which people speak their own language but are able to understand the language of their interlocutors.

Despite books with titles like *English-only Europe?* (Phillipson 2003), Backus et al. state that many other languages are used as lingua francas in Europe, including German over a wide area and Russian (at least by older people) in the former Soviet Union and Warsaw Pact countries. On other continents, many other major languages—mainly those that de Swaan (2001: 5) describes as 'supercentral' languages, one rung down from 'hypercentral' English in 'the global language system'—also serve as regional lingua francas, including Chinese, Swahili, Spanish, Portuguese, French, Hindi, and Bahasa Indonesia. However, the use of a lingua franca can sometimes be circumvented where people understand more than one language.

Towards the end of *The Search for the Perfect Language*, Eco (1995) states, 'Today, more than ever before [. . .] European culture is in need of a common language that might heal its linguistic fractures' while also remaining a continent of different languages, 'each of which, even the most peripheral, remains the medium through which the genius of a particular ethnic group expresses itself, witness and vehicle of a millennial tradition' (pp. 344–5). Eco suggests that receptive multilingualism could reconcile these two needs: people could 'meet each other and speak together, each in his or her own tongue, understanding, as best they can, the speech of others,' with the result that 'even those who never learn to speak another language fluently could still participate in its particular genius, catching a glimpse of the particular cultural universe that every individual expresses each time he or she speaks' (p. 351).

Receptive multilingualism is obviously easier for speakers of typologically similar or cognate languages. In many parts of Europe (probably the continent in which receptive multilingualism has the greatest potential), this applies to many speakers of neighbouring Romance, Germanic, and Slavic languages, who can expect (when listening) to find sound correspondences, cognate lexis, and morphological and syntactic regularities common to the language family. Where there has been L2 learning, receptive multilingualism can also function with typologically dissimilar languages; examples here might include French or Italian and German in Switzerland, French and Flemish in Belgium, Finnish and Swedish in Finland, and *any* language combination in cross-generational communication in migrant families, most often with the younger generation speaking the majority language and the older generation speaking the minority (or heritage) language (Rehbein et al. 2011). Receptive multilingualism has long been practiced in Europe, especially in cross-border communication by people with similar dialects in geographical dialect continua (see Trudgill 2002: 115–21), but it was greatly reduced by the homogenizing language and education policies of modern nation-states. Today, however, it remains a definite possibility for many people.

Receptive knowledge of a language is a dynamic phenomenon, and something that can be taught and acquired. Rehbein et al. (2011: 249) have proposed *lingua receptiva* ('LaRa') as an alternative name for receptive multilingualism, one which specifically relates to its receptive component: 'the ensemble of those *linguistic*, *mental*, *interactional* as well as *intercultural competencies* which are *creatively* activated when interlocutors listen to linguistic actions in their "passive" language or variety.' However speakers are not disregarded: their perception of the hearer's response influences the way they construct their utterances, and they 'apply additional competencies in order to monitor the way in which hearers activate their "passive knowledge" and thus attempt to control the ongoing process of understanding.' Hence—as in the use of ELF—speakers can attempt to simplify their language; reduce communicative asymmetries; reformulate, repair, recapitulate, and rephrase as necessary; and make phonological, lexical, morphological, and syntactic adaptations towards what they imagine hearers are better able to understand.

Hearers can use both non-verbal and verbal signals to steer the speaker's production as well as adopting what Firth (1996: 243) calls the 'let it pass' principle (see Chapter 1). Rehbein et al. further state that 'LaRa draws on the inference-making machine' (p. 258), but of course, as relevance theory (Sperber and Wilson 1986/1995) demonstrates, *all* verbal communication does this.[4] It also draws on 'available plurilingual resources and idiomaticity that exists between the languages involved' (pp. 258–9) but still with only one language being produced (and understood) at a time; Rehbein et al. make no mention of dynamic interferences as described by Grosjean (see Chapter 2).

Yet to what extent such jointly negotiated interaction allows the expression of what Eco calls the 'particular genius' and 'cultural universe' of a language remains debatable. All in all, Rehbein et al. (2011) make several somewhat unverifiable claims for LaRa. For example, they assert that both codeswitching and code-mixing 'focus on speaker-oriented linguistic activities' and that ELF too 'presupposes a focus on speaker' (p. 258), whereas LaRa focuses on the hearer. Perhaps it does—but on a hearer obliged to listen to a language he or she does not speak. Matthey (2008: 115), in contrast, suggests very plausibly that passive bilingualism seems to be entirely in the service of the *speaker's* expressive needs rather than the co-construction of meaning. Rehbein et al. also claim, with no attempt at justification, that 'in LaRa, the interactants use L1 to verbalize what they would not be able to verbalize in ELF' (p. 258), indirectly implying that LaRa might only be used when speakers' English is inadequate to a task. They argue that because LaRa involves the simultaneous (or at least consecutive) use of two languages, it promotes the idea of cultural and linguistic diversity, whereas Lüdi et al. (2010: 75) suggest, on the contrary, that receptive multilingualism is 'another manifestation of a monolingual ideology in the sense that accepting to understand another language could be the condition for refusing to speak it actively.' There is, unfortunately, an inherent inequality in receptive multilingualism or LaRa. Although ELF interactants often differ in their proficiency in this additional language, in receptive multilingualism each participant is by definition required to activate comprehension processes in a language they master less fully than the speaker (if not, they would not need to use receptive multilingualism). As Matthey (2008) argues, receptive multilingualism is hard to reconcile with the awareness that cooperative intercultural communicators generally try to accommodate to each other's uses or to converge towards a common language whenever possible. (The same logic of convergence also explains how less prestigious minority languages disappear as speakers choose to use the language of the majority.) If using only one language is not possible, making *some* attempt to use the interlocutor's language, if only briefly, by mixing languages and codeswitching, generally goes down well.

In non-conflictual situations, many speakers adjust their accents, dialects, lexis, grammar, phraseology, and so on, or (if they are bilingual) even change language completely, to approximate the patterns of interlocutors. Trudgill (2010: 189) describes accommodation as 'a deeply automatic process [. . .] the result of the fact that all human beings operate linguistically according to a powerful and very general maxim,' which (as we have seen in the preceding chapters) Keller (1994: 100) phrases as 'talk like the others talk.' Trudgill states that

> Keller's maxim, in turn, is the linguistic aspect of a much more general and seemingly universal (and therefore presumably innate) human tendency to 'behavioural coordination,' 'behavioural congruence,' 'mutual adaptation' or 'interactional synchrony,' as it is variously called in the literature. This is an apparently biologically given drive to behave as one's peers do.
>
> (Trudgill 2010: 189)

On the contrary, speaking different languages, using receptive multilingualism or interpreting, can provoke a 'them and us' feeling, especially in contexts where there are underlying linguistic tensions (such as Belgian and Canadian institutional settings). The will to use receptive multilingualism is clearly affected by what Rehbein et al. (2011) call 'ideological barriers,' which may be asymmetrical between speakers of a pair of languages. For example, receptive multilingualism seems to be used frequently and to work well enough in many institutional settings in peacefully multilingual Switzerland,[5] whereas in the Dutch-German border area, Beerkens and ten Thije (2011) found that it was only used in 8.3% of cases, most often in face-to-face encounters in the workplace, by a minority of people with 'a very positive attitude towards the neighbouring country, language and people' and 'a very positive view on receptive multilingualism as a language mode' (p. 114). What Beerkens and ten Thije do not mention is that it is only middle-class speakers in this border area who might *need* to use receptive multilingualism. As Trudgill (2002: 30) says, '[T]his is a border without an isogloss,' and speakers on either side 'speak dialects which are the same or very similar; this has meant that for generations there has been ready and easy cross-border communication, as there continues to be today.' But the dialect continuum only exists among working-class dialect speakers; as a result of standardization and the denigration of dialects, and consequent dialect death, middle-class Dutch and Germans now speak standard languages that are not effortlessly mutually comprehensible. They are also likely (particularly on the Dutch side) to have a fairly good knowledge of English.

This is not only the case in the Netherlands and Germany. Here are some further examples, limited to countries with which I have some familiarity: despite huge phonological, lexical, and grammatical similarities among Scandinavian languages, many Scandinavians seem to prefer speaking English to using receptive multilingualism; many Spanish speakers insist that they cannot understand Portuguese; in Belgium, English seems to diffuse latent Flemish-French linguistic animosity; in Switzerland, despite the best efforts of the education system, many young French and Swiss-German speakers choose to converse with each other in English; and so on.[6]

For most people, receptive multilingualism probably has more potential for *reading* than speaking, and it is claimed that a mere 30 to 50 classroom hours are needed to learn to read (at one's own speed) a typologically similar language (Blanche-Benveniste 2008; Grin 2008: 94; Janin 2008: 65), which is certainly far fewer than the 600 or more classroom hours estimated to be necessary to learn to understand and produce a neighbouring language in conventional language teaching.[7] Yet although this may be true for some pairs of typologically similar languages—for example, Catalan and Spanish, Czech and Slovak, Danish and Swedish, Estonian and Finnish, French and Italian—it is not true for others. As any number of German teachers could confirm, it is clearly *not* the case that most English speakers could learn to read German in 50 hours.[8] Moreover, estimations by receptive multilingualism researchers (or Francophone *intercompréhension* researchers) of *how much* of the target language needs to be understood for successful reading to take place seem to be considerably lower than those of Anglophone researchers into foreign language reading comprehension. For example, Meissner (2008: 233) suggests that a comprehension threshold of 70% is necessary (i.e., 70 elements out of 100 must be easily identified), whereas Nation (2001) states that adequate reading comprehension requires a recognition rate of over 98%.[9]

Whatever the word recognition rate, many people *do* find reading a typologically similar or cognate language easier than speaking it or understanding it being spoken, but in today's world a reading knowledge of *English* is necessary for many academic qualifications and jobs (see Chapter 6), even if it is in no way related to the reader's L1. In short, although there are contexts in which receptive multilingualism or 'LaRa' is a potential alternative to the use of a common language or translation, these are relatively limited in scope. Receptive multilingualism can indeed be part of a multilingual speaker's 'toolkit' for certain circumstances but probably in addition to English rather than as an alternative to it.

5.4 Codeswitching and Language Mixing

Contrary to a popular perception in some large and officially monolingual countries, monolingual humans are probably in a minority. As mentioned in Chapter 2, many writers on multilingualism (e.g., Grosjean 2010: 13) claim that more than half of the world's population is bilingual, although in the absence of accurate statistics, some add qualifications such as 'arguably' (e.g., Cook 2002a: 2). Some linguists then proceed to disregard the monolingual minority, claiming, for example, that today, 'individuals' (not *some* individuals) require 'sets of languages' to 'perform the essential functions of communication, cognition and identity' (Aronin and Singleton 2008: 4). But unlike interactants in 'LaRa,' who are said to occupy a succession of clear-cut monolingual speaker and hearer positions (Rehbein et al. 2011: 258), most bi- or multilingual speakers tend, at least some of the time, to mix their languages.

Grosjean's (2010) 'bilingual or holistic view of bilingualism' and his account of bilinguals' 'language modes' were outlined in Chapter 2. Grosjean argues that even in the monolingual speech mode, a bilingual's other language is never totally deactivated, resulting in dynamic interferences even in the most monolingual of situations. But quite apart from accidental interferences, bilinguals who are consciously in the bilingual speech mode—that is, communicating with interlocutors whom they know (or believe) to share the same languages—can codeswitch (shift to another language for a word, a phrase, a sentence, or more) for multiple reasons. There might be concepts that have no equivalent in a particular language or merely turns of phrase in one language that seem more appropriate or expressive; there might be motivations involving identity or status or solidarity or interpersonal intimacy; speakers can repeat things in two languages for added clarity or emphasis; and they can switch languages to report someone else's speech. Linguistic knowledge can also play a part: there might be domains in which even fairly balanced bilinguals habitually use one language and lack vocabulary in others—as Grosjean (2010: 29) says, 'If all languages were used in all domains, there would probably be much less reason to be bilingual'; and speakers who are migrants may have fragmented and truncated language repertoires and find that there are ideas they can only express in a particular language (Blommaert 2010: 9). Furthermore, in extensively bilingual communities, it seems that sometimes there might not really be a reason, and bilinguals just 'switch for the sake of switching' (Gardner-Chloros 1991: 156).

Hence multilinguals often switch between two or more languages. Lüdi et al. (2010: 65) give some delightful examples of language mixing recorded in the Swiss army (in an office rather than on a battlefield), including someone saying '*Ah. Voilà, allora questo è il, der Titel? auch vielleicht, l'abbiamo elaborato assieme*' and so on. (The chief-of-staff explains that they deliberately don't use English 'because we already have four languages in Switzerland.')

Yet codeswitching and language mixing are often confined to relatively informal situations, the established norm in more formal domains tending to be the exclusive use of a single language. Backus et al. (2011: 20), however, argue that this need not be the case: if codeswitching functions 'for daycare centers, some classroom interaction in schools, community organizations, shops and markets, work settings, and public transport,' there is no good reason why it could not also be used in 'classrooms, official services (city hall, police, tax office, etc.), staff meetings in business, parliament sessions, and written media.' Otheguy et al. (2015), who describe multilingual speakers as 'translanguaging' (see Chapter 2), would call this selecting features from a single mental grammar, or deploying one's full linguistic repertoire without regard for 'watchful adherence' to the socially and politically defined labels and boundaries of named languages, rather than codeswitching. Yet Backus et al. are forced to concede that as well as good reasons for mixing languages, there are *bad* reasons for not doing so: speakers (e.g., government officials) are *not* invariably maximally cooperative, especially 'when they are not communicating on their own behalf but as a representative of an organization, a nation or some other collective group.' In such formal and institutional circumstances, 'the need to assert authority, superiority, authenticity, priority or some other contested kind of social identity' often gets in the way of taking the option 'most likely to lead to successful communication' (p. 8). In other words, they stick to the official local language when codeswitching might produce better results.

5.5 Mandarin Chinese

It is almost universally accepted (among linguists) that languages spread either because of the attitudes and choices of language users or because of the power of the nations in which dominant languages are spoken (and the 'empowerment' new speakers of the languages expect to gain). Factors such as clarity, elegance, and logic play no part (*pace* an infamous tradition of such claims emanating from France),[10] and neither does ease of acquisition. Today it is often claimed by journalists, or 'people from outside academic linguistics' (Trudgill 2014a: 387), that a serious potential rival—or successor—to English as a global lingua franca is Mandarin Chinese, because of the number of native Mandarin speakers,[11] sizeable Chinese emigration, and the growth of the Chinese economy.

Trudgill brusquely dismisses this as 'obviously a facile and unrealistic view' (p. 388).

Graddol (2006: 63) reported that '[a]n estimated 30 million people are already studying Mandarin worldwide,' and a quick web search throws up numerous newspaper articles citing rising numbers of students learning Chinese in southeast Asia, the US, and Europe, and increasing numbers of parents sending their children to early immersion bilingual schools with Chinese, because it is thought that it will increasingly bestow linguistic capital (Bourdieu 1991) on its non-native speakers. Oddly, this widely shared perception that Mandarin might come to rival or even replace English around the world in the coming decades has not led the commentators who see English as the Trojan horse of American cultural imperialism and neoliberal market economics, imposed on subjugated nations and ingenuous individuals, to develop a parallel grand narrative of Mandarin as the insidious vector of non-democratic, oppressive, one-party state capitalism.

Yet notwithstanding all the evidence that languages and lingua francas are spread by military or economic might, irrespective of their level of difficulty for non-native learners, there *are* reasons to believe that despite its perceived utility for cross-cultural communication, many (adult) speakers of languages that are typologically very distant from Chinese will find learning Mandarin an overly daunting prospect. Learning to read Chinese involves learning several thousand characters—primary school leavers are expected to know about 2,500, and university graduates at least 3,500, while highly educated adults may know up to 10,000 characters—and learning these takes time, for example, 30% of primary school curriculum time in Hong Kong, plus lots of homework (Kirkpatrick 2010: 15–16). This level of difficulty would seem to count against Mandarin becoming a *written* global lingua franca. Mandarin is also a tonal language, which presents its share of difficulties for speakers of non-tonal languages, and it has (compared with most languages) an enormous number of homophones. For example, the syllable *ji* has 35 different meanings in the first (level rise) tone alone (p. 16), while the morpheme *yi* with a falling tone has 149 different characters, although most of these are parts of multisyllabic expressions (Taylor and Taylor 2014: 29–30), which is why Chinese is ill-suited to an alphabetic script.[12] The U.S. Foreign Service Institute classifies Chinese (alongside Cantonese, Korean, Japanese, and Arabic) as 'exceptionally difficult for native English speakers' and estimates that it takes a native English speaker 2,200 classroom hours (with the second year in-country) to reach professional fluency (compared with 600 hours for most Romance and Germanic languages, with the exception of German, which requires 25% more).[13] Mandarin can be expected to present a similar level of difficulty to speakers of most other non-East Asian languages, which might seem to count against it becoming a *spoken* global lingua franca.

A partially mitigating factor might be that Mandarin is generally considered to have a very simple grammar, and indeed McWhorter (2007, Ch. 5) argues that Mandarin (compared, e.g., with Cantonese) has undergone a process of simplification analogous to that of English (see Chapter 4) because of extensive non-native acquisition and interrupted transmission in the seventh to ninth centuries CE. And a Chinese speaker might point out that the supposedly simplified English language is not in fact that simple: it has a more extensive vocabulary than most languages, largely because of the Norse and Norman invasions of Anglo-Saxon England; inconsistent verbal morphology; inconsistent and irregular orthography;[14] and idiosyncratic phonetics—a large vowel system, consonants that are difficult for speakers of many other languages, seemingly arbitrary and unpredictable word stress, complex intonation patterns, and so on (see Wells 2005: 102–3).

Yet despite these difficulties, English *has* spread around the world, and for the moment, despite the tens of millions of people learning Mandarin (as opposed to the hundreds of millions of Chinese learning English), the Chinese seem to be having more success in, and more enthusiasm for, learning English than most of the rest of the world has for learning Chinese. For example, in the domain of science, Montgomery (2013: 84) suggests that 'by about 2025, perhaps sooner' there may be as many peer-reviewed articles in English written by Chinese scientists as by Americans. This seems to indicate that English has grown to a point where it is self-perpetuating and no longer dependent on the geopolitical standing of the United States. Many millions of people around the world, not just in China, have invested a great deal of time, effort, and money in learning to speak, write, and publish in English. Montgomery shows how previous prestigious scholarly lingua francas, such as Latin and Arabic, far outlasted the power of the conquerors that imposed them, and remained storehouses of texts and knowledge for many centuries. Thus there are good reasons to believe that English will remain the major language of knowledge for the conceivable future (see Chapter 6) as well as a majority of people's first choice as a global lingua franca.

Parenthetically, the case of Chinese scientists publishing in English is a prime example of how the recent spread and maintenance of English can be seen as the consequence of socioeconomic 'pull' (or 'demand-side') factors rather than 'push' factors, at least those involving language policy (e.g., inexplicably powerful plotters in British Council offices or wherever). Notwithstanding Phillipson's (1992, 2009) account of 'linguicism' and 'linguistic imperialism,' it seems to be the pragmatic pursuit of social and economic advancement, via a shared language of wider communication—in short empowerment rather than subjection to a foreign power—that is driving the global use of English.[15]

5.6 Conclusion

As argued, there is a limited range of contexts—chiefly among neighbouring, cognate, and/or typologically similar languages—in which receptive multilingualism and codeswitching (and perhaps 'translanguaging') are possible and could indeed be bolstered by training and official encouragement. But for broader international communication (without translation), regional lingua francas and a more widespread lingua franca remain necessary. There have been many lingua francas over history, usually based on the languages of conquerors, which have inevitably benefitted their native speakers (Ostler 2005, 2010). Despite the intrinsic unfairness of this state of affairs, it seems unlikely that language policy will overturn it in the foreseeable future. Ferguson (2007: 33) argues that 'the spread of English [. . .] is substantially a market-driven bottom-up process not amenable to control by any one country or organisation,' but the same is almost certainly true of whole alliances of countries and organizations. Machine translation is unlikely to change things either. Hence English as an international lingua franca probably has a long future ahead of it as a major component of multilingual communicators' repertoires. This is not without consequences, including the imposition of constraints in academic and scientific research and publishing, which is discussed in the following chapter, and the inevitable influence of English on other languages, which is the subject of Chapter 7.

Notes

1 See the discussion of multicompetence, translanguaging, and so on in section 2.3.

2 Then again, if we are to believe the sublimely negative Ortega y Gasset (1937/1992: 98), humans haven't been much better: 'almost all translations done until now are bad ones.'

3 At the time of writing, Google Translate's phrase-based system is being replaced by neural-network-based translation, in which computers—artificial 'neural networks'—'learn' by trial and error, 'rewiring' themselves (or altering numerical relationships among artificial neurons) and making predictions (or ever-improving guesses) about how to translate longer chunks or whole sentences according to patterns perceived in the data (see Lewis-Kraus 2016). Translation based on machine learning or artificial intelligence is clearly an enormous advance on translation restricted to pre-programmed parallel dictionaries and grammar rules, but it remains fallible.

4 '[L]anguages do not encode the kind of information that humans are interested in communicating. Linguistically encoded semantic representations are abstract mental structures which must be inferentially enriched before they can be taken to represent anything of interest' (Sperber and Wilson 1986/1995: 174), and 'an utterance will be understood as loose or metaphorical unless nothing less than a fully literal interpretation will do' (Wilson and Sperber 1988: 144).

5 Such settings include the Federal Parliament, as well as *Lettres/Philosophische* faculty meetings at the University of Fribourg/Freiburg, although here, sadly, if we are to trust Robert Rehder's (2009) exquisite poem 'The Gam,' not even the joint use of French and German can prevent the establishment of new world records in boredom!

6 No statistics exist in this area. For example, the European Commission's Eurobarometer statistics giving people's self-assessed language knowledge do not cover receptive multilingualism.

7 For example, it is often stated that it requires about 200 'guided learning hours' to reach CEFR level A2, and another 200 hours to reach each successive level, so that B2 requires approximately 600 hours and C1 800 hours. See https://support.cambridgeenglish.org/hc/en-gb/articles/202838506-Guided-learning-hours.

8 Although there is *some* cognate lexis—see, for example, the splendid 'Appendix of Teutonic (English-Swedish-Danish-Dutch-German) Cognates' at the end of Bodmer (1944/1985) and the *Vocabulaire parallèle des 39 langues d'Europe* in Kersaudy (2001)—German is still full of words that are not instantly recognizable to Anglophones.

9 All in all, receptive multilingualism seems to lead people into making hyperbolic and unfounded claims. For example, Cassen (2005), quoted in the 'Préface' to Conti and Grin (2008: 15), informs us that if all speakers of Romance languages mastered *l'intercompréhension*, in the year 2025, there would be 1.5 billion Chinese speakers, 1.04 billion English speakers, and 1.3 billion 'Romanophones' able to understand each other and thus 'considered and counted as speakers of the same language' (my translation). And the sky would be filled with *porci volatilis*. Moreover, official figures for the number of L2 French speakers worldwide (included in Cassen's 1.3 billion) are wholly fanciful (not to say fraudulent); see Chaudenson (2003).

10 Spectacularly uninformed claims about the superiority of the French language go back more than 250 years, including the egregious but hilarious Rivarol (1784), although he also said wise things about translation (see Chapter 7). Unfortunately they continue to this day; see Wright (2006), and Lodge (1998).

11 The number of Mandarin speakers should not be confused with the number of people in China; there are millions of speakers of Cantonese and the Shanghai dialect, as well as speakers of many other mutually incomprehensible Chinese dialects, plus 54 official minority languages and many minority groups.

12 Hagège (2012: 145) states that *English* is ill-suited to its role as an international language because many words have several meanings, giving rise to 'fatal ambiguities' (p. 153). He does not comment on this characteristic of Chinese.

13 See http://web.archive.org/web/20071014005901/www.nvtc.gov/lotw/months/november/learningExpectations.html. See also Odlin (1989: 39).

14 Hagège (2012: 142) states (without giving a source) that English uses 1,120 graphemes (letters or combinations of letters that represent a phoneme) to write 62 possible phonemes. Other scholars give rather lower figures, for example, Caravolas (2006: 500), citing Carney (1994), gives about 210 graphemes for 44 phonemes.

15 Rebuttals of Phillipson's notion of *linguistic* imperialism (e.g., Conrad 1996; Brutt-Griffler 2002; Spolsky 2004, Ch. 6; Edwards 2011, Ch. 8) tend not to engage with his arguments about imperialism *tout court* (in terms of transnational corporations, the IMF and the World Bank, American military interventions, 'McDonaldization,' etc.).

6 Academic English, Epistemicide, and Linguistic Relativity

> 'Our language is of no consequence in the rest of the world. Every student has to know English, French and German. Without them you can't complete a degree. Because of this our own language has sunk to the level of some sort of patois, a medium for apprentices. The most advanced studies are written in foreign languages. The great minds come to us in English by way of English textbooks—a language we can read quite easily, but which we can seldom speak or write without making mistakes. I notice it even now, as I am trying to explain this to you. If I were speaking Norwegian, I could be more subtle, more precise.' [. . .]
>
> 'Don't any good books get translated into Norwegian?'
>
> 'Of course they do, there are plenty of translations. But you can't get away from the fact that you're not reading the real thing. Some people find that depressing.' [. . .]
>
> 'If you're a small country,' he says, 'where politics and fashion and film and cars and machines and practically everything else is imported from abroad, and if beyond that practically all essential books, that is to say the books that are better than most local books, the "founding books" so to speak—if those books are all foreign, then the countries producing them will regard you the same way as colonial powers regard their colonies, and city folks regard the provinces.'
>
> Willem Frederik Hermans, *Beyond Sleep* [1966], trans. Ina Rilke (2006: 79–81)

6.1 Dealing With the Dominance of English

Speakers of the 'smaller' languages of north-west Europe have long been used to the dominance of English. Advanced study requires a knowledge of English, and despite abundant translations, people still encounter the ideas of many famous thinkers in books written in English. Some (or perhaps many) people resent this situation, like the character in this extract, a fictional Norwegian geologist whose conversation in English with a Dutch colleague was in fact written in Dutch by Willem Frederik

Hermans 50 years ago (and more recently translated into English).[1] Hermans's novel also includes an American living in Europe who laments the way European manufacturers invent American-sounding brand names and how Europeans imitate American music or write in English or use American expressions and try to put on American accents—and all this half a century ago.

In the intervening decades English has reinforced its position as the world's 'hypercentral' language (de Swaan 2001), and it has become increasingly necessary for researchers to write in English when publishing for an international audience. In the natural sciences, for example, whereas national languages are still used for technical work and journals in many countries, it is estimated that English is now used globally for more than 90% of communication aimed at an international audience. This includes books and articles as well as research institute websites, private sector research and development, international patents, statistical and data archives, grant applications, job advertisements, job interviews, conferences, visiting lectures, and a lot of graduate-level teaching (Montgomery 2013: 3, 168). The prestigious research journals in most fields have switched to English-only publication, and the major citation indices only include articles in English or at the very least with abstracts and references in English. Ammon (2003) states that more than 80% of articles in the social sciences and humanities are written in English too, although he concedes that such figures may be skewed by the fact that they rely heavily on English-language databases and citation indices.[2] Across Europe, universities have introduced courses taught in English in pursuit of fee-paying foreign students and enhanced international prestige and contacts (and also to develop their staff and students' English-language skills).

In this chapter I will discuss the consequences of the almost obligatory use of not just the English language but also, in the human sciences, of an argumentative style that can safely be called English Academic Discourse (EAD). This form of discourse is sometimes described as being 'writer-responsible,' as opposed to more indirect and inductive forms of writing that are supposedly 'reader-responsible' and inherently more difficult to understand. I will argue, from the perspective of relevance theory, that this notion is false and based on an etic or outsiders' view. I will also consider the claim that the dominance of EAD is a form of 'epistemicide' that effectively kills other forms of knowledge, and discuss the consequences for writers of other languages of having to write in or be translated into English.

Despite widespread bilingualism it is still evident (as argued in the previous chapter) that many people are more at ease working in their first or dominant language and have a lesser facility of expression, less grasp of stylistic differences, less command of constructions and rhetorical strategies, and so on, in foreign or additional languages. Writing is often more laborious and time-consuming in an L2, and there is the unavoidable risk of unwanted L1 transfer. *Bien pensant* attempts to abolish the notion of 'native speaker' are not helpful in this regard; it is obvious that native speakers of English are advantaged in global academic discourse and can, *ceteris paribus*, more easily produce polished texts and speak confidently at conferences. Cogo and Jenkins (2010: 275) insist that ELF is 'an additionally acquired language system' for native English speakers as well as for non-natives because 'they are no longer the norm providers,' but it is not an additionally acquired *language*, and the fact remains that native English speakers do *not* generally have to learn a foreign language to communicate internationally. Many of them also use ENL without any concessions to their international audience.

As argued in the previous chapters, there is an increasing awareness among L2 English speakers, and (one hopes) an increasing acceptance among native English speakers too, that when used as a lingua franca, English is no longer related to any given speech community in which particular ways of speaking and writing are appropriate. Yet whereas *spoken* ELF contains a huge amount of linguistic variation and non-standard forms, formal *written* communication tends to resemble standard, educated native English to a much greater extent. This is especially so of academic work, in which more careful formulation and revision and re-reading are expected.

Academic language is difficult to read and write—native English speakers also need to learn these registers to integrate a professional community of practice—and putting it in a foreign language obviously increases the difficulty and entails costs in energy, editing, and correction. Even if many non-native English-speaking scientists are just as used to thinking and writing in English as in their mother tongue in their professional domain, as a consequence of reading and perhaps teaching in this language, it remains an L2. As Nygaard argues, whereas native speakers (in the human sciences) are often concerned about 'authorial voice' or even playing with the language and challenging generic conventions, researchers writing in English as an additional language are often simply concerned about 'getting it right.'[3]

Some researchers continue to write in their L1 and pay for a translation—so that ENGLISH becomes €NG£I$H[4]—but most researchers write directly in L2 English, even though, as Chan (2016) states, this often involves 'self-translation' from the L1, with all the crosslinguistic interference this entails. On the other hand, as long as researchers self-translate rather than think and write in English as fully functioning bilinguals, the L1 is not endangered. If everyone thinks and writes directly in English, there is clearly the possibility of domain loss, in which other languages (potentially *all* other languages) gradually lose lexical and stylistic resources through disuse or, in Bourdieusian terms, are dispossessed of linguistic capital. If a language lacks the terminology to express recent scientific concepts without massive recourse to loanwords, it ceases to be an adequate vehicle for doing research and teaching at advanced levels or even for explaining what such work is about.

The other side of the coin is that science, which aims at universal acceptance and thus a global audience, is now more international (while also more monolingual) than ever before. L2 English-speaking scientists in developing countries that were marginally involved in research a generation ago now have full access to the knowledge of their chosen fields and can disseminate their findings to colleagues around the world. Furthermore, although the current level of dominance by a single language is historically unprecedented, there have been many earlier scientific lingua francas in different parts of the world, including Greek, Syriac, Arabic, Persian, Sanskrit, Chinese, and Latin (Ostler 2005). In a book called *Does Science Need a Global Language?*—might that be a leading question?—Montgomery (2013: 125) suggests that the development of science, whether in ancient Egypt, Greece, India, China, the Islamic Empire, or in medieval and Renaissance Europe, has always 'depended to a considerable degree on the existence of a lingua franca.' Indeed the period between about 1680 and 1970, when science was written in a number of vernacular languages, was an anomaly, 'the only period of major advancement *without* a single, true lingua franca' (p. 134). Hagège (2012: 118) suggests that the period in the late 19th and early 20th centuries when many major scientists published in either English, French, or German (and often had a reading knowledge of the other two languages, despite the widespread use of translation) was an extremely fecund one for science precisely because different languages offer different routes to conceptual and terminological innovation (whereas monolingualism stifles innovation). This hypothesis cannot be proved, however, and it still disregards or marginalizes speakers of first languages other than this scientific trinity. Proponents of linguistic diversity such as Hagège (who not infrequently confuse diversity with the use of French) would prefer a multilingual landscape, with perhaps three or more dominant languages of science, but just like today, this would still require a great number of researchers to learn at least one foreign language.

Yet it is undeniable that huge advantages accrue to native speakers of English (and to highly competent non-native speakers who achieve 'native-like' proficiency). Many scientists seek them out for international collaborations to the clear professional advantage of the Anglophones, who are free-riders benefitting from the learning and use of English by non-native speakers. Competence in English rather than science can lead to professional advancement. Even if English used as a lingua franca is international and supposedly 'cultureless,' it is still the English language and closer to the culture of native speakers of English than any other. As a result, many L2 English speakers choose (or need) to go to inner circle countries to improve their language skills, and more than a few choose to stay, leading to a massive 'brain drain' or the asymmetric flow of human capital to the inner circle countries.[5] Native English speakers also benefit from education systems that can put more money into advanced science education because they don't invest in foreign language teaching.[6]

So what can be done? Given that the dominance of English is likely to continue, various initiatives to help researchers write in English *as well as* in their L1 have been suggested by Ammon (2007), Ferguson (2007), Salager-Meyer (2008), and Montgomery (2013), among others, which would go some way to countering the disadvantages incurred by non-Anglophone researchers and the dangers of domain loss:

- English needs to be fully integrated into the science curriculum, as a core subject, like mathematics. Universities need to offer graduate students courses in English for research publication purposes as well as editing, revising and proofreading services for academic staff. Montgomery believes that 'where the funds and facilities exist to teach science adequately, there should be the capacity to teach languages, too' (p. 174), so 'it shouldn't be thought excessive to ask that students who reach a graduate level in a field as complex as geochemistry or molecular genetics be able to acquire functionality in a foreign tongue'—which also applies 'to monolingual Anglophones' (p. 128).
- Scientific journals need to add more non-native English speakers to their editorial boards, and editors and reviewers need to show greater tolerance towards deviations from native English norms, where these don't compromise intelligibility, and to provide more editorial support for non-Anglophones, probably by employing language editors. In a much-cited article, Ammon (2000: 111) insisted that non-native English-speaking scientists should have the right to their 'linguistic peculiarities' when writing for the international community,[7] and Montgomery (2013: 98) states that this has indeed come to pass in the natural sciences: 'linguistic peculiarities' *are* increasingly accepted, and there is 'a significant flexibility in what is now acceptable as written scientific English' without this leading to any 'serious problems of meaning.'
- It should be possible to present conference papers in major languages other than English, with interpreting being made available, financed by the conference fees of those who benefit from it (although reviewing conference proposals in languages other than English presents its own set of problems).
- To counter domain loss authors can potentially write in their L1s and be translated into English or indeed write in English (perhaps with editorial assistance) and be translated into their L1, although there are of course prohibitive questions of cost and complex copyright issues (Montgomery, p. 179). Hagège (2012: 118) argues that scientists (or at least Francophone scientists) should write in their L1,

with an official body circulating abstracts in English, even though this would presumably decrease the readership of such articles. Yet where authors with other L1s do write in English, universities and national science associations could easily insist on comprehensive L1 summaries of doctoral dissertations, articles, and so on.

6.2 Rhetorical Strategies and Epistemicide

Chan (2016: 173) suggests that dual-language publishing with translation is particularly applicable to the humanities, in which the form of discourse is often inextricably related to the content and the language of expression. This leads us to a far broader issue than the acceptability of non-native 'peculiarities,' or non-standard constructions, phraseology, and lexis in English, which is the acceptability, or otherwise, of 'non-Anglo' argumentative and rhetorical structures. In fact the dominance of English in academic writing poses a number of epistemological questions. Are non-native English-speaking researchers being forced to restrict themselves to paradigms, methods, procedures, and discourse strategies that are familiar to their Anglophone colleagues? To what extent can or should academic English encompass *rhetorical* flexibility and variation as well as the variation of surface lexicogrammatical features? Can or should researchers expect their readers to accommodate to patterns of text organization that are uncommon in native English? How far do 'Anglo' discourse norms constrict alternative styles of thinking and impose near-homogeneous practices?

Text organization and argumentative structure in research papers in the natural sciences are relatively uncontentious. The IMRD (or IMRAD) structure, standing for introduction, methods, results, and discussion, is used for reporting laboratory work in many disciplines, and there are other normalized verbal and visual forms for reporting fieldwork, theoretical investigations, methodological innovations, mathematical modelling, and so on. While these forms largely derive from 20th-century Anglophone (British and North American) and western European scientists, they are now broadly international, although they seem to allow minor cultural differences. For example, Montgomery (2013: 186) suggests that there is a broad East Asian style involving more indirect ways of expressing doubt and criticism, forestalling disagreement until credibility has been established, or indeed totally avoiding a dialogical or adversarial stance in relation to the work of other researchers. Chinese researchers, heirs to a tradition stressing respect for authority and precedent, often include citations of renowned scientists even if they are not immediately relevant to the work at hand (p. 108). All in all, for some scientific domains, Montgomery foresees the emergence of 'a global variety of professional English that incorporates or allows for elements from many local discourses—a kind of broad, forgiving world standard' (p. 60).[8]

Rhetorical norms in the humanities and social sciences are less uniform, although even here there are many journals (including in applied linguistics) whose positivist reviewers call for empirical data and testable hypotheses and decry anything that looks essayistic, introspective, and so on. Yet to be published in English-language academic journals in the human sciences, authors (whether native or non-native English speakers) are generally expected to use a particular type of writing and text organization.

That this type of writing is not universal can easily be ascertained by reading in other languages or by reading research (in English) on contrastive or intercultural rhetoric. In 1966, Kaplan famously illustrated various patterns of paragraph and text organization—as revealed by the compositions of international ESL students in American universities, rather than in published research—with a series of squiggles or doodles depicting what he called rhetorical patterns that differ from established English ones. To the native English-speaking reader, these appear to be 'out of sync' and lacking organization and cohesion if transferred to English expository prose.

According to Kaplan (1966/1972: 249), English expository essays follow a linear development: ideally 'the flow of ideas occurs in a straight line from the opening sentence to the last sentence,' probably with the main argument stated in the first paragraph.[9] Writers of Romance languages and Russian, on the contrary, are said to use digressions and introduce extraneous material and parenthetical amplifications of subordinate elements, while Chinese and Korean writing is indirect—Kaplan says of one paper written by a Korean student that it 'arrives where it should have started'—with paragraphs that can be described (borrowing from Yeats's poem 'The Second Coming') to be 'turning and turning in a widening gyre' (or perhaps an expanding circle!) around the subject, showing it from a variety of tangents but never directly (p. 253). In short, Kaplan describes the writing of outer and expanding circle users as 'employing a rhetoric and a sequence of thought which violate the expectations of the native reader' (p. 247). His article is about what 'the English reader expects to be an integral part of any formal communication,' but he was referring to the native English reader (specifically the ESL composition teacher), whereas today, to a far greater extent than in 1966, the readership of academic work in English is global.

Contrastive rhetoric à la Kaplan, not unlike orthodox EFL/ESL theory, is clearly a deficit model rather than a celebration of ESL (or ELF) writers' multilingual resources, and it eventually provoked an equal and opposite body of work decrying the reductionist, essentialist, and deterministic notion of discrete, static, monolithic, homogeneous cultures and discourse patterns. Many theorists criticized the cultural stereotyping and 'othering' of the ESL learner and the implicit assumption of the superiority of native English writers and writing, usually described in terms of virtues such as linearity, logic, directness, clarity, coherence, deductive reasoning, individualism, critical thinking, and audience awareness (see, e.g., Zamel 1997; Pennycook 1998; Atkinson 1999; Kubota 1999).[10] Kubota and Lehner (2004) call for a 'critical cultural rhetoric' that celebrates multiculturalism and 'transculturation.' Canagarajah (2013) champions *codemeshing*—the textual realization of *translanguaging*, or the ability of multilingual speakers to shuttle between the diverse languages that form their repertoire, treating them as an integrated system (see Chapter 2). In response to these criticisms, rhetorical analysts (e.g., Connor 2004, 2008; Li 2008) now tend to use the term 'intercultural rhetoric' and to insist that they treat learners and writers as multilingual and multicultural agents, and cultures as dynamic systems.

Yet 'critical' work in ESL theory, with its postmodern leitmotifs of diversity, hybridity, interculturality, liminality, pluralism, reflexivity, and so on has not affected the gatekeeping practices of English-language academic journals in article selection, reviewing, and copy-editing. Bennett, who has carried out a detailed survey of English academic style manuals (2009), offers a full account of the linear 'Anglo' style, which she calls 'English Academic Discourse' or EAD. I cannot improve on her summary of its underlying principles:

> The discourse needs to be above all clear and coherent, and based upon a structured rational argument supported by evidence; the language should be generally impartial and objective, with fact clearly distinguished from opinion, and there should be general caution and restraint about all claims made; current theory will be incorporated through citation and referencing. The text should be organized into sections with a clear introduction, development and conclusion, each of which should be subdivided into paragraphs, and there will be a hierarchical organization on all these levels (general statement of theme, followed by development, etc.). In terms of style, the prose should be lucid, economical and precise, avoiding vagueness, verbosity and circumlocution, and will make use of complete sentences with straightforward syntax. Impersonal structures, such as the passive and nominalized forms, will predominate in many disciplines, and there will be an absence of figurative language (though this is less marked in the humanities) allowing the focus to fall firmly on the object of study.
>
> (Bennett 2007: 161)

This hegemonic EAD, which has effectively become 'the discourse of modernity' (Halliday and Martin 1993: 84), clearly encapsulates a particular view of the world, and Bennett (2007: 154) describes it as the 'predatory' agent of 'epistemicide' and 'symbolic genocide'—'the systematic destruction of rival forms of knowledge.'[11] 'Knowledges' that are grounded on radically different ideologies are 'silenced completely'—starved of funding and remaining unpublished—as their form is unacceptable to journal editors and publishers (see Uzuner 2008; Lillis and Curry 2010), whereas 'knowledges' that have some overlap with the dominant one are 'bullied or cajoled into an acceptable shape.' If authors do not oblige—by a form of self-censorship that makes their work more rational, clear, succinct, terse, plain, logical, linear, and objective, and less emotional and verbose—their work is likely to be rejected by journal editors. If they write in their L1 and submit their work to Anglophone translators, it will almost certainly be adapted and given a structure that is acceptable in EAD because 'any attempt to diverge from the norm in translation is likely to be received as incompetence by editors and peer reviewers and rejected out of hand' (Bennett 2013: 180).

Thus the hegemony of EAD rather dampens the optimistic claims by ELF researchers about the freedom of non-native English speakers to use non-standard forms or even to 'display systematic new patterning' (Mauranen et al. 2010a: 188): a sprinkling of morphosyntactically non-standard 'ELF variants' are rather insignificant compared to an imposed overall rhetorical structure. Mauranen (2006b: 276) claims that ELF is 'a more important means of academic communication than its standard native varieties' because there is more of it than work written by native English speakers, but the non-native English-speaking authors are still expected to conform to the epistemological bases and presuppositions of EAD, a style of academic discourse largely developed by native English speakers.

Many researchers have described discourse styles that do *not* coincide with EAD. For example, Clyne (1980) discusses German writers' traditional preference for digressions (*Exkurse*) which introduce 'extraneous,' 'parenthetical,' or 'subordinate' material into linear argumentation.[12] Mauranen (1993) finds that Finnish academics tend to prefer end-weight strategies. They provide background materials (hypotheses, facts, or other research) and an interpretive framework before making a claim (probably under the influence of the German academic tradition) and present claims as a conclusion rather than as a point of departure, necessitating inferential work by the reader en route. Finnish writers tend not to make explicit transitions between sections or to provide signposts or coherence markers which, it is felt, could be rather patronizing or overly condescending to the reader.

Finnish academic writing thus shares with some Asian rhetorical forms what Hinds (1990: 98) calls 'delayed introduction of purpose': placing the thesis statement in final position after a lot of contextual detail has been presented. Hinds describes a 'quasi-inductive' four-part structure often used in expository prose, such as newspaper editorials, in Chinese, Japanese, and Korean. Originating in Classical Chinese poetry, this structure—called *qi-cheng-zhuan-he* in Chinese, *ki-shoo-ten-ketsu* in Japanese, and *ki-sung-chon-kyul* in Korean—is notable for a sudden topic shift in its third part, which introduces an unexpected element, with a connection but not a direct association to the major theme, into an otherwise normal progression of ideas. The fourth part, the conclusion, does not need to be decisive but can indicate a doubt or ask a question. Hinds (1983) gives examples of Japanese newspaper editorials using this structure that were translated sentence by sentence for the English-language edition, and Scollon and Scollon (1997) show how this structure is used in both Chinese- and English-language newspapers in Hong Kong, so it clearly isn't dependent on anything inherent to the linguistic or cognitive structures of a given language.

Similarly Yamuna Kachru (1995: 28) suggests that Indian and Chinese writers often give a great deal of background information without ever relating it directly to the topic under discussion as a politeness strategy, with the indirectness allowing readers to reach their own conclusions. Kirkpatrick and Xu (2012), however, argue that whereas Chinese writing has always shown a preference for inductive reasoning (which gives an impression of indirectness and obliqueness), deductive reasoning and mixed methods of argument have always existed alongside it too. Canagarajah (2002: 149) asserts that 'local' or 'periphery' scholars in Sri Lanka treat the reader as being intelligent enough to understand an evolving argument without heavy-handed guidance from the author. They provide sufficient data to allow readers to make the necessary inferences and to make up their minds as to the acceptability of the argument without being led by the nose. This accords with Hall's description of indirect communication in what he calls 'high-context' cultures (such as those of East and South Asia), in which interlocutors rely on shared background knowledge and contextual information:

> When talking about something that they have on their minds, a high-context individual will expect his interlocutor to know what's bothering him, so that he does not have to be specific. The result is that he will talk around and around the point, in effect putting all the pieces in place except the crucial one. Placing it properly—this keystone—is the role of his interlocutor. To do this for him is an insult and a violation of his individuality.
>
> (Hall 1977: 113)

Indirect communicative strategies such as these might also be explained in terms of protecting the reader's autonomy and 'negative face'—'the basic claim to freedom of action and freedom from imposition'—whereas 'Anglo'-style writers are concerned to promote their own 'positive face'—'positive self-image and the desire that this self-image be appreciated and approved of' (Brown and Levinson 1987: 61).

Hinds (1987) describes indirect forms of writing as 'reader-responsible,' meaning that the reader has to make an effort and use inductive logic to provide the transitions and logical links between the sentences and paragraphs, unlike in 'writer-responsible' cultures such as the United States and the UK, in which readers expect writers to use coherence devices and textual transitions to make the connections between arguments explicit. However, the notion that inductive rhetorical strategies necessarily impose additional interpretive effort on the reader would appear to be an outsider's view. Pragmatic theories of language—most notably relevance theory, which shows that *all* verbal communication is, in part, inferential—include an economic component which states that interpretive effort should be matched by adequate cognitive effects. Consequently we must assume that communicators in supposedly 'reader-responsible' cultures are not imposing excessive and unnecessary processing costs on their receivers, who are expected to understand an author's intended meanings, expressed according to the culture's chosen rhetorical forms, by following the path of least effort and expending a minimum of processing effort. This is particularly the case if we accept Sperber and Wilson's (1986/1995: 260) cognitive and communicative principles of relevance, such that '[h]uman cognition tends to be geared to the maximisation of relevance' and that '[e]very act of ostensive communication communicates a presumption of its own optimal relevance.'

According to relevance theory, what is optimally relevant (and meaningful and readily interpretable) depends on the mutual cognitive environment of the communication partners. Thus to describe the non-linear, inductive, four-part structure of some Chinese, Japanese, or Korean expository prose—and in particular its third part (*zhuan*, *ten* or *chon*)—as incoherent, and requiring readers to interpret more and generally work harder than readers of linear, deductive English texts, is to reveal an etic perspective.[13] Difficulty lies in the eye of the beholder.[14] Analysts from so-called writer-responsible cultures imagine the processing cost or effort, or the amount of inference, that would be necessary to make sense of a supposedly 'reader-responsible' text in *their own* cognitive environment and attribute this effort to readers in 'reader-responsible' cultures, with their wholly different cognitive environment.[15]

Clearly different cultures, languages, and genres *do* have preferred compositional forms, and most readers have expectations about the ordering of ideas and understand and recall information more readily when it is presented in a manner that meets these expectations.

Yet in recent decades there has been a dramatic increase in the number of outer and expanding circle academics who have been trained in inner circle countries and use Anglo-American conventions, not only in English but also when writing in their L1 (see Eggington 1987). More and more Asian and European scholars seem to be turning to deductive reasoning, with an explicit statement of purpose and the main idea outlined at the beginning of articles. In some cases this may be the result of training at school: Japanese schoolchildren, for example, are now trained in 'logical thinking,' which is considered to be necessary in international communication, and in an 'Anglo' style of organizing paragraphs and arguments (Kubota 2002). As Cameron (2002: 70) points out, this is clear evidence of the existence of dominant and subaltern cultures: 'Finns do not run workshops for British businesses on the virtues of talking less; Japanese are not invited to instruct Americans in speaking indirectly.'

Despite this trend, however, the use of native English discourse styles is clearly *not* a necessity in a language used as a lingua franca for an international readership. Non-native English-speaking writers should have the option of transferring the overall rhetorical patterns of their own linguaculture into their written English—which is effectively ELF—because thought and discourse patterns are more fundamental than surface 'peculiarities' or lexicogrammatical variation. Certainly non-native English speakers need to learn to read and understand 'Anglo' rhetorical patterns, or they will not have access to a huge body of writing only available in English. But native English speakers also need to become competent in reading rhetorical modes and forms of writing other than the dominant one. They need to become accustomed to articles in the human sciences that do *not* begin by stating their thesis and then systematically develop and support it, even though many reviewers for academic journals continue to complain that such a style entails a lack of perspective, coherence, and conviction (see, e.g., Canagarajah 2002, Ch. 4). They need to accommodate to papers with literary vocabulary and figures of speech, as well as delayed introduction of purpose, in which some points may only be implicit and the ideas only loosely connected, without explicit cohesive devices linking topics from one sentence and paragraph to the next.[16] They need to accept rhetorical styles that give space to a lot of additional background information, and tangential and peripherally related arguments, perhaps all leading to a relatively non-assertive conclusion, as such strategies do *not* intrinsically impose additional processing effort on readers who are familiar with them.

Ideally, all users of academic English should be able to understand both direct and indirect uses of language, and a range of deductive, inductive, and quasi-inductive rhetorical styles. Given the range of writers and readers of research written in English, a more hybrid approach—somewhere between the sign-posted, deductive style and the inductive style that invites the reader to follow the evolving argument without too much heavy-handed authorial guidance—may eventually emerge. Indeed Mauranen et al. (2010b) already see timid signs of hybridization, cross-cultural heterogeneity, and diversity in academic English. In short, writing for an international audience, researchers should feel free to transfer the rhetorical patterns of text organization of their choice into English, depending on their perception of their readers' expectations.

6.3 Domesticating and Foreignizing Translation

Although overall patterns of text organization are not language specific, particular sentence structures usually are, which clearly has consequences for translation. Bennett (2007) gives examples of the work of Portuguese scholars in the humanities and social sciences who favour an elaborate style that is radically different from EAD. These writers use a rich literary vocabulary and figures of speech and are not afraid of abstraction, ambiguity, paradox, and digression. Bennett describes the syntax of the meandering sentences of the Portuguese humanities style (which has counterparts in the other Romance languages) as having a 'tendency to cultivate verbal foliage that, to English eyes, only obscures the main trunk of the argument,' and as 'anything but clear and linear, with a sprouting of subordination that defies translation into a language like English' (p. 156). English translators of such work are faced with a choice between producing a faithful, source-oriented translation that readers unfamiliar with this style of argumentation will presumably find unclear and obscure, or a target-oriented translation that 'Anglifies' or domesticates the text. Yet this second option—which generally involves adding connectors, splitting up sentences, and replacing 'flamboyant emotive terms' with 'more matter-of-fact equivalents' and 'familiar-sounding collocations' (p. 157)—comes at the cost of eradicating the text's 'underlying ideology' and destroying its 'entire infrastructure' (by restructuring it), which clearly has 'far-reaching consequences as regards the worldview encoded in it' (p. 155).

Bennett illustrates her argument with both literal, source-oriented translations and (published) target-oriented translations of the same passages from articles by Portuguese humanities scholars, stating that the alterations in the published versions 'were necessary because the texts would not have been comprehensible to the English reader otherwise, and as such would not be acceptable for publication in an English language journal' (p. 158). She does not specify whether she means the native Anglophone reader or the global community of readers of academic work written in English, but I agree that readers of most L1s other than Romance languages would find non-domesticated translations of Romance academic texts hard to read (though not actually incomprehensible). It is easy to argue, as Kirkpatrick and Xu (2012: 5) do, that '[w]e need to create an environment in which the ideas of others can flow through to the Anglo-American world,'[17] but some forms of expression do not seem to work very well in English.

Bennett (2013) also gives the example of an academic text in a Romance language that *wasn't* domesticated in its English translation, namely Foucault's *L'archéologie du savoir*. This was translated as *The Archaeology of Knowledge* (by Alan Sheridan Smith, who translated a number of Foucault's books, although his name doesn't appear in this one) in a very source-oriented fashion, closely following French discourse patterns, in a way that Bennett describes as 'quite difficult to understand' (p. 181). She quotes a 140-word sentence (from Foucault 1972/2002: 59) in which the subject is deferred until the fourth line and that has so many subordinate clauses that 'the main point is not clearly discernible at first reading.' Furthermore the succeeding sentence, beginning with 'But' is actually ungrammatical, appearing to be a subordinate clause that has come detached from the previous sentence. This is acceptable in Romance languages, in which 'periodic sentences' can have a period or full stop followed by a final detached subordinate clause for rhetorical effect, but not in English. Foucault was presumably translated into English in this style in the 1970s because he had such a reputation that the publisher and translator felt that the English version should retain his style and his 'voice,' which suggests that Romance-style academic writing is *not* actually incomprehensible in English but merely difficult to understand.

Here is another example—what would have been the final 177-word sentence (and paragraph) of Bernard-Henri Lévi's *American Vertigo* but for a postscript inspired by Hurricane Katrina. The mostly word-for-word English translation, 185 words long, is by Charlotte Mandel:

> De ce pouvoir implacable et souvent invisible qu'est devenu l'empire modern maintenant qu'il n'est plus le stade suprême de la puissance d'un Etat, de ce panoptique sans œil et sans origine qui ne nous fait plus le cadeau, chaque matin, de nous livrer sur un plateau d'argent le nom d'un suspect, la tête d'un coupable ou le plan d'une Bastille, de ce Maître, en un mot, dont un lacanien eût dire qu'il est pur signifiant et dont je disais moi-même, il y a trente ans, dans *La Barbarie à visage humain*, qu'il est l'autre nom, sinon du monde, du moins de tout ce qui, en ce monde, travaille à l'asservissement des hommes, l'Amérique n'est pas le démiurge; elle n'en est plus, si elle le fut jamais, le cerveau; on ne peut plus dire, ni qu'elle est le noyau malin de l'Empire, ni qu'elle est l'empire du Mal; ou alors, oui, on peut le dire; mais il faut se résigner, alors, à ne rien comprendre ni à l'Empire, ni au Mal, ni à l'Amérique.
>
> (Lévi 2006a: 482)

> Of this implacable and often invisible power that the modern empire has become now that it no longer represents the ultimate stage of state power; of this eyeless and originless panopticon that no longer offers us the name of a suspect, the head of a guilty man, or the map of a Bastille on a silver platter every morning, now that it is no longer the "master"—a notion that is a pure signifier, about which Lacan would say (and about which I myself wrote, almost thirty years ago, in *Barbarism with a Human Face*) that it is the other name if not for

> the world then at least for all that, in this world, works toward the enslavement of men—America is not the demiurge; it is no longer, if it ever was, the mastermind; you can no longer say either that it is the malignant nucleus of empire or that it is the empire of evil; or else, yes, you may well say so, but if you do, then you'll need to resign yourself to understanding nothing whatsoever about empire, evil, and America.
>
> (Lévi 2006b: 298–9)

Assuming that the translator was not in a position simply to delete this sentence, a somewhat arbitrary list of things that is America is *not*, and assuming, in an EAD-like fashion, that the author might have wanted to be comprehensible in English, it would probably be better to rearrange it and cut it up, possibly moving the subject from the 122nd word to the first ('America is not the demiurge of this implacable and often invisible power'). This could be followed by an anaphoric sentence beginning: 'The modern empire has become an eyeless and originless panopticon,' a third beginning 'It is no longer the "master",' and a short anaphoric fourth sentence: 'It is no longer, if it ever was, the mastermind.' This might be followed by two further sentences beginning 'You can no longer say either' and 'Or else, yes, you may well say so, but.' The clauses could also be rearranged in various other ways. But calquing the source text's syntax is of course easier for the translator than adapting it to the dominant style of EAD or the usual sentence patterns of English.

To use a term revived by Venuti (2008: 15), the English translation of Lévi's *American Vertigo*, like that of Foucault's *L'archéologie du savoir*, might be described as a *foreignizing* one. Venuti was drawing on the much-cited distinction between the two 'ways' (or paths) open to a translator proposed by the German theorist Schleiermacher (1813/2004: 49)—'Either the translator leaves the author in peace as much as possible, and moves the reader toward him; or he leaves the reader in peace as much as possible and moves the writer toward him.' Schleiermacher's two paths later came to be referred to as *verfremdende* (foreignizing) and *einbürgernde* (naturalizing or domesticating) translation. Schleiermacher preferred the former path, 'bending' the target language to create a deliberate foreignness or strangeness, reproducing, where feasible, lexical and syntactic features from the source text. (Schleiermacher assumes that readers of translations are monolingual or at least lack a knowledge of the foreign language being translated; today many readers of academic texts translated into English are multilingual and so may not actually experience any text not transformed into 'EAD' as irredeemably 'foreign.')

Schleiermacher was not in fact saying anything remarkably new but essentially paraphrasing Goethe, who had stated some months previously, in a funeral oration for the famous German Shakespeare translator

Wieland, that there are 'two maxims in translation': either the author of a foreign nation is 'brought across to us in such a way that we can look on him as ours,' or 'we should go across to what is foreign and adapt ourselves to its conditions, its use of language, its peculiarities' (Goethe 1813/1977: 39). Unlike Schleiermacher, Goethe did not take this dichotomy to be absolute, quickly adding that Wieland 'looked for the middle way in this, tried to reconcile both.' Goethe, in turn, was paraphrasing Herder (1767–8), who had distinguished between an 'accommodating' approach, meaning accommodating to the source text, and a 'lax' approach. Herder, similarly, was doing little more than adding a new pair of adjectives to the age-old debate about faithful versus free translation.[18]

Venuti (2008) proposes an updated version of Schleiermacher's account of foreignizing translation, the attempt to 'register the linguistic and cultural difference of the foreign text, sending the reader abroad' (p. 16). He indicts the Anglo-American publishing industry, which is 'imperialistic abroad and xenophobic at home' (p. 13), with 'imposing English-language cultural values on a vast foreign readership, while producing cultures in the United Kingdom and the United States that are aggressively monolingual, unreceptive to the foreign' (p. 12). He is consequently concerned to 'develop a theory and practice of translation that resists dominant values in the receiving culture so as to signify the linguistic and cultural differences of the foreign text' (p. 18). But Venuti is particularly interested in making foreignized translations of stylistically innovative and experimental literary texts, calling for translations that shift between standard and non-standard dialects, registers, and styles; use convoluted syntax, awkward phrasings, unidiomatic constructions, and polysemous words; and juxtapose colloquialisms, archaisms and neologisms, jargons, and foreign borrowings, all the while foregrounding the signifier, calling attention to words as words and transgressing the prevailing cultural codes of English. Although his critical frame of reference includes a lot of French theoretical writing, Venuti is *not* calling for the translation of those particular texts in a way that would preserve their Francophone style and 'epistemology.'

Many Anglophone poststructuralists and cultural critics choose to write English as if it were French, with long, noun-heavy, end-weighted sentences, having seemingly interiorized French discursive patterns or more likely been influenced by non-domesticated English translations of Foucault, Barthes, Derrida et al. As Bellos (2011: 182) says, 'English language translations of French critical theory from the 1960s to the 1990s [. . .] have made abstract discourse about literature in English sound much more like French than it ever did before.'[19] Thus in this domain, the problem of epistemicide and the destruction of texts' underlying ideologies hardly seems to arise. But the fact remains that languages, and their grammatical constructions and preferred discourse patterns, *are* different, and what seems natural and appropriate in one language is not necessarily so, or necessarily possible, in another. Sound patterns—rhymes, rhythms, and alliterative and assonant word combinations—notoriously get 'lost in translation,' but so do grammatical structures, and with them discourse patterns. Complex syntax, for example, is facilitated by inflected languages like French and Portuguese, which can explicitly mark many grammatical relations that have to be inferred in English, which lost most of its inflections many centuries ago. Thus although as Kaplan (1987:10) says, '[A]ny native speaker of any particular language has at his disposal literally hundreds of different mechanisms to signify the same meaning,' and all rhetorical modes are theoretically feasible in every language, 'each language has certain clear preferences, so that while all forms are possible, all forms do not appear with equal frequency or in parallel distribution.'

Parks (2014: 217) describes this as 'a paradox at the heart of translation'—the text we are translating 'is also the greatest obstacle to expression. Our own language prompts us in one direction, but the text we are trying to respect says something else, or the same thing in a way that feels different.' If it is too different, experienced translators will choose to change it.[20] Thus as Bennett (2007: 156) concedes, the preferred style of writing of Portuguese academics in the humanities (perhaps excluding literary theory) 'defies translation into a language like English,' leading translators to reconstruct source texts, probably destroying their underlying ideology and worldview in the process. 'Epistemicide' does not only occur because of the hegemony of EAD but also because some discourse styles, and certainly sentence structures, are hard to transfer from language to language.[21]

6.4 Linguistic Relativity

Given that discourse styles and sentence patterns differ from language to language, the question arises whether being obliged to write in another language ineluctably changes what one wants to express. Different languages have different constructions or grammatical structures, and their lexicons divide up the universe in different ways, and it has long been argued that this imposes cognitive constraints and affects the way speakers perceive and think about the world. As Montgomery (2000: 272) says, 'The movement of scientific knowledge across cultural-linguistic borders has always involved substantive change—the creation of new vocabularies; the deletion and addition of epistemological matter; [. . .] alterations in logic and organization; shifts in style of persuasion.'

In the 19th century, Humboldt (1820/1904: 27) argued that the differences among languages are not a matter of sounds and signs but of 'differing world views' [*Weltansichten*]. Humboldt's ideas were rediscovered and reformulated in the United States in the 20th century by Boas, Sapir, and Whorf. Boas (1966: 289) argued that 'the categories of language

[. . .] impose themselves upon the form of our thoughts'; Sapir (1949: 10) stated that the forms of language 'predetermine for us certain modes of observation and interpretation' and that '"the real world" is to a large extent unconsciously built up on the language habits of the group,' which 'predispose certain choices of interpretation' (p. 162); and Whorf (1956: 213) asserted that '[w]e dissect nature along lines laid down by our native languages' and posited the 'linguistic relativity principle' such that 'users of markedly different grammars [. . .] must arrive at somewhat different views of the world' (p. 221). Fishman (1982: 12, note 1) states that the basic notions of the linguistic relativity hypothesis—which these days generally goes under the name of the 'Sapir-Whorf hypothesis'—and also of the stronger version, linguistic determinism, are in fact much older and 'occur several times throughout two-and-a-half thousand years of Euro-Mediterranean language-related speculation [. . .] and are probably of at least similar vintage in India, China, and perhaps even elsewhere.'

It does seem likely that the way speakers construe experience and select and structure information for verbalization depends on the grammatical categories available in a language, especially those expressing tense and aspect. Speakers fit their thoughts into conventional linguistic frames (e.g., the progressive, perfective, or imperfective aspect) and are likely to pay attention to aspects of events or situations that can be readily encoded in the language they habitually speak (Talmy 2000). Consequently Slobin (1996: 76) suggests that 'in acquiring a native language, the child learns particular ways of thinking for speaking.' As argued in Chapter 2, lower-level L2 learners are likely to express themselves according to patterns derived from the L1, leading to non-native-like categorizations and descriptions of experience, although proficient bilinguals are likely, notwithstanding a certain amount of transfer, to acquire two ways of thinking for speaking or two ways of looking at the world.

For example, Hagège (2012) broadly endorses the notion of linguistic relativity and highlights some of the grammatical and conceptual dissimilarities between English and French as part of his argument that Francophone researchers should write in French. One of the differences he elaborates on (pp. 157–62) is ways of describing motion in satellite-framed languages, which include Chinese as well as most Indo-European languages, except the Romance ones, and verb-framed languages, which include the Romance languages, Arabic, Hebrew, Turkish, and Japanese (Talmy 1985). In the former the main verb typically encodes the *manner* of motion, whereas the path or direction of motion is expressed in 'satellites' (e.g., *the ball rolled down the hill*; *he ran up the stairs*); in the latter the main verb encodes the *path* of motion, whereas the marking of manner is optionally expressed in a 'satellite' (*entrer/monter en courant, entrar/subir corriendo*). In fact most languages actually allow *both* types of constructions, so this classification only refers to a *preferred* construction; as Mounin (1955/1994: 33–40) argues, the grammatical forms available in French (just like those available in English) are in fact extraordinarily supple and generally allow considerably more than one way of saying the 'same' thing.[22] Yet a Francophone zoologist is likely to write *Les zèbres traversent la rivière à la nage* (the zebras cross the river by swimming), whereas an Anglophone would write *The zebras swim across the river*. Whether this is in fact an important conceptual distinction, so that a sentence written in or translated into English expresses something very different from the equivalent sentence in French, is clearly a matter of opinion.

Despite such conceptual differences among languages, translators generally develop habitual ways of translating particular structures from a source to a target language. In a much-quoted article, Jakobson (1959/2004: 140) argued (in total opposition to Humboldt, Sapir, and Whorf) that '[a]ll cognitive experience and its classification is conveyable in any existing language' and that '[a]ny assumption of ineffable or untranslatable cognitive data would be a contradiction in terms' (p. 141). For Jakobson, grammar does not cause problems for translation because '[i]f some grammatical category is absent in a given language, its meaning may be translated into this language by lexical means.' He is equally sanguine about the translation of lexis, arguing that '[w]henever there is deficiency, terminology may be qualified and amplified by loan-words or loan-translations, neologisms or semantic shifts, and finally, by circumlocutions' (p. 140). However, leaving aside circumlocutions, it is evident that an individual translator cannot impose a semantic shift on a language, or use a neologism or loan translation and expect it to be immediately understood in the target language if the underlying linguistic concept doesn't already exist, and besides, using loanwords is not actually translating. Translating lexis is actually a rather more delicate matter than Jakobson admits. Moreover, even where a ready-made 'translation equivalent' of a source language word exists, it is very unlikely to carry the same range of connotations.

For this reason Venuti (2013: 110) talks about both losses and gains: translators 'attempt to compensate for an irreparable loss'—of the sound and order of the words in the source text and all the resonances and connotations and allusions they carry for the reader in the source culture—'by controlling an exorbitant gain.' Each word in a translation has its own resonances and connotations and allusions, giving additional meanings which 'inhere in every choice the translator makes' (p. 110)—and of course 'the translator has chosen every single word in the translation, whether or not a source-language word lies behind it' (p. 111). So translation is necessarily transformative: 'any translation will at once fall short of and exceed whatever correspondence a translator hopes to establish by supporting different meanings, values, and functions for its receptors' (p. 193). To put it another way, '[a] translation always communicates an interpretation, a foreign text that is partial and altered, supplemented with features peculiar to the translating language' (1998: 5).

Well-known examples of differing connotations are to be found in two widely anthologized articles on translation. In 'The Task of the Translator,' Benjamin (1923/2004: 78) argued that *Brot* and *pain* (bread) 'signify something different to a German or a Frenchman,' while in 'The Misery and the Splendor of Translation,' Ortega y Gasset (1937/1992: 96) declared that 'it is utopian to believe that two words belonging to different languages, and which the dictionary gives us as translations of each other, refer to exactly the same objects,' and that there is an 'enormous difference' between 'the thing the Spaniard calls a *bosque*' (forest) and what 'the German calls a *Wald*.'[23]

Yet despite his *bosque/Wald* example, Ortega y Gasset would have us believe that when a Spaniard and a German use *scientific terminology*, such problems do not arise. He states that science books 'are easier to translate from one language to another' because 'in every country these are written almost entirely in the same language' (p. 95), as 'the author himself has begun by translating from the authentic tongue in which he "lives, moves and has his being" into a pseudolanguage formed by technical terms, linguistically artificial words which he himself must define in his book.' Montgomery, in *Science in Translation* (2000: 286), demurs, saying he 'can hardly resist the urge, for example, to contemplate replacing Benjamin's *Brot* and *pain* with words like *Sauerstoff* and *oxygène* or *Trägheit* and *inertie*.' Although these terms signify the same basic phenomena, Montgomery denies that they are precise equivalents of *oxygen* and *inertia*, 'with the same exact mixture of denotative and connotative significance.' If this is the case with terms from the natural sciences, it is all the more so in the humanities and social sciences. Cassin et al. (2014) show how the supposed translation equivalents across European languages of about 400 philosophical terms are partially inadequate and do not overlap. For example, *Geist* is not the same as *mind*, which is not the same as *esprit*, and so on. Similarly Hagège (2012: 125) points out that Weber's key term *Herrschaft* (domination) is part of a semantic field including *Gewalt*, *Gewaltsamkeit*, *Herrschaft*, *Macht*, and others, which is not structured the same way as the French semantic field of *domination*, *force*, *pouvoir*, *puissance*, and so on or the English grouping of *domination*, *power*, *force*, *strength*, and so on. Examples like these could be multiplied at will.[24]

As argued in Chapter 2, the partial nature of translation equivalents is not necessarily a problem for bilinguals. 'Coordinative' bilinguals (if they actually exist) will have separate conceptual representations, one for each word in the two (or more) languages. 'Compound' bilinguals, on the contrary, will have a single fused or undifferentiated conceptual system linked to the two lexicons, containing all the information and connotations connected with the corresponding words in the different languages. Consequently they are likely to use words in either their L1 or an L2 intending to communicate nuances (parts of combined conceptual representations) that are in fact incommunicable (or merely sound odd) to monolinguals who do not share the bilingual's language combination. This *is* a problem for a bilingual writer. For example, a German academic obliged to write in English might write, say, *bread*, *forest*, *oxygen*, *spirit*, or *domination* 'intending' to communicate connotations of *Brot*, *Wald*, *Sauerstoff*, *Geist*, or *Herrschaft* that may not be inferred by Anglophone readers. This will also be the case if he or she uses the German words as loanwords. For this reason Bordet (2016) argues that calques or newly coined 'dynamic' translation equivalents are preferable to loanwords, especially metaphorical ones, which are inevitably transplanted into a language shorn of their source language connotations and their multifarious links with a network of related concepts in a lexical field. Using target language words to translate a term potentially releases connotative meanings and linkages with a native semantic field, even though these will differ from the source language ones.

The same problem arises if, for example, a German speaker chooses to write in German and reaches non-Germanophone readers in translation; there is *no* way of communicating the precise meanings of words in languages other than English to readers of English who do not know the language in question. The only guaranteed way to comprehend the nuances of another language is to learn it. As Kuhn (2000: 61) puts it, '[A]nything which can be said in one language can, with imagination and effort, be *understood* by a speaker of another. What is prerequisite to such understanding, however, is not translation but language learning.' Importantly '[l]anguage learning and translation are [. . .] very different processes: the outcome of the former is bilingualism, and bilinguals repeatedly report that there are things they can express in one language that they cannot express in the other' (p. 238).

Kuhn's interest in incommensurability and untranslatability is diachronic: he is concerned with the hermeneutic problem of understanding historical texts (including translations) using scientific terms that now have different meanings, notably the writings of Aristotle, Newton, Volta, Bohr, and Planck. What happens in periods of 'revolutionary science' is that different scientists 'are presented with different data by the same stimuli' (Kuhn 1977: 309) and begin to use old words with new meanings. (Words—or their English translations—that have radically changed their meanings in the history of science include *motion*, *force*, *star*, *planet*, *gravity*, *matter*, *mixture*, *compound*, *atom*, *electron*, *particle*, and *wave*.) In such situations communication can only be partial as there is no neutral language that scientists can use in the same way in which to state their new theories. In his 1969 postscript to *The Structure of Scientific Revolutions*, Kuhn (1962/2012: 175) urges that 'men[25] who hold incommensurable viewpoints be thought of as members of different language communities and that their communication problems be analyzed as problems of translation.' But translation only goes so far: a new theory will only prosper if a majority of scientists 'find that at some point in the language learning process they have ceased to translate and begun instead to speak the language like a native' (1977: 339). Hence (*pace* Ortega) 'the problems of translating a scientific text, whether into a foreign tongue or into a later version of the language in which it was written are far more like those of translating literature than has generally been supposed' (2000: 62).

Non-native English-speaking researchers who are obliged by the language's international dominance to write in English are thus likely to develop a complex conceptual system containing mental representations of words of (at least) two languages. Some people argue that active bilingualism and a bilingual lexicon are advantageous for a researcher, and enhance the capacity for creativity and innovation, because the different cognitive potentials of different languages broaden one's concepts, vocabulary, and expressive possibilities, stimulate the imagination, and so forth (Coulmas 2007). Others focus on the losses inherent to translation. For example, Hagège, despite being a truly remarkable polyglot, still seems to assume that monolingualism is the norm and that professional researchers are *incapable* of mastering a non-native language, even though most countries (including Anglophone ones) are full of multilingual research teams. He takes it as axiomatic that L2 users need to simplify their thought, depriving themselves of the nuances and intuitions they could exploit in their dominant language, and that L2 English speakers are unable to explain or defend their work adequately to grant-awarding bodies, whose non-Anglophone members do not have the linguistic competence to present any objections they might have, and so on (2012: 121). This is a remarkably pessimistic and somewhat ungenerous way of seeing the world, which runs counter to the optimistic claims made by most proponents of multilingualism outlined in Chapter 2. It also echoes Schleiermacher, who despite his preference for foreignizing translations, still believed that '[o]ne must be loyal to one language or another, just as to one nation, or else drift disoriented in an unlovely in-between realm,' and that aiming 'to write equally as well and as originally in [a] foreign tongue as in one's own' is 'a wicked and magical art' and an attempt to 'mock the laws of nature' (1813/2004: 58; see Pym 1995).

In fact many researchers *are* able to operate in more than one language and do not have to deform their thoughts because they are written in English—at least, that is, if their thoughts are largely compatible with the accepted forms of EAD or with other non-language-specific forms of argumentation (such as more inductive styles) that are transferable to English. Preferred L1 sentence structures may well have to be jettisoned, and many L1 connotations may get lost if L2 English is used, but these are ineluctable consequences of communicating (directly or via translation) to speakers of other languages, which would arise even if English was not the dominant language of science and academic research.

A further consequence of widespread bilingualism with English is the inevitable effect of English on non-native English speakers' L1s, which is the subject of the next chapter.

Notes

1 — Onze taal telt in de wereld nauwelijks mee. Iedere student moet Engels, Frans en Duits kennen. Zonder die talen zou je geen enkele academische studie kunnen voltooien. Onze eigen taal wordt daardoor een soort lagere taal, een leerlingentaal. De hoogste wijsheid is in vreemde talen geschreven. De leermeesters spreken tot ons in het Engels, in Engelse leerboeken. Een taal die wij wel goed kunnen lezen, maar toch meestal niet zonder fouten spreken of schrijven. Ik merk het zelfs al op dit ogenblik, nu ik jou dit probeer uit te leggen. Kon ik Noors tegen jou spreken, mijn woordkeus zou meer subtiel, meer nauwkeurig zijn. [. . .]

— Worden er dan geen boeken in het Noors vertaald?

— Natuurlijk, een heleboel. Maar al zijn die boeken vertaald, dan weten we toch dat het geen eigen werk is. Daar gaat op sommige mensen een deprimerende werking van uit. [. . .]

— Als je een klein land bent, zegt hij, als de politiek en de mode en de films en de auto's en de machines en bijna alles uit het buitenland komt. Als dan ook nog bijna alle essentiële boeken, dat wil zeggen de boeken die gelijk hebben, de boeken die de waarheid bevatten, de boeken die beter zijn dan de meeste inheemse boeken, dat wil zeggen de vaderboeken, als die in vreemde talen geschreven zijn, dan krijgt zodoende het buitenland een positie tegenover je als het moederland tegenover de kolonie, als de stad tegenover het platteland.

Willem Frederik Hermans, *Nooit meer slapen* (1966/1997: 73–5)

2 For the politics, ethics, constraints, and so on of academic publishing in English, see Swales (1997); Ammon (2000); Ammon (2001); Gazzola and Grin (2007); Lillis and Curry (2010); Ferguson et al. (2011); Jenkins (2013). See Canagarajah (2002) on the iniquities and absurdities of academic journal publishing requirements for periphery scholars working, for example, in war zones without regular electricity, batteries, computers, photocopiers, adequate paper, typewriter ribbons, recent books and journals, a reliable postal service, or even a sample issue of the journal or its style sheet, and so on. This inevitably leads to the marginalization and disenfranchisement of 'periphery' or 'local' scholars. See Bennett (2014) on the 'semiperiphery' of southern, central, and eastern Europe.

3 This is from a conference paper: L. Nygaard, 'Running with blades: How Norwegian peace researchers view publishing in English' (2015); see https://ppriseal.webs.ull.es/Nygaard_Running.pdf.

4 Attributed to Roman Tetil, a translator in Kraków; quoted in Salager-Meyer (2008).

5 The United States, Canada, and Australia, which together comprise 5% of the world's population, have 75% of the world's expatriate university graduates (Van Parijs 2011: 159). According to the World Bank, in 2000, the Organisation for Economic Cooperation and Development (OECD; essentially the rich countries) had a net surplus of about 12 million brains, but

the six Anglophone OECD countries had a surplus of 14 million, meaning that millions of people from the non-Anglophone OECD countries had also moved to the English-speaking ones. About 100,000 Africans working in science, technology, medicine, and nursing move to OECD countries every year, and more than a quarter of the medical workforce in Britain, the United States, Canada, and Australia come from developing countries (Salager-Meyer 2008).

6 For example, France spends about four times more per capita on foreign language teaching than Britain (Grin 2005: 88–91) and Switzerland about 40 times more per capita than the United States (Maurais 2003: 32). Then again, although the possession of native English as a resource is 'unfair,' so is the global distribution of natural resources and climates that allow ample food production, encourage the development of a tourist industry, and so on.

7 Insisting that ELF is *different from* but not *inferior to* native English, Jenkins (2005: 153) unhelpfully reproaches Ammon for describing ELF variants as 'peculiarities' and daring to suggest that non-native English speakers might be linguistically 'disadvantaged.'

8 This rather contrasts with Montgomery's (2000: 257) earlier claim that different localized forms of English 'to an important degree, make for different sciences' so that rather than a single unified science, we have 'different epistemological dialects' (p. 267).

9 Linearity may, however, be in the eye of the beholder. Canagarajah (2002) very reasonably describes as 'circular' the 'structure of anticipating the conclusion at the beginning, and then reaching the same point in the conclusion' (p. 122), 'with the reader brought back to the starting point at the end of the paper' (p. 147).

10 As Bennett (2007, 2011, 2014) likes to point out, most of these can easily be seen as *protestant* values.

11 The term 'epistemicide' originates with the Portuguese sociologist Boaventura de Sousa Santos. See, for example, Santos (1998: 103).

12 Clyne gives the notable example of Schütze's two-volume *Sprache soziologisch gesehen* (1975), which is more than 1,000 pages long and includes sentences that are more than a page long, as well as myriad digressions, and digressions from digressions, even in the conclusion.

13 McCagg (1996) analyzes the newspaper article that serves as an example in Hinds (1987) and disputes the claim that Japanese writing is more difficult to follow for a Japanese reader, but more on the grounds of shared cultural knowledge and experience, and shared conceptual metaphors, than on argument structure as such. Kubota (1999: 15) denies that 'Japanese written discourse is characterized by culturally specific features such as *reader responsibility*, *ki-shoo-ten-ketsu*, and *delayed introduction of purpose*,' but Hinds (1983: 183) does not suggest that *all* Japanese discourse displays these features but merely that *ki-shoo-ten-ketsu* is 'an expository writing style for Japanese compositions which is consistently evaluated highly' and used in at least one well-known popular newspaper column.

14 The fact that perceptions of inherent linguistic difficulty (of either comprehension or production) usually emanate from outsiders is demonstrated by the drift of many languages from a synthetic to an analytic structure under the influence of non-native adult learners, as described in Chapter 4.

15 As mentioned in the acknowledgements, I am greatly indebted here to the thoughts of Ernst-August Gutt. See Gutt, in reply to a question of mine on the Relevance Theory List (November 2013) at www.phon.ucl.ac.uk/home/relevance/relevance_archives_new/0890.html.

16 Whereas Mauranen (1993) suggested that the inductive, end-weighted approach of some Finnish academics would be improved by the addition of explicit textual transitions, connectors, discourse markers and so on, today she is more circumspect, arguing that 'Anglo-American rhetoric is not necessarily the most effective, comprehensible, or "natural" choice for structuring academic texts even if we use English' and that '[i]t goes without saying that it is not more "scientific"' (2012: 242).

17 Strangely, they follow this assertive sentence with a much more tentative one: 'We need to debate the proposition that ideas and research which do not conform to Anglo-American rhetorical principles might be presented and published in varieties of English.'

18 Goethe read his funeral elegy on 25 January 1813, and Schleiermacher delivered his lecture 'On the Different Methods of Translating' on 24 June of the same year. Goethe (1813/1977: 39) also said of Wieland that 'as a man of feeling and taste he preferred the first maxim [bringing across the author of a foreign nation] when in doubt,' thus taking the opposite position to Schleiermacher. Inventing binary oppositions to describe antithetical types of translation is a popular pastime among translation theorists; recent examples (all of which have their uses) include formal equivalence versus dynamic equivalence (Nida 1964, excerpted in Venuti 2004), *sourcier* versus *cibliste* (Ladmiral 1979), overt translation versus covert translation (House 1981), adequate translation versus acceptable translation (Toury 1995), and documentary translation versus instrumental translation (Nord 2005).

19 Indeed not heeding the American philosopher Brand Blanshard's (1954: 52–3) warning that '[p]ersistently obscure writers will usually be found to be defective human beings,' some literary and cultural theorists insist that what they write cannot afford to be easily readable but *needs* to be difficult, full of jargon, allusions, and syntactic complexity; Culler and Lamb (2003: 9) complain that some theoretical writers actually 'aren't difficult enough' and issue a 'call to difficulty.'

20 At this point I should mention that until recently I earned a living, at least in part, by teaching (or perhaps bullying) Anglophone translation students *not* to leave long, noun-heavy, end-weighted Romance sentences intact in English.

21 Bennett does not mention that Santos, who coined the term 'epistemicide,' also writes extensively in English as well as in Portuguese (and Spanish), and that in English he often uses a style that is very much like EAD. A number of Santos's writings are freely available online via his website, www.boaventuradesousasantos.pt/pages/en/homepage.php.

22 One might add that the range of grammatical forms available in French could be augmented by importing structures from other languages, for example in translations, as suggested by Rivarol, Herder, Schleiermacher, Goethe, and others (see Chapter 7), although this possibility would probably not appeal to Hagège.

23 Damrosch (2003: 290) points out that Ortega's reference to Balzac's novel *Splendeurs et misères des courtisanes* links translation with prostitution.

24 See Wierzbicka (2006, 2014) for numerous (and usually convincing) examples of how the semantics of many English words differ from those of near-equivalents in other languages.

25 Kuhn invariably uses the word *men* to refer to scientists. He does, very infrequently, mention female philosophers, including the splendidly named Margaret Masterman, although in her case he also states that he had been forewarned that 'she was a madwoman' (2000: 299).

7 Bilingualism, Translation, and Anglicization

All around the world, there is a very long history of language contact leading to language change. Notwithstanding the linguists who insist that contact rarely induces change (see Chapter 3), it has repeatedly been shown that over the long term—the *very* long term—neighbouring languages often tend to become more similar as regular contact among contiguous speech communities leads bi-or multilingual speakers to replicate linguistic features. This is particularly the case in oral cultures. In literate cultures *translations* from a dominant or prestigious language can help diffuse borrowed or replicated elements without much direct contact, let alone societal bilingualism. And with today's globalized media, societal bilingualism no longer necessarily involves geographically neighbouring languages or contiguous or overlapping populations.

In many countries the dominant language now providing the model for replication is English. The lexical influence of English has long been evident in many languages, but there is often, to a lesser extent, also an influence on syntactic constructions and discourse structures. Hence whereas the previous chapters have been concerned with 'source language agentivity'—the influence of speakers' L1s on L2 English (and potentially on native English)—this chapter examines the contrary process, 'recipient language agentivity,' that is, the incorporation of features from English into other languages, by their native speakers.

7.1 Bilingualism and Linguistic Convergence

The tendency of neighbouring languages to converge as bilingual speakers consciously or unconsciously calque or replicate grammatical patterns across languages was already mentioned in Chapter 3. The most salient aspects of language use are probably pronunciation, which is often emblematic of individual and group identity, and lexis. This might incline speakers to resist using words that are easily identifiable as originating in another language. But speakers are generally rather less aware of syntax, and hence of syntactic changes, such as the progressive replication of grammatical structures from another language. In cases of intensive long-term contact, some bilingual speakers spontaneously make what Weinreich (1953: 7) called 'interlingual identifications.' They manipulate existing grammatical forms in their L1 to create new patterns that replicate grammatical concepts or structures in an L2, where these prove to be useful, without borrowing any specific grammatical forms. Thus unlike in cases of language *shift*, in which the 'shifting speakers who introduce interference features typically do not speak the target language fully,' here it is native speakers of the borrowing language with a good knowledge of the L2 'who introduce the interference features' (Thomason and Kaufman 1988: 348, note 1). The replication of structures by way of loan translations can gradually lead to a partial convergence of lexical, semantic, and structural systems, and a certain degree of levelling and uniformity across a linguistic region.

Ross (1996, 2003), investigating Melanesian languages, coined the term *metatypy* for the change in morphosyntactic type and grammatical organization (as well as semantic patterns) that a language undergoes as a result of its speakers' bilingualism in another language. Metatypy or structural replication can completely change a language's typological profile and lead to a large degree of mutual intertranslatability between a model and a replica language. If more than two languages are involved, metatypy gives rise to a *Sprachbund* (language union or linguistic area) in which languages become increasingly structurally similar.[1] Sprachbunds (or *Sprachbünde*) are found on every continent (Thomason 2001, Ch. 5). Dixon (1997), writing about Australia, describes how the languages of a given area gradually become more similar and converge towards a common prototype, as linguistic features diffuse across them. He states that two Australian languages with very little common lexis that come into contact will gradually borrow in both directions until about 50% is shared, at which point the lexis stabilizes. In Europe, convergence seems to have been on a much smaller scale, but linguists long ago described the Balkan Sprachbund, evoking a number of morphosyntactic and phonological similarities among Greek, Macedonian, Albanian, Romanian, Bulgarian, and some Serbian dialects, resulting from long-term contact from the Byzantine period onwards, which led to borrowing, imperfect learning during language shift, convergence, and so forth.

More recently it has been suggested that there is a much larger European Sprachbund, with languages and dialects having become increasingly alike as a result of cultural, social, economic, and political exchanges across borders as well as migrations of speakers of Germanic, Romance, and Slavic languages in late antiquity and the early Middle Ages (Heine and Kuteva 2006). Borrowing a well-known term from Whorf (1956: 138), Haspelmath (1998: 271) describes a 'Standard Average European' (SAE) linguistic area in which 'languages such as French, German, Italian, English, as well as (to a lesser extent) Swedish, Polish and Modern Greek share a substantial number of structural features in their grammars.'[2] Haspelmath describes the *nucleus* of SAE as comprising Dutch, German, French, and northern Italian dialects; van der Auwera (1998) makes a similar grouping and calls it the 'Charlemagne Sprachbund.' For Haspelmath, the *core* (bigger than the nucleus) of SAE contains the Romance and Germanic languages as well as the West and South Slavic and Balkan languages, whereas the *periphery* includes East Slavic, Baltic and Balto-Finnic languages, and Hungarian as well—'perhaps'—as Basque. Thus language contact and the areal spread of linguistic features are said to override genealogical accounts of family trees and posited typological universals. SAE includes many Indo-European languages (but not all of them—the Celtic, Indic and Iranian subgroups are clearly excluded) as well as non-Indo-European languages like Finnish, Estonian, and Hungarian, which now have many SAE syntactic features that render them typologically fairly different from the other Finno-Ugrian languages. From an entirely different (Chomskyan) theoretical perspective, Lightfoot (2003: 101) courageously argues that today, 'English grammars may be more similar to Italian than to German, and French grammars may be more similar to German than to Spanish. There is no reason to believe that structural similarity should be even an approximate function of historical relatedness.' Of course the languages in this SAE Sprachbund share only a few structural properties out of the thousands of different ones represented in their grammars,[3] but the processes of replication and diffusion outlined here show how, in the present day and in the future, calques of English grammatical structures could spread across Europe and beyond.

One should, perhaps, also sound a note of caution here. Although Heine and Kuteva (2005: 261) insist that the extent of grammatical replication is underestimated because it is much more difficult to identify than the borrowing of actual form-meaning units, one might also argue that it is all too easy to identify—or postulate—as similarities between languages may also be the result of language-internal factors (see Chapter 3).[4] Language contact is certainly not the only explanation for similarities among languages: for example, similar lexical items can take on metaphorical meanings and acquire grammatical functions in comparable ways across many languages, according to regular processes of grammaticalization, without any language contact taking place (again, see Chapter 3).

Sprachbunds are usually several centuries in the making, and the global influence of English only dates back a century or so, and widespread bilingualism with English much less. But the effects of English can already be seen. In a paper written in the 1980s, Kachru (1994: 139) stated—'recapitulat[ing] the obvious'—that 'within the traditional levels of lexis, grammar, phonology, and orthography [. . .] Englishization has left hardly any major language (or, for that matter, any minor language) untouched.' In many multilingual outer circle countries, the prestige of English and its dominant role in politics, administration, education, and the media has inevitably resulted in crosslinguistic interaction. In many expanding circle countries, bilingualism with English is on the increase, but English can also influence other languages by way of innumerable translations, which can spread both borrowed (i.e., untranslated) and calqued lexis, as well as calqued syntactic structures, or at least lead to changes in the frequencies of use of alternative structures. The influence of English on European lexis scarcely needs to be demonstrated; see, for example, Görlach (2001, 2002); Anderman and Rogers (2005); Furiassi et al. (2012). There is also an English influence in the domain of idioms; see Piirainen (2016). The influence of English in the replication of grammatical and discourse structures is more subtle, but can be discerned in many languages.

7.2 Translation as Enrichment and Impoverishment

English can influence the way even monolingual speakers use their L1s, as a consequence of the hegemony of Anglo-American publishing houses and the economics of publishing. There are very unequal flows of translations, with many more books being translated from English than into it. But what translations there are into English are often used as the relay for further translations, potentially—and insidiously—Anglicizing the third language version. Translations can of course transfer ideas from one culture to another, and also enhance the target language and its literary forms, but after a certain point calques of terminology, phraseology, and syntactic patterns can potentially begin to turn a borrowing language into a reflection of the dominant one. A parallel contemporary development is the increase in the number of writers (particularly novelists) in various languages who deliberately simplify their style and eschew local cultural references to facilitate translation into English as a gateway to the global market.

The conviction that translations (or imitations) of important works, notably the Greek and Roman classics, can greatly enrich the signifying and expressive potential of a national language and its literary traditions, and indirectly serve to bolster the nation, was current in Europe for many centuries, notably in Tudor England, Classical France, and Romantic Germany. It was principally theorized in the late 18th and early 19th centuries. For example, Rivarol (1785) argued that French was merely part of an 'alloy' that would only achieve perfection by 'trading' with its neighbouring languages and digging into the classical tongues. Schleiermacher (1813/2004: 62)—whose preference for foreignizing translations was outlined in the previous chapter—argued that the German language could 'flourish and develop its own strength only through extensive contact with the foreign,' and that 'much in our language that is beautiful and strong was developed, or restored from oblivion, only through translation.' The very Germanophile Germaine de Stael argued in 'The Spirit of Translation' (1816/2006: 279) that 'the greatest service we can render literature is to transport the masterpieces of the human intellect from one language to another,' and that 'naturalized beauties' deriving from translations 'imbue a national literary style with new turns of phrase and original expressions' (p. 280). And Goethe (1828/1921: 92) wrote that '[l]eft to itself every literature will exhaust its vitality, if it is not refreshed by the interest and contributions of a foreign one,' while in conversation with Eckermann (Goethe 1827/1850: 350–1), he famously declared that '[n]ational literature is now a rather unmeaning term; the epoch of world literature [*Weltliteratur*] is at hand, and everyone must strive to hasten its approach.'

In a short passage in the 'Notes and Queries for a Better Understanding,' appended to his *West-östlicher Divan* (1819/2004), a collection of lyrical poems inspired by the Persian poet Hafez (whom he had read in a German translation), Goethe describes three 'kinds' or 'epochs' of translating, which with canonical works often succeed each other. The first kind is a simple transfer of hitherto foreign content, generally in plain, artless prose, to be used 'for a quick reading, which would open up the essential meaning of the work' (p. 65). This is often followed by a second translation which today, following Venuti (2008: 15), would most likely be described as 'domesticating,' in which foreign ideas are reproduced in a language's native style. Like Schleiermacher, de Stael, and many others before him, Goethe associates this procedure primarily with the frivolous French (possibly excluding Rivarol):

> The French make use of this style in the translation of all poetic works [. . .] In the same way that the French adapt foreign words to their pronunciation, they adapt feelings, thoughts, even objects; for every foreign fruit there must be a substitute grown in their own soil. (p. 64)

In Goethe's third epoch—'the finest and the highest of the three'—the translator's goal 'is to achieve perfect identity with the original, so that the one does not exist instead of the other but in the other's place' (p. 65). In producing a work that would 'correspond to the different dialects, rhythms, meter, and prosaic idioms in the original,' the translator 'more or less gives up the uniqueness of his own nation, creating this third kind of text, for which the taste of the masses has to be developed.' The third kind of text is to be understood as having enhanced the target language.[5]

Well into the 20th century, there was still a widespread conception that 'minority' languages and literatures had a great deal to gain from translations of the world's classics. For example, there was a huge amount of translation into the renascent Hebrew in the decades following the establishment of Israel. The Israeli translation scholar Even-Zohar (1990a: 47) describes literature and translation in terms of 'polysystems' in a broader culture and society and argues that countries with a 'young,' 'peripheral,' or 'weak' literature tend to be receptive to translations of texts from older and more hegemonic literatures, which can add new linguistic and poetical elements to the target-language repertoire. This is a wholly asymmetrical relationship; as Even-Zohar (1990b: 62) points out, 'A target literature is, more often than not, interfered with by a source literature which completely ignores it,' because countries with established, vigorous literary traditions translate far fewer foreign texts, and what translations there are tend to occupy a marginal or peripheral position. Furthermore, their translators tend to follow local literary and linguistic models rather than importing foreign norms.

But there is a counter-argument, which is that adding new (borrowed or replicated) linguistic elements to minority languages does not help them retain their specificities and their differences from more dominant languages. The survival of minority languages and cultures might in fact be aided by domesticating or naturalizing translations rather than foreignizing ones. After a certain point, if too many foreign structures are calqued and assimilated into the target language, it begins to contract rather than diversify. As Cronin puts it,

> Minority languages that are under pressure from powerful languages can succumb at lexical and syntactic levels so that over time they become mirror-images of the dominant language. Through imitation, they lack the specificity that invites imitation. As a result of continuous translation, they can no longer be translated. There is nothing left to translate.
>
> (1998: 147–8)

This is the consequence of what Cronin calls *translation as reflection*—'the unconscious imbibing of a dominant language that produces the numerous calques that inform languages from Japanese to German to Irish' (p. 148), to which he opposes *translation as reflexion*—'second-degree or meta-reflection [. . .] the critical consideration of what a language absorbs and what allows it to expand and what causes it to retract, to lose the synchronic and diachronic range of its expressive resources' (p. 148). Cronin states that this process of absorbing and normalizing loanwords or calques occurs in media translation, because of the speed with which translations are needed for breaking news stories,[6] as well as in scholarly discourses, which in minority languages gradually turn into replicas of the dominant discourse (which is to say EAD).

Bennett's account of the hegemony of EAD, and what this imposes on English translators of academic work, was set out in the previous chapter. Bennett also argues, however, that translation *from* English into other languages contributes, perniciously, to epistemicide. Given that researchers are increasingly obliged to write in English, or get their work translated for Anglophone journals, translations from English tend to be things like textbooks for schools and universities—'secondary works aiming at the dissemination of knowledge that has already been accepted by the relevant academic community' (Bennett 2013: 171). According to Bennett, what happens here is that 'the English original is perceived to have such authority and prestige that translators feel little need to adjust the discourse to suit the linguistic habits of the target culture' (p. 171). This can lead to English structures being calqued onto and absorbed into the target language. Rather than flourishing, and developing their own strength through extensive contact with the foreign, as Schleiermacher put it, languages are simply Anglicized. Thus for Bennett, both heavily domesticated translations into English and source-oriented, foreignizing translations from English are 'vehicles of colonization' (p. 188) that 'serve to reinforce the dominance of English by erasing the particularities of the other discourse, effectively silencing alternative forms of construing knowledge' (p. 171).

One might object that some of these claims are overstated and that some features attributed to EAD, such as clarity and comprehensibility, are not necessarily bad things per se nor unique to writing in English. But EAD-style clarity should not be the only game in town, and Bennett argues that translators, as cultural mediators, have a role to play in *raising awareness* of these issues and de-reifying the dominant discourse. Hence trainee translators should be equipped with 'the mediation skills that can enable them to negotiate solutions able to achieve the stakeholders' [authors, publishers, conference organizers, etc.] real world goals while avoiding complete effacement of the subaltern discourse' (p. 187).

Cronin, too, is given to exaggeration. There may be, as he states, a lot of calques in Japanese and German, but (unlike Irish) these are scarcely minority languages, and (unsurprisingly) he does not give an example of a language that has become an imitation of another (such as English) to the extent that it 'can no longer be translated' because 'there is nothing left to translate.' And in fact, as well as calques, speakers of minority languages such as Irish and Welsh generally use a lot of loanwords from the dominant language (in this case English). *Contra* Cronin, one might well argue that the way to help minoritized languages spoken by bi- or multilingual communities is not to attempt to preserve or maintain or revitalize a 'pure' version but an 'impure' one that the minority community finds valuable (Crystal 2000, Ch. 4; Otheguy et al. 2015).

For the moment, the translation-induced effects of English on other languages are still relatively minor, as the global influence of English is recent. In Europe the influence of Church Latin and Greek, and of French in the 18th century, was longer lasting, but not nearly long enough to turn any language into what Cronin calls a 'mirror-image' of another one. This parallels my argument in Chapter 4 about the influence of ELF on native English: so far the timescale is insufficient for it to have had any major effects.

One example of the effect that English *has* had on many languages, in a short period of time, is the modified use and semantic extension of the passive construction, seemingly resulting from the translation of news. Kachru (1994) states that this process has occurred in Africa and Asia, in both the outer and expanding circles. Here (as elsewhere) the media get a lot of their information in the form of English-language dispatches from news agencies. These are swiftly translated into local languages, with 'very close adherence to the text,' with the result that structures which 'originally appeared as a close translation from English gradually became institutionalized in a particular register and, then, slowly found [their] way into wider use' (p. 142).

In Hindi, for example, the passive generally occurs without the agent (e.g., the equivalent of *the letter was sent*), but under the influence of administrative, journalistic, and academic English, the passive with agent (the equivalent of *the letter was sent by my assistant*) has become more common (Kachru 1994: 142). Similarly, in the expanding circle, the Korean expression '...*e uihan*' (translating *by*) has been transferred from English. Kachru also states that in Chinese, Japanese, and Thai, among other languages, the passive construction was traditionally only used in the context of unpleasant states, but now, under the influence of (translated) English, it is no longer restricted to adversative connotations. The increased use of the passive, under the influence of English, has also been observed in Swahili (p. 143). In India and East Africa, translation from English is found alongside varying levels of societal bi- or multilingualism with English; in the expanding circle countries mentioned, the effect of translation may well be greater than that of English spoken as a lingua franca. In a detailed study of French news agency journalists translating dispatches from English, McLaughlin (2011) finds that they also frequently replicate the prototypical English passive as *être* + past participle, especially in reported speech, leading to a concomitant decrease in the use of alternative constructions.

Literary translation can also be a conduit for calques. In Swedish, for example, translations of novels from English are said to have led to the growing use of the construction 'subject + verb of diction + manner adverbial' after direct speech, calquing constructions like *'No,' she replied calmly*, which Gellerstam (2005) describes as a 'fingerprint' left behind by translation. In Italian it is widely argued that the greatly increased use of *stare* (be, continue to be) + the gerund to express processes (e.g., *sto andando*, I'm going; *sta accadendo*, it's happening) as well as states (*sto aspettando*, I'm waiting) in all stylistic levels since the early 20th century was influenced by the English progressive form (*be* + *ing*) by way of translations (books and films) of detective and spy stories (Durante 1981: 268–9, quoted in Brianti 1992: 238–9). McLaughlin found that

French news agency journalists too use significantly more present participles with *-ant*, translating the English progressive *-ing* form, than are found in non-translated written French.

Gallitelli (2013) has identified a set of stylistic differences between English-language novels translated into Italian and novels originally written in Italian, and the areas in which recent translated English fiction shows clear evidence of transfer are constructions that are already available in the target language. There are nearly twice as many adverbs ending with *-mente* (translating adverbs with *-ly*) than in fiction written in Italian, and a much greater use of the periphrastic present progressive, which is particularly easy for translators from English to copy. Musacchio (2005: 71) also states that 'on close inspection syntactic loan constructions often turn out to be pre-existing Italian constructs which become more widely used as a consequence of contact with a foreign language.' Other changes in Italian that seem to derive from English, and which are used by many journalists and (non-literary) translators, include the use of possessives rather than articles for parts of the body and the more frequent use of subject pronouns (Parks 2014: 200).

But translators also have the possibility of consciously resisting source-language influence. Apart from the examples just mentioned, Gallitelli shows that contemporary Italian translators of English fiction tend to *avoid* English calques, and also to shun the more oral forms used by native Italian novelists, in favour of a hyper-correct, conservative, standardized, formal literary style that has gone out of fashion elsewhere. Literary translators make great use of the subjunctive, the conditional, and the future, which elsewhere in Italian are being edged out by the indicative, the imperfect, and a present-tense construction. The translated novels from recent decades in Gallitelli's corpus are also lexically richer than Italian novels, thus disproving the belief that translations are inevitably lexically impoverished compared with non-translated language.[7]

McLaughlin's journalism corpus also shows that 'translation as reflection' by unthinking translators is not necessarily the source of calques. For example, she finds very little use of adjectives placed before the noun (13% in the corpus compared to a global rate of 35% in present-day French), which contradicts the widely held view that the influence of English is leading to more preposed adjectives in French (and the other Romance languages).[8] On the contrary there appears to be a *negative contact effect*, with the journalists choosing the structure that least resembles the English one in their French translation and underusing constructions that could be considered as calques. Mounin (1955/1994: 59) long ago described 'hypertranslation,' resulting from a dread of word-for-word renderings, when translators choose a form that is as different as possible from the one in the source text.

Thus various minor structural calques or replications, attributed to the influence of translations from English, have been identified in many languages. These rarely seem to be especially shocking, either because they involve the increased usage of already existing constructions, but previously stylistically marked and infrequent ones, or because, as Thomason and Kaufman (1988: 54) put it, the 'transferred features' tend to be those that 'fit in well typologically with corresponding features in the recipient language.' Certainly no language is actually turning into a 'mirror-image' of English.

Some (European) languages also incorporate semantic calques, transferring English meanings to existing words. For example, some French speakers now use *contrôler*, *ignorer*, and *opportunité* with the sense of their English cognates (as well as with their older French meanings—to check or inspect, not to know about something, and appropriateness), while some Italian speakers use *assumere*, *approcciare*, and *realizzare* to mean to suppose, to address a problem, and to realize (as well as with their older meanings—to accept responsibilities, to come near to something, and to achieve). This can lead to great anguish and calls to the barricades. For example, Myard et al. (2000: 8) believe that the occasional Anglified verbal choices of their Francophone compatriots constitute a mortal threat to their (Myard et al.'s) human rights, whereas Rollason (2005: 53) proclaims—farcically—that American English is undermining 'the creative and generative capacities of French,' which is destined to 'lose its autonomy and become a subsystem' of American English. *Honi soit qui mal y pense!* A counter-argument is that a language like French that has, for example, one word for *conscience* and *consciousness*, *experience* and *experiment*, *fly* and *steal*, *sense* and *direction*, and *wife* and *woman* can surely cope with a few more polysemous words, especially when this does not even involve the importation of foreign words, sounds, or phonotactic atrocities.[9] But of course lexical prejudices are not rational; I still wince every time I hear someone use *disinterested* in the sense of uninterested, and shudder when I hear *imply* used in the sense of infer, but laugh my head off at the fools of the previous generation who insisted that *hopefully* can only mean 'full of hope' and not 'it is to be hoped that.'

It is harder for native English speakers—or at least *this* native English speaker—to get too worked up about foreign words coming into the language, given that more than 70% of the vocabulary of modern English is borrowed,[10] including 14 Scandinavian and 13 French words out of Swadesh's (spurious—see Dixon 1997: 36) list of 206 'unborrowable' core words (Matras 2009: 166). This is not particularly unusual—for example, more than half of Japanese and Korean words are from Chinese, a lot of Urdu words come from Persian and Arabic, and there are also a large number of loanwords in Persian, Turkish, and so on—although such cases (as well as some cases of slight structural borrowing) generally result from the influence of a prestigious literary (or religious) language, 'often known to the borrowers primarily or only in its written form' (Thomason and Kaufman 1988: 66). There *was* a time when

English purists resisted fancy foreign (Latinate) multisyllabic coinages, which were stigmatized as 'inkhorn terms' as they took too much ink from the inkwells (made of horn) in which writers dipped their quills. But this was more than 450 years ago,[11] and English still has more than 100,000 words ultimately deriving from classical sources (Hughes 2000: 370). (I leave it to the reader to locate a single paragraph in this book that has more Germanic than Romance vocabulary.)

In short, language contact and convergence by way of grammatical replication and lexical borrowing have been going on for millennia all over the world and are not going to stop. Today's dominant language is English, and the growth of bi- or multilingualism with English, along with the influence of the media and translations from English, are leading to minor changes in many other languages. However, these changes are (so far) on nothing like the scale of the many instances of radical convergence, metatypy, and replication that have been recorded around the world. And the influence of English in translation merely follows on from the earlier influence of Latin and Greek in most of Europe, and Sanskrit, Persian, and Arabic in parts of Asia. There is, nonetheless, every reason to believe that the gradual but relatively slight Anglification or Anglicization of many other languages will continue as long as English remains the world's dominant lingua franca.

7.3 Translation Into English: Weary, Stale, Flat, but Potentially Profitable

Although translations *from* English appear to be a vector of crosslinguistic influence, the same cannot be said for translations *into* English. On the contrary, translations into English often seem to *subtract* from the standard language rather than adding anything to it, least of all foreignizing elements from source texts.

This is partly a consequence of the pluricentric nature of the language and the many small differences existing among the major native and nativized varieties. David Bellos (2011: 191) explains what happens to his French-English fiction translations. He writes the way he likes, although he has to 'make choices in every paragraph about what variety of written English to use' (essentially, one presumes, British or American). Then a copy editor makes his prose conform to the style appropriate to the publishing house's target audience, which is usually international. A translation of fiction into English consequently loses all 'quirks of language that mark it as belonging to any geographical variety.' Bellos calls this language, stripped of all regional vocabulary and turns of phrase and thus not a representation of a language actually spoken or written anywhere at all, 'Tranglish' and 'English-*minus*.' If copy-editing like this incidentally removes some of a writer or translator's poetic effects (rhythm, alliteration, assonance, etc.), this also renders the prose less interesting.

It is commonly argued that translated language in general displays 'universal features' (or at the very least regularities or tendencies), such as a tendency towards explicitation, a tendency towards disambiguation and simplification, a strong preference for grammatical conventionality, a noticeable cleaning away of repetitions occurring in source texts, and the joint tendencies to over-represent typical features of the target language so that they appear more frequently in translations than in texts originally written in the target language and to under-represent rare or unique items in the target language (Mauranen and Kujamäki 2004).[12] Most of these universals or tendencies lead to a distinct stylistic flattening.[13]

Berman (1984/1992: 5) defined a bad literary translation as one 'which, generally under the guise of transmissibility, carries out a systematic negation of the strangeness of the foreign work,' but he did not envisage authors trying to remove any strangeness from their work *before* it was even published and translated. Yet Kazuo Ishiguro has explained in multiple interviews how he changed the way he wrote early in his career, when his novels began to be translated into many languages. After what seems to have been a particularly traumatic time cloistered in a hotel room explaining his work to Norwegian literary journalists, Ishiguro says he started to think, 'I can't write that, because the Norwegians wouldn't understand' (2008: 145). This applies first of all to puns and wordplay, which—notoriously—tend to be 'lost' in translation: 'So the kind of language that relies very much on wordplay, on brilliant use of linguistics, pleasurable and great as it might be in the English language [. . .] you suddenly think: "Well, it will be just nothing in Norway"' (p. 145). It also applies to cultural references: Ishiguro says that describing a character in terms of what London neighbourhood he lives in and what designer clothes he wears will mean nothing to the dreaded Norwegians, or indeed to Londoners ten years after the novel is written, 'so you stop using this technique. You don't describe your characters in terms of such local signals' (p. 145).

Pace Ishiguro, I suspect that many more people know what 'Notting Hill' and 'Paul Smith suits' signify from journalism and fiction than from first-hand experience of the neighbourhood or the clothes in question, and that a large proportion of our knowledge of cultural trivia comes from stories of various kinds. One might think that a writer with an established reputation and a loyal readership could, on the contrary, specialize in such 'local signals' (which don't involve any *translation* difficulties)—but only the author knows how tedious it is to spend days on end on long book tours explaining such things to literary journalists.

One of the ironies of Ishiguro's post-translation epiphany is that he made his reputation with two novels with (compellingly unreliable) Japanese narrators, which necessarily involves intriguing linguistic choices. Etsuko, in *A Pale View of Hills* (1982), speaks English as a second language, and as Ishiguro says, '[P]articularly when she's reproducing Japanese dialogue in English, it has to have a certain foreignness about it,' while Ono in *An Artist of the Floating World* (1986)

> is supposed to be narrating in Japanese; it's just that the reader is getting it in English. In a way the language has to be almost like a pseudotranslation, which means that I can't be too fluent and I can't use too many Western colloquialisms. It has to be almost like subtitles, to suggest that behind the English language there's a foreign language going on. I'm quite conscious of actually figuring these things out when I'm writing, using a certain kind of translationese.
>
> (2008: 13)[14]

Ishiguro is, of course, perfectly aware of the broader implications of his position:

> I think a lot of writers, without ever having a clear policy on it are starting to write differently, because of the Norwegians! And I think, if it is a problem for an English-language writer, it must be much more of an issue for—say—a Norwegian writer who has a sense that in order to have anything like a large significant readership, in order to find his or her place on the literary platform, they will have to be translated primarily into English and French and German. They would have to address their readers through these other, larger languages and this does something quite crucial and profound to what is actually produced. And I think there are good things and bad things. It is good in a way that writers address the whole world and they don't look inward, they perhaps have an outgoing, international viewpoint.
>
> But what is very dangerous of course, is that something very crucial and vital disappears here, in this homogenization of literature; some of the very great energies that come out of someone's knowledge of their own locale, the language that is used in their own culture. All these things will perhaps somehow be ironed out. [. . .] you can see that effect [. . .] a McDonald's kind of effect, even with serious literary fiction. [. . .] I am very affected by it, and I think many writers I meet now are very conditioned by these forces.
>
> (p. 146)[15]

Tim Parks, who regularly reviews translated European fiction in the *New York Review of Books*, suggests that many novelists today are writing in a particularly straightforward style to make their work easier to translate into English, which is often used as the relay language for further translations. For example, he compares English translations of recent

Norwegian and Dutch novels with the belated translation of a novel from the 1960s by the Flemish writer Hugo Claus and says:

> it seemed that the contemporary writers had already performed a translation within their own languages; they had discovered a lingua franca within their own vernacular, a particular straightforwardness, an agreed order for saying things and perceiving and reporting experience, that made translation easier and more effective. One might call it a simplification, or one might call it an alignment in different languages to an agreed way of going about things.
>
> Inevitably, there is an impoverishment [. . .] but there is also a huge gain in communicability, particularly in translation where the rhythm of delivery and the immediacy of expression are free from any sense of obstacle.
>
> (Parks 2014: 199)

Unsurprisingly Parks infers that the 'skeleton lingua franca beneath the flesh of these vernaculars' is basically English: 'seeking maximum communicability,' Continental novelists have internalized English ways of expressing things, which 'can be absorbed and built into other vernaculars so that they can continue to exist while becoming more easily translated into each other—or into English itself' (p. 200). Thus alongside all the academic researchers and scientists who replicate 'Anglo' rhetorical structures, there appear to be novelists imitating English discourse structures in general. This results in what might be called literature *for* translation rather than literature *in* translation. But the more the readership of fiction 'is diluted or extended, particularly if it includes foreign-language readers, the more difficult it is for a text of any stylistic density to be successful' (p. 89). In the long run, Parks argues, either through the choices of writers, or just by 'a process of natural selection, it seems inevitable that style will align with what can be readily translated more or less into multiple languages and cultural settings, or into a readily intelligible international idiom' (p. 90).

Most novels published in most Continental European countries are translations (between 50 and 80% of them), and given the Anglophone hegemony in international fiction publishing, most of these (about 75%) are from English (Parks 2014: 67, 205). Consequently most European novelists grew up reading translations and are accustomed to reading fiction about other countries, particularly the United States, and naturally conceive of their own readership as international. Furthermore, given the continuing fall in sales of fiction in recent years, novelists *need* to sell abroad to make a living. Although wholly dissimilar languages and complicated literary styles *can* be translated, self-consciously difficult or experimental writing (which flourished in the 1960s and 1970s) that exploits the phonetic, lexical, semantic, and syntactic resources of a given language presents much more of a challenge. Getting translated is more easily achieved by writing in a straightforward style about characters who could be living anywhere and saying very little about the culture of the country in which the novel is set. Parks suggests that American authors such as Jonathan Franzen and Philip Roth 'can write about Americans for Americans (which is no doubt as it should be) and nevertheless expect to be read worldwide,' even while detailing the minutiae of American culture, because of 'the huge pull the country exercises on the world's imagination' (p. 192). On the other hand the German-speaking Swiss author Peter Stamm—who 'writes in the leanest prose imaginable' (p. 189) in a style that is 'absolutely translatable' (p. 190)—'has been obliged to write about everyman for everyone everywhere' (p. 192) to attract an international public. Parks also mentions the German novelist Siegfried Lenz, the Norwegian writer Per Pettersen, the Dutch author Gerbrand Bakker, the Italian thriller writer Giorgio Faletti, and 'many other French and Italian authors' as being particularly straightforward and translation friendly (p. 200). Writers no longer identify with a particular speech community or participate in current social or political debates in their home country—unless they are American. Instead we get 'literature that may give pleasure but rarely excites at the linguistic level, rarely threatens, electrifies, reminds us of, and simultaneously undermines the way we make up the world in our own language.'[16]

By way of example, here is the opening of a story by Peter Stamm, the Swiss author who Parks picks out (although it is a first-person narration by a Swiss rather than 'everyman'):

> Ich war mit dem Abendzug aus dem Welschland nach Hause gekommen. Damals arbeitete ich in Neuchatel, aber zu Hause fühlte ich mich noch immer in meinem Dorf im Thurgau. Ich war zwanzig Jahre alt.
>
> Irgendwo war ein Unglück geschehen, ein Brand ausgebrochen, ich weiß es nicht mehr. Jedenfalls kam mit einer halben Stunde Verspätung nicht der Schnellzug aus Genf, sondern ein kurzer Zug mit alten Wagen. Unterwegs blieb er immer wieder auf offener Strecke stehen, und wir Passagiere begannen bald, miteinander zu sprechen und die Fenster zu öffnen.
>
> Es war die Zeit der Sommerferien. Draußen roch es nach Heu, und einmal, als der Zug eine Weile gestanden hatte und das Land um uns ganz still war, hörten wir das Zirpen der Grillen.
>
> Es war fast Mitternacht, als ich mein Dorf erreichte. Die Luft war noch warm, und ich hatte die Jacke nur übergehängt. Meine Eltern waren schon zu Bett gegangen. Das Haus war dunkel, und ich stellte nur schnell meine Sporttasche mit der schmutzigen Wäsche in den Flur. Es war keine Nacht zum Schlafen.
>
> (from *Am Eisweiher*, part of *Blitzeis, Erzählungen*, 1999)

> I had come home on the evening train from the French part of Switzerland. I was working in Neuchatel at the time, but home was still my village in the Thurgau. I was just twenty.
>
> There had been an accident somewhere, a fire, I don't remember what. At any rate, the train came from Geneva half an hour late, and it wasn't the normal express but a short train with old cars. It kept stopping in the middle of nowhere, and the passengers got into conversation with each other, and opened the windows.
>
> It was summer, vacation time. Outside, it smelled of hay, and once, when the train had stopped somewhere for quite some time and the country around was very quiet, we heard the screaking of cicadas.
>
> It was almost midnight when I got to my village. The air was still warm, and I slung my jacket over my arm. My parents had already gone to bed. The house was dark, and I did nothing more than dump my carrier bag full of dirty clothes in the corridor. It didn't feel like a night for sleeping.
>
> (from *Black Ice, a story sequence*, translated by Michael Hofmann, in Stamm 2006)

The prose and the narrative style are wholly unadventurous and, as Park says, readily translatable. If you can read German, you can largely translate this word for word in your head, give or take the basic differences of German and English word order.

Analogous arguments have been made about poetry. The Sinologist Stephen Owen (1990: 28) has complained that non-Western poets, imagining (and wishing for) an international audience reading them in translation, produce poetry designed to be 'free of all local history' but which turns out to be 'a version of Anglo-American modernism or French modernism.' Consequently 'an essentially local tradition (Anglo-European),' which the poets have encountered in (often mediocre) translations, 'is widely taken for granted as universal.' Whereas 'poetry has traditionally been built of words with a particular history of usage in a single language—of words that cannot be exchanged for other words,' the desire to be translated creates 'a pressure for an increasing fungibility of words.' So we get 'world poetry that anyone can write and that can be translated into something still recognizable as poetry,' with universal images and just a smattering of local colour. Many American poets, on the contrary, use a lot of current slang and popular cultural references so that their wordplay and allusions may be incomprehensible even to American audiences 50 years hence. Owen discusses an English translation of the work of the Chinese poet Bei Dao and complains that the poems 'could just as easily be translated from a Slovak or an Estonian or a Philippine poet' and that 'most of these poems translate themselves' (p. 31). Far from running the risk of being 'lost in translation,' Dao's poetry is 'poetry written to travel well' (p. 31).[17]

Damrosch (2003: 289), using Goethe's term, describes 'world literature' as consisting of works that easily leave their origins behind and 'gain on balance in translation' as stylistic losses are 'offset by an expansion in depth as they increase their range.' But the kind of writing that Parks variously describes as 'literature *for* translation,' 'the dull new global novel,' and 'literature without style' seems to lack both poetic features that could be lost and depth that could be expanded. Rather than world literature we get literature from nowhere. One can easily come up with a list of recent and contemporary authors who do *not* fit Parks's pattern (without being as 'difficult' as the writers he mentions from the middle of the last century)—for example, Gianni Celati, Elena Ferrante, Michel Houellebecq, Karl Ove Knausgård, Jonathan Littell, and W. G. Sebald—and it is possible that some of the authors Parks cites would insist that their lean prose about everyman was a purely artistic choice (à la Hemingway). It is not entirely certain whether we are dealing with a Western European fictional Sprachbund or a fictional Western European Sprachbund, but it *does* seem plausible that the quest for readability, and translatability into English, is quenching or at least lessening the literary creativity of many writers.

Another option open to novelists who decline to write about their own society and culture is to set their stories in the United States. However, unlike fiction about 'everyman,' outsiders' portrayals of America have the potential to irritate American readers. A notable example of this is the Swiss author Joel Dicker's *La Vérité sur l'Affaire Harry Quebert* and its English translation *The Truth About the Harry Quebert Affair*.[18] This novel won major French literary prizes in 2012 and quickly sold over 1.5 million copies in French and another 1.5 million in nearly 40 translations. But although Penguin bought the U.S. rights for half a million dollars, based on the book's French success, the English translation was savaged by the majority of American reviewers and was not a commercial success.

The plot is a murder mystery, and (if you can stomach the writing) the book is a 'page turner' that also contains meta-narratives (four levels of books within books) and reflections on writing. The narrator is an American author, seemingly describing American life and culture from the inside, and his descriptions were evidently convincing enough for a Francophone readership, with some reviewers suggesting that the book seemed so American that one checked to see that it wasn't a translation. But, as Besser (2015) points out, whereas French readers experienced a foreign form (essentially an imitation of an American crime novel) and a description of a foreign culture filtered through a European (or Francophone) viewpoint, the relationship between the foreign and the familiar is just the opposite for American readers of an English translation. Here the subject matter and the form are domestic, but attenuated or distorted by a foreign perspective, even though the foreignness was played down by the publisher: Penguin packaged and promoted the book as an American thriller because translated books in the United States are widely considered to be off-puttingly literary, exotic, foreign, inaccessible, and so on.

But whereas French reviewers were highly impressed with Dicker's European take on America—it was even compared to Nabokov's portrayal of 1950s America in *Lolita*—most American reviewers found it clichéd, stereotyped, simplistic, exaggerated, distorted, lumbering, mistaken, and so on, despite a fair amount of deliberate 'Americanization,' adaptation, and pruning of unnecessary explanations of American cultural practices by the translator and editor. It was widely assumed that the book's French reputation as high-quality literary fiction derived from the fact that its main characters are writers, and that French reviewers and prize juries were inordinately impressed by the meta-fictional tricks that struck American reviewers as mere pretention.

And indeed to readers more familiar with the United States than Dicker was when he wrote it, the book often appears risible. Most of the characters are archetypes or caricatures, beginning with an inexcusably cartoonlike Jewish mother. The universities attended by many characters are mentioned, but apart from the narrator, *everyone* went to either Yale or Harvard. No-one ever eats *anything* that isn't typically American—T-bone steaks, hamburgers, hot dogs, donuts, apple pie, deli sandwiches, and so on. The narrator lives in 'a plush apartment in the Village' (even French readers are expected to know which 'Village' this is), and rents 'an office close to Central Park,' and so on. But perhaps a writer who can sell 3 million copies in 40 languages of a novel about a *faux*-America doesn't particularly *need* to be loved and successful in the United States itself. To steal some adjectives from Hamlet, this kind of prose, both in the source text and the English translation, may be weary, stale, and flat but not at all unprofitable.

Just by way of comparison, here is an example of the kind of stylistically interesting contemporary writing that *does* present multiple challenges to translators: the opening of Ali Smith's recent novel *Autumn* (2016).

> **It was the worst of times, it was the worst of times.**
> Again. That's the thing about things. They fall apart,
> always have, always will, its in their nature. So an
> old old man washes up on a shore. He looks like a
> punctured football with its stitching split, the leather
> kind that people kicked a hundred years ago. The
> sea's been rough. It has taken the shirt off his back;
> naked as the day I was born are the words in the head
> he moves on its neck, but it hurts to. So try not to
> move the head. What's this in his mouth, grit? it's
> sand, it's under his tongue, he can feel it, he can hear it
> grinding when his teeth move against each other,

> singing its sand-song: I'm ground so small, but in the end I'm all, I'm softer if I'm underneath you when you fall, in sun I glitter, wind heaps me over litter, put a message in a bottle, throw the bottle in the sea, the bottle's made of me, I'm the hardest grain to harvest
>
> to harvest
>
> the words for the song trickle away. He is tired. The sand in his mouth and his eyes is the last of the grains in the neck of the sandglass.
>
> Daniel Gluck, your luck's run out at last.

There are intertextual references, beginning with the first sentence, an adaptation of the famous anaphorical antithesis that opens Dickens's *Tale of Two Cities*. This is quickly followed by a reference to a well-known line from Yeats's poem 'The Second Coming' ('Things fall apart; the centre cannot hold'). There are deliberately used clichés or fixed expressions—*That's the thing about*; *the shirt off his back*; and *naked as the day I was born*. There are long, rhythmic sequences of monosyllables, which are quite difficult to write (try it) and impossible to replicate in translation (except perhaps in Chinese and southest Asian languages)—37 in a row beginning with *as the day I was born* in the eighth line, and another 19 lower down beginning with *The sand in his mouth*. There is a play of words (requiring a knowledge of the German word for *luck*) involving the protagonist Gluck, a German-born songwriter, who seems to compose a song in his dream that he's washing up on the shore, with its (somewhat forced) rhymes (*small—all—fall*, *glitter—litter*, and *sea—me*). There are also repetitions (*always have, always will*), alliterations (*stitching split/kind that people kicked/singing its sand-song/hardest grain to harvest*), metaphors (the sand in his teeth singing its sand-song; words trickling away; life as a sandglass), the alternation of long and short sentences, and so on. The rest of the novel contains a lot of elaborate puns and wordplay, lists of potential rhymes in the songwriter's head, intertextual citations, references to British artists and contemporary and past political events, and so on. We can safely assume that unlike Ishiguro (if he is to be taken at face value), Smith does *not* have a Norwegian translator in her head as she writes.

Yet while the Anglophone market for fiction is large enough to embrace playful and experimental writers like Ali Smith, it no longer seems to have room for translations of Smith-like writers in other languages. This might seem surprising, given the number of L2 English speakers around the world. Grosman (2000) imagines a counterfactual world that is the exact opposite of the one that Parks describes. Rather than writing bland, delocalized fiction, or setting their stories in the United States, hoping to make a living by being translated for native English speakers, novelists could continue to write about their local culture, hoping to be translated for an international readership of *non-native* English speakers. Grosman asks whether it is 'too utopian to expect the ever-growing community of non-native speakers of International English [. . .] to develop an interest in reading the English translations of such literary works as are not available in their mother tongue' (p. 29). She imagines translations that 'would not need to be targeted at any particular literary system,' in which the translator could 'endeavour to preserve more culture-specific textual features, thus offering readers more of the original and unappropriated otherness of the source text' (p. 30). Such translations would need to be done by 'native-like (i.e. still non-mother tongue) speakers of English with profound understanding of their own culture, its tradition, and relationships with other cultures, and with a well-developed intercultural awareness' (p. 30), but with 'follow-up reading and editing by a native speaker,' presumably to make sure that nothing is *too* foreignized (and hence incomprehensible) for the international, non-native English-speaking readership, with its broad range of hybrid varieties, or similects, of English.

In the same collection of essays, Kovačič (2000) makes an analogous argument regarding film subtitling. Subtitles for 'minor' languages are often made via a relay translation into English. But it is quite possible that the source language culture and the target language culture share common traditions, values, and language properties that are not shared by the relay language (English), so Kovačič suggests that the relay translation should preserve literal translations of source language idioms and add footnotes or parenthetical explanations of culture-bound concepts, historical names, institutions, slang, jargon expressions, and so on for the benefit of the third-language subtitler, rather than produce an intermediary translation that reads as a British or American text.

Unfortunately, however, it appears that Grosman's vision of an international audience for foreignized English translations of fiction is indeed 'too utopian.' This market does not seem to exist. As Parks (2014: 197) says, sales of translated fiction suggest that although many people are content to read scientific or academic work in English, they tend to prefer reading fiction translated into their L1. This is even the case where a translated novel has passed through English as a relay language, thereby losing even more of the specificities of the source text. The economics of subtitling also make Kovačič's very logical demand for relay subtitles that are not wholly 'Anglified' an unlikely proposition.

Thus it seems that translations into English will continue to lose most traces of the 'otherness' of the source language, where the author hasn't already tried to diminish these in pursuit of translatability. Meanwhile, for better or worse, translations from English—in combination with an ever-increasing number of multicompetent L2 English speakers around the world—are helping transfer a limited number of English constructions (words, idiomatic expressions, and phrasal patterns) to other languages. In short, it appears that English is currently influencing other languages rather more than speakers of other languages are influencing English.

Notes

1 The German term *Sprachbund*, a calque from Russian, was introduced in an article (in French!) by the Russian linguist Trubetzkoy in 1928.

2 As Heine and Kuteva (2006: 23, note 16) point out, Whorf did not use 'Standard Average European' as a term of linguistic typology or even define it by means of linguistic properties. He meant a shared European culture, consisting of similar ways of thinking that were very different from those of the Hopi.

3 Haspelmath (1998, 2001) lists (among others) the definite article (grammaticalized from a demonstrative pronoun) and the indefinite article (grammaticalized from the numeral *one*); relative clauses with relative pronouns; the periphrastic perfect using a transitive verb of possession (*have*) and a passive participle; nominative experiencers; a passive construction formed from a passive participle plus an intransitive copula-like verb (such as *be* or *become*); dative external possessors (although not in English, possibly as a result of imperfect learning; see Chapter 4); negative pronouns instead of verbal negation; particle comparatives (*bigger than*); and verb fronting (or subject-verb inversion) in polar questions. Van der Auwera (1998: 815–6) offers a largely different list of 12 'SAE-features' identified by earlier linguists, some of them very general: analytic expression formats; simplified case paradigms; definite and indefinite articles; use of *have* and *be* as auxiliaries; non-Pro-Drop character; relatively fixed sentence level word order (V2 and VSO); phrasal word order with prepositions and postposed genitives; accusativity; finite verb-subject agreement; passives with the agent; non-identical agent and subject; and lexical and phraseological similarities. This still leaves *a lot* of grammatical features that are *not* shared across the different languages.

4 For example, Bybee (2015: 249) complains that Heine and Kuteva (2005) 'simply assert that languages were in (close) contact without having or supplying information about the extent and nature of the contact.'

5 All of this, of course, wholly disregards possible complaints by the source language community about 'cultural appropriation.' As Steiner (1998: 244) suggests, 'there is in every act of translation—and especially where it succeeds—a touch of treason. Hoarded dreams, patents of life are being taken across the frontier.'

6 News *is* translated quickly: McLaughlin (2011: 103) observed French news agency translators working at an average of just over 17 words per minute, with 10% of dispatches being translated at speeds greater than 30 words per minute. In comparison the fortunate translators at the United Nations and the other international organizations in Geneva are generally expected to do about 1,650 words a day (which is more than five times slower).

7 This is argued, for example, by Berman (1985/2004), who describes both qualitative and quantitative lexical impoverishment as 'deforming tendencies' in literary translation. Quantitative impoverishment can be shown by a simple type/token ratio—the number of different words (types) compared to the total number of words (tokens).

8 Placing an adjective before or after a noun in French can lead to differences of meaning: see Coppieters (1987)—and test your French!

9 France, famously, has a body (the *Académie française*) that creates officially sanctioned neologisms to replace Anglicisms and other borrowings, but it obviously can't oblige the public to adopt them. (Similarly Spain has the *Real Academia Española*, which was established in 1713 primarily to defend Spanish against the invasion of Gallicisms!) The spread of a few new word meanings borrowed from English in France is rather less drastic than

the incursion of *thousands* of Anglicisms into the Acadian French dialects of Prince Edward Island in Canada (including verbs like *watcher*, *starter*, and *feeler* and adjectives like *botheré* and *overfishé*); see the slightly startling appendices in King (2000).

10 This figure is quite widely quoted. Pei (1967: 92) states that 12,000 of the 20,000 words in 'full use' in English are of Latin, Greek, and French origin, to which must be added loans from other languages. Williams (1975: 68) gives 33% of words of English origin out of 10,000 different words in a corpus of business letters. Tadmor (2009: 56) gives a lower figure of 41% of loans from a list of 1,460 *basic* lexical meanings in the World Loanword Database (http://wold.clld.org) compared with an average of 24.2% across the 41 languages studied.

11 For example, Sir John Cheke translated the *Gospel of St. Matthew* in 1550, using words such as *byword*, *crossed*, *foresayer*, *gainrising*, and *hundreder*, where Tyndale's *Bible* (1526), and the later *Authorized Version* (1611), largely based on Tyndale, used *parable*, *crucified*, *prophet*, *resurrection*, and *centurion* (Baugh and Cable 2002: 214). Such sentiments were not confined to the 16th century; 300 years later William Barnes, a self-taught philologist, proposed replacing a number of Greek and Latin words by coinages with Germanic roots, such as *birdlore* for *ornithology*, *inbringing* for *importation*, *landfolk* for *people*, *speech-craft* for *grammar*, and *workstead* for *laboratory* (Bailey 1991: 193–4).

12 Mauranen and Kujamäki's corpus-based description of translated language is presented neutrally, and Mauranen (2012: 117) very plausibly suggests that the similarities between the lexical simplification frequently found in both learner language and ELF and in translated language result from the memory constraints involved in bilingual processing. Berman (1985/2004: 280), however, offers a critical account of the many unconscious 'deforming tendencies' in literary translation, including qualitative and quantitative lexical impoverishment (already mentioned), rationalization, clarification, expansion, ennoblement or rhetorization, the effacement of the superimposition of languages, and the destruction of rhythms, underlying networks of signification, expressions and idioms, linguistic patternings, and vernacular networks (or, in this last case, on the contrary, their exoticization), all of which 'lead to the same result: the production of a text that is more "clear," more "elegant," more "fluent," more "pure" than the original' and 'the destruction of the letter in favour of meaning.'

13 Lefevere (1992: 107) uses the word 'flattening' in this context, whereas Toury (1995: 304) writes about 'standardization,' and Chesterman (1997: 72) mentions the tendency of translations to be 'less idiosyncratic' and 'more conventionalized' than the source text.

14 Interview with Gregory Mason (1986), in Ishiguro (2008: 3–14).

15 This is perhaps Ishiguro's fullest discussion of this issue, in an interview with François Gallix (1999), in Ishiguro (2008: 135–55). The theme of being 'haunted by the Norwegians' (p. 146) also appears in other conversations in the same collection. Of course, despite his deliberate stylistic austerity and his general avoidance of current sociopolitical issues, there is a huge amount to admire in Ishiguro's Nobel-winning writing, particularly the range of genres he exploits and his fascinating first-person narrators, with all their fallible memories, self-deceptions, and peculiar perceptions. Moreover, I can (wholly gratuitously) assure readers that Ishiguro's prose is better than the songs he wrote and performed at the University of Kent's fortnightly Wednesday evening folk club in 1974–5!

16 This is from the last paragraph of a *New York Review of Books* piece (www.nybooks.com/daily/2013/11/07/literature-without-style/), omitted from the version in *Where I'm Reading From*. Parks's overall argument, partly outlined in the final chapter of the second edition of *Translating Style* (2007), is encapsulated in the titles of four blog pieces he wrote for the *New York Review of Books* (collected in Parks 2014), from which I am quoting liberally here: 'Your English is showing,' 'Ugly Americans abroad,' 'The dull new global novel,' and 'Literature without style.' Parks is heavily involved in the Global Literature and Translation (GLINT) project at the Libera Università di Lingue e Comunicazione (IULM) in Milan (www.iulm.it/wps/wcm/connect/iulmit/iulm-it/ricerca/progetti-di-ricerca/progetti-di-ateneo/letteratura-globalizzata).

17 Dao's poems obviously *don't* 'translate themselves,' and Damrosch (2003: 22–4) compares alternative translations, showing that even the words of 'world poetry' are far from being 'fungible.'

18 This section draws on an excellent unpublished MA thesis by Margaret Besser (2015) at the Translation and Interpreting Faculty of the University of Geneva.

8 Conclusion

Language Contact and the Future of English

English, like most languages, has been in contact with other languages for its entire history, and today it is in contact with all the world's 'larger' languages and a huge number of 'smaller' ones. The different varieties of native English (English, Welsh, Scottish, Irish, American, Australian, etc.) have all been shaped, to a greater or lesser extent, by contact with other local languages—which is largely why they are different varieties (Kirkpatrick 2007: 5–7). As outlined in Chapter 1, in many countries in Asia and Africa in which English has an official second language role, contact with local languages has also led to the development of indigenized or nativized or acculturated (and codified) local varieties, often known as New Englishes or World Englishes. In much of the rest of the world, where English is used as an additional language or a lingua franca for international and intercultural communication, speakers of many first languages have predictable and recognizable ways of speaking English, influenced by interaction with or transfer from their L1. In ELF, these hybrid, L1-influenced varieties, for which Mauranen has coined the useful term 'similects,' 'come together much like dialects in contact' (Mauranen 2012: 30).

It appears that the more frequent lexicogrammatical forms shared by many similects (as well as by many New English varieties) are diffusing (or have already diffused) into common ELF usage as interlocutors accommodate to each other's ways of speaking. But because ELF is used by speakers of a vast number of different L1s, with varying levels of proficiency in this additional language, it still shows a great deal of variation—as indeed do most supposedly focused and stable varieties of spoken native English. Yet the variation to be found in ELF includes a lot of non-standard morphosyntax, lexis, and phraseology that is not used in native English varieties, which Widdowson (2003: 48) describes as exploitation of 'the *virtual* language,' as opposed to the forms that have been actualized by the language's native speakers.

The main question I have addressed in this book is whether the more stable and widely shared usages of non-native or L2 speakers are likely to be diffused among speakers of native English varieties. And the answer

I have given is a negative one. Although L2 speakers of English far outnumber L1 users, they mostly use English with each other in the absence of the language's native speakers. Meanwhile, unlike the first few centuries after the Anglo-Saxons settled in England, when they were in contact first with large numbers of indigenous Celts and later with invading Vikings, today's native English speakers are in a large majority in the inner circle countries. While many L1 English speakers *are* exposed to a range of L2 varieties, they are not usually confronted with the critical mass of non-native speakers that might result in them accommodating to—or 'giving in to' (Thomason and Kaufman 1988: 43)—their lexicogrammatical forms, especially where these remain variable and unpredictable. Similarly, increasing intercultural contact among speakers of different native varieties of English has led to very little convergence.

I argued (somewhat uncontroversially) in Chapter 5 that the widespread use of ELF is likely to continue, sometimes alongside 'translanguaging,' receptive multilingualism, and so on. There is little sign of it being displaced by another language, and newspaper reports of the 'vast numbers' of people learning Mandarin are generally exaggerated. There is equally little chance of spoken ELF being displaced by machine translation because, despite huge advances in speech recognition, natural languages do not lend themselves particularly well to reliable automatic translation, and because most people will probably continue to find face-to-face communication in a shared language or languages preferable to relying on electronic gadgets for getting things done, socializing, making friendships, and so on.

But non-native speakers will, in the vast majority of cases, continue to use languages differently from their native speakers. Post-adolescent second language learners will continue to learn languages imperfectly or incompletely, according to native usages, for all the reasons outlined in Chapters 1 and 2. One can, uncontroversially, describe this as failure to attain full mastery of all the grammatical and phonological features of the native speakers' Basic Language Cognition (Hulstijn 2015). Alternatively, one can avoid reference to imperfection and (monolingual) native norms and talk about 'difference' and 'multicompetence.' Attempts to do away with the conventional distinction between native and non-native speakers, or L1 and L2 users, are generally well-intentioned, designed to counter the marginalization of non-native speakers, and assert their legitimacy and their ownership of the languages they use. But however well-intentioned such arguments may be, the differences between the usages of most L1 and most L2 speakers are going to persist. Moreover, as argued in Chapter 3, where ELF is concerned it is possible that some conscious language change is at work, alongside imperfect learning, with some ELF speakers deliberately avoiding some constructions they know to be used by native speakers, in the aid of clarity, enhanced expressivity, and general communicative effectiveness with other L2 speakers.

Lingua franca settings without any native speakers are particularly propitious for deliberate changes of usage of this type. Yet the factors that make such changes effective for L2 speakers—explicitness, simplification, regularization, reduced redundancy and ambiguity, and so on—do not apply to L1 speakers of English with their extensive experience of the native language. As mentioned in Chapter 1, Cameron-Faulkner et al. (2003) estimate this experience at roughly 50 million meaningful utterances heard by the age of 20, or perhaps 49 million or so reasons to use English differently from non-native speakers who only began learning the language in school. There are well-documented reasons why speakers adapt the way they talk and accommodate to other people's usages, involving identification, attributions of prestige, the perception of enhanced expressivity, and so on. But as argued in Chapter 4, these processes are only marginally at play in most ENL-ELF/ESL interactions.

There are widespread examples of teenagers in multi-ethnic neighbourhoods playing with language and choosing to mix forms from languages spoken by their friends, but such usages tend to be temporary and not to spread to the speech community at large. Some claims have been made for ESL-influenced features being disseminated among a native-speaking population (e.g., Hundt and Vogel [2011] writing about New Zealand), but in general, non-native usages seem to be having little influence on native speakers. As McWhorter (2011: 17) has pointed out, the days when English was influenced by contact with Celts and Vikings, and its transmission was 'interrupted' by incomplete non-native acquisition, preceded 'widespread literacy, education, and language standardization.' Today, on the contrary, the massive presence of the standard native version of the language in print, in the media, and in education ensures that it 'can survive endless waves of second-language acquisition intact.'

And it *is* the native version of the language that continues to dominate in print and education, despite the huge number of L2 speakers writing in English. In Chapter 6 I argued that academic written English *should* be open to the influence of non-native users, although more in terms of text organization, argumentative structure, and rhetorical patterns than lexicogrammatical variation. At the lexicogrammatical level, the standard forms of academic discourse in English are obviously attuned to the language's syntactic patterns. Different languages favour different ways of structuring sentences, and most competent translators habitually adapt and 'domesticate' source texts in ways that enhance their readability in the target language. Similarly, competent bilingual authors write differently according to the language they are using. One cannot write in English the way one writes in, say, Arabic, Chinese, French, Japanese, or Russian. Here it seems more likely that the English language, and the favoured argumentative and rhetorical norms of English academic discourse, will have more influence on the work of L2 writers than L2 writers will influence the way academic English is written. Unfortunately writing in English (or being translated into English) is *imposed* on many non-Anglophone academics, who are not interested in exploring the linguistic possibilities of more than one language, à la Beckett, but merely in publishing their research. It is up to the global research community—some 5.5 million people, according to Lillis and Curry (2010: 1)—to engage with the gatekeepers of academic publishing to ensure that the dominance of the English language does not inevitably lead to what Santos (1998:103) and Bennett (2007: 154) call 'epistemicide'—the 'murder' or 'systematic destruction of rival forms of knowledge.'

A further consequence of the dominance of English is the incorporation of features from English into other languages by their native speakers. Notwithstanding competing language-internal explanations of change (some of which were outlined in Chapter 3), there is a very long history of language contact and grammatical replication across languages all around the world, sometimes leading to Sprachbunds, including what Haspelmath (1998) calls the 'Standard Average European' linguistic area. In many parts of the world, English is currently the dominant language in contact, borrowing, and replication. This is most obvious at the lexical level, but in many languages it is also apparent—although usually quite minimally—in syntax and discourse structures. Commonly cited causes are widespread (asymmetrical) bilingualism with English, which automatically results in borrowing and calquing, which are widely attested consequences of bilingualism (or 'multicompetence'), and a huge amount of (asymmetrical) translation from English. There also appears to be an inverse process, with writers in various languages, particularly novelists, choosing to simplify their style, or make it 'Anglo-compatible,' to facilitate translation into English and access to the global market (Parks 2014).

Whether one sees the impact of English as a positive or negative development, or merely a neutral process, probably depends on one's fondness or otherwise for linguistic purity and one's attitude to English and/or the countries in which the major native varieties are spoken. But all in all, contrary to the claims and predictions of some proponents of ELF, it seems that English is currently having a greater influence (or at least a more immediately visible one) on other languages than the usages of the ever-growing number of L2 English speakers are having on native varieties of English. Because this book has 'the future' in the title, I will hazard that this state of affairs will continue for some time—although that is just one more 'some' to go along with the sprinkling of hedges and qualifiers (some, many, most, perhaps, possible, and probably) in this conclusion.

Bibliography

All websites (including those in the footnotes to the chapters) last accessed 24 August 2017.

Abrahamsson, N. and Hyltenstam, K. (2009) 'Age of onset and nativelikeness in a second language: Listener perception versus linguistic scrutiny', *Language Learning* 59(2): 249–306.

Adams, D. (1979) *The Hitchhiker's Guide to the Galaxy*, London: Pan Macmillan.

Adrados, F.R. (2005) *A History of the Greek Language: From Its Origins to the Present*, trans. F. Rojas del Canto, Leiden: Brill.

Aitchison, J. (2013) *Language Change: Progress or Decay?* 4th edn, Cambridge: Cambridge University Press.

Ammon, U. (2000) 'Towards more fairness in international English: Linguistic rights of non-native speakers?' in R. Phillipson (ed.) *Rights to Language: Equity, Power, and Education*, Mahwah, NJ: Lawrence Erlbaum, pp. 111–16.

Ammon, U. (ed.) (2001) *The Dominance of English as a Language of Science*, Berlin: Mouton de Gruyter.

Ammon, U. (2003) 'The international standing of the German language', in J. Maurais and M. Morris (eds.) *Languages in a Globalising World*, Cambridge: Cambridge University Press, pp. 231–49.

Ammon, U. (2007) 'Discussion: Global scientific communication: Open questions and policy suggestions', in A. Carli and U. Ammon (eds.) *Linguistic Inequality in Scientific Communication Today*, *AILA Review* 20: 123–33.

Anderman, G. and Rogers, M. (eds.) (2005) *In and Out of English: For Better, for Worse?* Clevedon: Multilingual Matters.

Aneja, G.A. (2016a) '(Non)native speakered: Rethinking (non)nativeness and teacher identity in TESOL teacher education', *TESOL Quarterly* 50(3): 572–96.

Aneja, G.A. (2016b) 'Rethinking nativeness: Toward a dynamic paradigm of (non)native speakering', *Critical Inquiry in Language Studies* 13(4): 351–79.

Aronin, L. and Singleton, D. (2008) 'Multilingualism as a new linguistic dispensation', *International Journal of Multilingualism* 5(1): 1–16.

Atkinson, D. (1999) 'TESOL and culture', *TESOL Quarterly* 33(4): 625–54.

Bachman, L.F. (1990) *Fundamental Considerations in Language Testing*, Oxford: Oxford University Press.

Backus, A., Maracz, L. and Ten Thije, J.D. (2011) 'A toolkit for multilingual communication in Europe: Dealing with linguistic diversity', in J.N. Jørgensen (ed.)

A Toolkit for Transnational Communication in Europe (Copenhagen Studies in Bilingualism 64), Copenhagen: Copenhagen University Press, pp. 5–24.

Bailey, R. (1991) *Images of English: A Cultural History of the Language*, Cambridge: Cambridge University Press.

Bamgboṣe A. (1998) 'Torn between the norms: Innovations in world Englishes', *World Englishes* 17(1): 1–14.

Barlow, M. (2013) 'Individual differences and usage-based grammar', *International Journal of Corpus Linguistics* 18(4): 443–78.

Barlow, M. and Kemmer, S. (eds.) (2000) *Usage-Based Models of Language*, Stanford: CSLI Publications.

Bauer, L. (1983) *English Word-Formation*, Cambridge: Cambridge University Press.

Bauer, L. and Trudgill, P. (eds.) (1998) *Language Myths*, London: Penguin.

Baugh, A.C. and Cable, T. (2002) *A History of the English Language*, 5th edn, London: Routledge.

Beckner, C. et al. (The 'Five Graces Group') (2009) 'Language is a complex adaptive system: Position paper', in N.C. Ellis and D. Larsen-Freeman (eds.) *Language as a Complex Adaptive System*, Oxford: Wiley-Blackwell, pp. 1–26 (also published as *Language Learning* 59, Supplement 1).

Beerkens, R. and Ten Thije, J.D. (2011) 'Receptive multilingualism in the Dutch-German border area', in J.N. Jørgensen (ed.) *A Toolkit for Transnational Communication in Europe (Copenhagen Studies in Bilingualism 64)*, Copenhagen: Copenhagen University Press, pp. 102–40.

Bellos, D. (2011) *Is That a Fish in Your Ear? Translation and the Meaning of Everything*, New York: Faber & Faber.

Benjamin, W. (1923/2004) 'The task of the translator', trans. H. Zohn, in L. Venuti (ed.) *The Translation Studies Reader*, 2nd edn, London: Routledge, pp. 75–85.

Bennett, K. (2007) 'Epistemicide: The tale of a predatory discourse', *The Translator* 13(2): 151–69.

Bennett, K. (2009) 'English academic style manuals: A survey', *Journal of English for Academic Purposes* 8(1): 43–53.

Bennett, K. (2011) 'The Scientific Revolution and its repercussions on the translation of technical discourse', *The Translator* 17(2): 189–210.

Bennett, K. (2013) 'English as a lingua franca in academia: Combating epistemicide through translator training', *The Interpreter and Translator Trainer* 7(2): 169–93.

Bennett, K. (2014) 'Introduction—the political and economic infrastructure of academic practice: The 'semiperiphery' as a category for social and linguistic analysis', in K. Bennett (ed.) *The Semiperiphery of Academic Writing: Discourses, Communities and Practices*, Basingstoke: Palgrave Macmillan, pp. 1–12.

Berdan, R. (1996) 'Disentangling language acquisition from language variation', in D. Preston and R. Bayley (eds.) *Variation in Second Language Acquisition*, Amsterdam: John Benjamins, pp. 203–44.

Berman, A. (1984/1992) *The Experience of the Foreign: Culture and Translation in Romantic Germany*, trans. S. Heyvaert, Albany: State University of New York.

Berman, A. (1985/2004) 'Translation and the trials of the foreign', trans. L. Venuti, in L. Venuti (ed.) *The Translation Studies Reader*, 2nd edn, London: Routledge, pp. 276–89.

Berns, M. (2008) 'World Englishes, English as a lingua franca, and intelligibility', *World Englishes* 27(3/4): 327–34.

Berns, M. (2009) 'English as lingua franca and English in Europe', *World Englishes* 28(2): 192–9.

Bernstein, B. (1964) 'Elaborated and restricted codes: Their social origins and some consequences', *American Anthropologist* 66(6): 55–69.

Berthoud, A-C., Grin, F. and Lüdi, G. (2011) 'The DYLAN project booklet', www.dylan-project.org/Dylan_en/dissemination/final/booklet/assets/DYLAN-Project_Final-Booklet_A4.pdf

Berthoud, A-C., Grin, F. and Lüdi, G. (2013) *Exploring the Dynamics of Multilingualism: The DYLAN Project*, Amsterdam: John Benjamins.

Besser, M. (2015) 'Too strange to fail: The European rise and American fall of *Les Bienveillantes* and *La Vérité sur l'Affaire Harry Quebert*', unpublished MA thesis, Faculté de traduction et d'interprétation, Université de Genève.

Bialystok, E. and Hakuta, K. (1994) *In Other Words: The Science and Psychology of Second-Language Acquisition*, New York: Basic Books.

Biber, D., Johansson, S., Leech, G., Conrad, S. and Finegan, E. (1999) *The Longman Grammar of Spoken and Written English*, London: Longman.

Biermeier, T. (2008) *Word-Formation in New Englishes: A Corpus-Based Analysis*, Münster: LIT.

Birdsong, D. (1992) 'Ultimate attainment in second language acquisition', *Language* 68(4): 706–55.

Birdsong, D. (1999) 'Introduction: Whys and why nots of the critical period hypothesis for second language acquisition', in D. Birdsong (ed.) *Second Language Acquisition and the Critical Period Hypothesis*, Mahwah, NJ: Lawrence Erlbaum, pp. 1–22.

Birdsong, D. and Molis, M. (2001) 'On the evidence for maturational constraints in second-language acquisition', *Journal of Memory and Language* 44(2): 235–49.

Björkman, B. (2008) '"So where we are?" Spoken lingua franca English at a technical university in Sweden', *English Today* 24(2): 35–41.

Blanche-Benveniste, C. (2008) 'Comment retrouver l'expérience des anciens voyageurs en terres de langues romanes?' in V. Conti and F. Grin (eds.) *S'entendre entre langues voisines: vers l'intercompréhension*, Chêne-Bourg: Georg, pp. 33–51.

Blanshard, B. (1954) *On Philosophical Style*, Bloomington: Indiana University Press.

Blommaert, J. (2010) *The Sociolinguistics of Globalization*, Cambridge: Cambridge University Press.

Bloomfield, L. (1933) *Language*, New York: Holt, Rinehart & Winston.

Boas, F. (1966) *Race, Language and Culture*, Chicago: University of Chicago Press.

Bock, J.K. (1986) 'Syntactic persistence in language production', *Cognitive Psychology* 18(3): 355–87.

Bod, R., Hay, J. and Jannedy, S. (2003) *Probabilistic Linguistics*, Cambridge, MA: MIT Press.

Bodmer, F. (1944/1985) *The Loom of Language: An Approach to the Mastery of Many Languages*, L. Hogben (ed.), New York: Norton.

Bolinger, D. (1976) 'Meaning and memory', *Forum Linguisticum* 1(1): 1–14.

Bolton, K. (2003) *Chinese Englishes: A Sociolinguistic History*, Cambridge: Cambridge University Press.

Bordet, G. (2016) 'Counteracting domain loss and epistemicide in specialized discourse: A case study on the translation of Anglophone metaphors to French', *Publications* 4, 18, www.mdpi.com/2304-6775/4/2/

Bourdieu, P. (1991) *Language and Symbolic Power*, trans. G. Raymond and M. Adamson, Oxford: Polity Press.

Braine, G. (ed.) (1999) *Non-Native Educators in English Language Teaching*, Mahwah, NJ: Lawrence Erlbaum.

Braine, G. (2010) *Nonnative Speaker English Teachers: Research, Pedagogy, and Professional Growth*, New York: Routledge.

Breiteneder, A. (2009) 'English as a lingua franca in Europe: An empirical perspective', *World Englishes* 28(2): 256–69.

Brianti, G. (1992) *Périphrases aspectuelles de l'italien: Le cas de andare, venire et stare + gérondif*, Bern: Peter Lang.

Britain, D. (2007) 'Grammatical variation in England', in D. Britain (ed.) *Language in the British Isles*, Cambridge: Cambridge University Press, pp. 75–104.

Brown, P. and Levinson, S. (1987) *Politeness*, Cambridge: Cambridge University Press.

Bruthiaux, P. (2003) 'Squaring the circles: Issues in modeling English worldwide', *International Journal of Applied Linguistics* 13(2): 159–78.

Brutt-Griffler, J. (2002) *World English: A Study of Its Development*, Clevedon: Multilingual Matters.

Brutt-Griffler, J. and Samimy, K. (2001) 'Transcending the nativeness paradigm', *World Englishes* 20(1): 99–106.

Buschfeld, S. (2013) 'English in Cyprus and Namibia: A critical approach to taxonomies and models of World Englishes and second language acquisition research', in S. Buschfeld, T. Hoffmann, M. Huber and A. Kautzsch (eds.) *The Evolution of Englishes: The Dynamic Model and Beyond*, Amsterdam: John Benjamins, pp. 181–202.

Butler, J. (1990) *Gender Trouble: Feminism and the Subversion of Identity*, London: Routledge.

Bybee, J. (2007) *Frequency of Use and the Organization of Language*, Oxford: Oxford University Press.

Bybee, J. (2008) 'Usage-based grammar and second-language acquisition', in P. Robinson and N.C. Ellis (eds.) *Handbook of Cognitive Linguistics and Second Language Acquisition*, London: Routledge, pp. 216–36.

Bybee J. (2015) *Language Change*, Cambridge: Cambridge University Press.

Bybee, J. and Hopper, P.J. (2001) 'Introduction to frequency and the emergence of linguistic structure', in J. Bybee and P.J. Hopper (eds.) *Frequency and the Emergence of Linguistic Structure*, Amsterdam: John Benjamins, pp. 1–24.

Bybee, J., Perkins, R. and Paglucia, W. (1994) *The Evolution of Grammar: Tense, Aspect, and Modality in the Languages of the World*, Chicago: University of Chicago Press.

Cameron D. (1995) *Verbal Hygiene*, London: Routledge.

Cameron, D. (2002) 'Globalization and the teaching of "communication skills"', in D. Block and D. Cameron (eds.) *Globalization and Language Teaching*, London: Routledge, pp. 67–82.

Cameron-Faulkner, T., Lieven, E. and Tomasello, M. (2003) 'A construction based analysis of child directed speech', *Cognitive Science* 27(6): 843–73.

Campbell, L. (1993) 'On proposed universals of grammatical borrowing', in H. Aertsen and R.J. Jeffers (eds.) *Historical Linguistics 1989: Papers From the Ninth International Conference on Historical Linguistics*, Amsterdam: John Benjamins, pp. 91–119.

Canagarajah, A.S. (2002) *A Geopolitics of Academic Writing*, Pittsburgh, PA: University of Pittsburgh Press.

Canagarajah, A.S. (2005) 'Introduction', in A.S. Canagarajah (ed.) *Reclaiming the Local in Language Policy and Practice*, Mahwah, NJ: Lawrence Erlbaum, pp. xiii–xxx.

Canagarajah, A.S. (2007) 'Lingua franca English, multilingual communities, and language acquisition', *Modern Language Journal* 91(5): 921–37.

Canagarajah, A.S. (2013) *Translingual Practice: Global Englishes and Cosmopolitan Relations*, London: Routledge.

Canale, M. and Swain, M. (1980) 'Theoretical bases of communicative approaches to second language teaching and testing', *Applied Linguistics* 1(1): 1–47.

Caravolas, M. (2006) 'Learning to spell in different languages: How orthographic variables might affect early literacy', in R.M. Joshi and P.G. Aaron (eds.) *Handbook of Orthography and Literacy*, Mahwah, NJ: Lawrence Erlbaum, pp. 497–512.

Carney, E. (1994) *A Survey of English Spelling*, London: Routledge.

Cassen, B. (2005) 'Un monde polyglotte pour échapper à la dictature de l'anglais', *Le Monde Diplomatique*, janvier: 22–3.

Cassin, B. et al. (eds.) (2014) *Dictionary of Untranslatables: A Philosophical Lexicon*, Princeton: Princeton University Press.

Cenoz, J. (2003) 'The additive effect of bilingualism in third language acquisition: A review', *International Journal of Bilingualism* 7(1): 71–87.

Chambers, J.K. (1998) 'TV makes people sound the same', in L. Bauer and P. Trudgill (eds.) *Language Myths*, London: Penguin, pp. 123–31.

Chambers, J.K. (2002) 'Dynamics of dialect convergence', *Journal of Sociolinguistics* 6(1): 117–30.

Chan, L.T. (2016) 'Beyond non-translation and "self-translation": English as lingua academica in China', *Translation and Interpreting Studies* 11(2): 152–76.

Chandrasekhar, A. (1978) 'Base language', *IRAL: International Review of Applied Linguistics in Language Teaching* 16(1): 62–5.

Chaudenson, R. (2003) 'Geolinguistics, geopolitics, geostrategy: The case of French', in J. Maurais and M.A. Morris (eds.) *Languages in a Globalising World*, Cambridge: Cambridge University Press, pp. 291–7.

Cheshire, J., Kerswill, P., Fox, S. and Torgersen, E. (2011) 'Contact, the feature pool and the speech community: The emergence of Multicultural London English', *Journal of Sociolinguistics* 15(2): 151–96.

Chesterman, A. (1997) *Memes of Translation*, Amsterdam: John Benjamins.

Clackson, J. and Horrocks, G. (2007) *The Blackwell History of the Latin Language*, Oxford: Wiley-Blackwell.

Clyne, M. (1980) 'Culture and discourse structure', *Journal of Pragmatics* 5(1): 61–6.

Cogo, A. and Dewey, M. (2006) 'Efficiency in ELF communication: From pragmatic motives to lexico-grammatical innovation', *Nordic Journal of English Studies* 5(2): 59–93.

Cogo, A. and Dewey, M. (2012) *Analysing English as a Lingua Franca: A Corpus-Driven Investigation*, London: Continuum.

Cogo, A. and Jenkins, J. (2010) 'English as a lingua franca in Europe: A mismatch between policy and practice', *European Journal of Language Policy* 2(2): 271–94.

Connor, U. (2004) 'Intercultural rhetoric research: Beyond texts', *Journal of English for Academic Purposes* 3(4): 183–95.

Connor, U. (2008) 'Mapping multidimensional aspects of research: Reaching to intercultural rhetoric', in U. Connor, E. Nagelhout and W. Rozycki (eds.) *Contrastive Rhetoric: Reaching to Intercultural Rhetoric*, Amsterdam: John Benjamins, pp. 299–315.

Conrad, A.W. (1996) 'The international role of English: The state of the discussion', in J.A. Fishman, A.W. Conrad and A. Rubal-Lopez (eds.) *Post-Imperial English: Status Change in Former British and American Colonies, 1940–1990*, Berlin: Mouton de Gruyter, pp. 13–36.

Conti, V. and Grin, F. (eds.) (2008) *S'entendre entre langues voisines: vers l'intercompréhension*, Chêne-Bourg: Georg.

Cook, V.J. (1991) 'The poverty-of-the-stimulus argument and multi-competence', *Second Language Research* 7(2): 103–17.

Cook, V.J. (1999) 'Going beyond the native speaker in language teaching', *TESOL Quarterly* 33(2): 185–209.

Cook, V.J. (2002a) 'Background to the L2 user', in V.J. Cook (ed.) *Portraits of the L2 User*. Clevedon: Multilingual Matters, pp. 1–28.

Cook, V.J. (2002b) 'Language teaching methodology and the L2 user perspective', in V.J. Cook (ed.) *Portraits of the L2 User*, Clevedon: Multilingual Matters, pp. 325–44.

Cook, V.J. (2013) 'ELF: Central or atypical form of second language acquisition?' in D. Singleton, J.A. Fishman, L. Aronin and M.Ó Laoire (eds.) *Current Multilingualism: A New Linguistic Dispensation*, Berlin: De Gruyter Mouton, pp. 27–44.

Cook, V.J. (2016) 'Premises of multi-competence', in V.J. Cook and L. Wei (eds.) *The Cambridge Handbook of Linguistic Multi-Competence*, Cambridge: Cambridge University Press, pp. 1–25.

Coppieters, R. (1987) 'Competence differences between native and near-native speakers', *Language* 63(3): 544–73.

Corder, S.P. (1967) 'The significance of learners' errors', *IRAL: International Review of Applied Linguistics in Language Teaching* 5(4): 161–9.

Corrigan, K.P. (2010) 'Language contact and grammatical theory', in R. Hickey (ed.) *Handbook of Language Contact*, Oxford: Wiley-Blackwell, pp. 106–27.

Coseriu, E. (1983) 'Adam Smith and the beginnings of language typology', *Historiographia Linguistica* 10(1/2): 1–12.

Coseriu, E. (1988) 'Linguistic change does not exist', in J. Albrecht, J. Lüdtke and H. Thun (eds.) *Energeia und Ergon. Sprachliche Variation—Sprachgeschichte—Sprachtypologie: Studia in Honorem Eugenio Coseriu; Band 1: Schriften Eugenio Coseriu (1965–1987)*, Tübingen: Gunter Narr, pp. 147–57.

Coulmas, F. (2007) 'English monolingualism in scientific communication and progress in science, good or bad?' in A. Carli and U. Ammon (eds.) *Linguistic Inequality in Scientific Communication Today*, *AILA Review* 20: 5–13.

Croft, W. (2000) *Explaining Language Change: An Evolutionary Approach*, London: Longman.
Croft, W. (2010) 'The origins of grammaticalization in the verbalization of experience', *Linguistics* 48(1): 1–48.
Croft, W. and Cruse, D.A. (2004) *Cognitive Linguistics*, Cambridge: Cambridge University Press.
Cronin, M. (1998) 'The cracked looking glass of servants: Translation and minority languages in a global age', *The Translator* 4(2): 145–62.
Crystal, D. (2000) *Language Death*, Cambridge: Cambridge University Press.
Crystal, D. (2003) *English as a Global Language*, 2nd edn, Cambridge: Cambridge University Press.
Crystal, D. (2008) 'Two thousand million?' *English Today* 24(1): 3–6.
Culler, J. and Lamb, K. (2003) 'Introduction: Dressing up, dressing down', in J. Culler and K. Lamb (eds.) *Just Being Difficult? Academic Writing in the Public Arena*, Stanford: Stanford University Press.
Cummins, J. (1984) *Bilingualism and Special Education: Issues in Assessment and Pedagogy*, Clevedon: Multilingual Matters.
Cummins, J. and Swain, M. (1986) *Bilingualism in Education*, London: Longman.
Curzan, A. (2014) *Fixing English: Prescriptivism and Language Change*, Cambridge: Cambridge University Press.
Dąbrowska, E. (1997) 'The LAD goes to school: A cautionary tale for nativists', *Linguistics* 35(4): 735–66.
Dalton-Puffer, C., Nikula, T. and Smit U. (2010) *Language Use and Language Learning in CLIL Classrooms*, Amsterdam: John Benjamins.
Damrosch, D. (2003) *What Is World Literature?* Princeton: Princeton University Press.
Darwin, C. (1871) *The Descent of Man, and Selection in Relation to Sex*, London: John Murray.
Davidson, D. (2005) 'A nice derangement of epitaphs', in *Truth, Language, and History*, Oxford: Clarendon Press, pp. 89–108.
Davies, A. (2003) *The Native Speaker: Myth and Reality*, Clevedon: Multilingual Matters.
De Angelis, G. (2007) *Third or Additional Language Acquisition*, Clevedon: Multilingual Matters.
De Angelis, G. and Selinker, L. (2001) 'Interlanguage transfer and competing linguistic systems in the multilingual mind', in J. Cenoz, B. Hufeisen and U. Jessner (eds.) *Cross-Linguistic Influence in Third Language Acquisition: Psycholinguistic Perspectives*, Clevedon: Multilingual Matters, pp. 42–58.
De Groot, A.M.B. (1993) 'Word-type effects in bilingual processing tasks: Support for a mixed representational system', in R. Schreuder and B. Weltens (eds.) *The Bilingual Lexicon*, Amsterdam: John Benjamins, pp. 27–51.
De Groot, A.M.B. (2011) *Language and Cognition in Bilinguals and Multilinguals: An Introduction*, New York: Psychology Press.
De Stael, G. (1816/2006) 'The spirit of translation', trans. J. Luzzi, *Romanic Review* 97(3/4): 279–85.
De Swaan, A. (2001) *Words of the World: The Global Language System*, Cambridge: Polity Press.
De Swaan, A. (2004) 'Endangered languages, sociolinguistics and linguistic sentimentalism', *European Review* 12(4): 567–80.

DeKeyser, R.M. (2000) 'The robustness of critical period effects in second language acquisition', *Studies in Second Language Acquisition* 22(4): 499–533.

Dicker, J. (2012) *La Vérité sur l'Affaire Harry Quebert*, Paris: Éditions de Fallois/ L'Age d'Homme.

Dicker, J. (2014) *The Truth About the Harry Quebert Affair*, trans. S. Taylor, New York: Penguin.

Dixon, R.M.W. (1997) *The Rise and Fall of Languages*, Cambridge: Cambridge University Press.

Doughty, C. and Williams, J. (eds.) (1998) *Focus on Form in Classroom Second Language Acquisition*, Cambridge: Cambridge University Press.

Durante, M. (1981) *Dal latino all'italiano moderno: Saggio di storia linguistica e culturale*, Bologna: Zanichelli.

Eckert, P. (2003) 'Dialogue—sociolinguistics and authenticity: An elephant in the room', *Journal of Sociolinguistics* 7(3): 392–431.

Eco, U. (1995) *The Search for the Perfect Language*, trans. J. Fentress, Oxford: Wiley-Blackwell.

Edwards, J. (2011) *Challenges in the Social Life of Language*, Basingstoke: Palgrave Macmillan.

Eggington, W.G. (1987) 'Written academic discourse in Korea: Implications for effective communication', in U. Connor and R.B. Kaplan (eds.) *Writing Across Languages: Analysis of L2 Text*, Reading, MA: Addison-Wesley, pp. 153–67.

Ellis, N.C. (2002) 'Frequency effects in language processing: A review with implications for theories of implicit and explicit language acquisition', *Studies in Second Language Acquisition* 24(2): 143–88.

Ellis, N.C. (2006a) 'Language acquisition as rational contingency learning', *Applied Linguistics* 27(1): 1–24.

Ellis, N.C. (2006b) 'Selective attention and transfer phenomena in L2 acquisition: Contingency, cue competition, salience, interference, overshadowing, blocking, and perceptual learning', *Applied Linguistics* 27(2): 164–94.

Ellis, N.C. (2008) 'The psycholinguistics of the interaction hypothesis', in A. Mackey and C. Polio (eds.) *Multiple Perspectives on Interaction: Second Language Research in Honor of Susan M. Gass*, New York: Routledge, pp. 11–40.

Ellis, N.C. (2012a) 'Frequency-based accounts of second language acquisition', in S. Gass and A. Mackey (eds.) *The Routledge Handbook of Second Language Acquisition*, London: Routledge, pp. 193–210.

Ellis, N.C. (2012b) 'What can we count in language, and what counts in language acquisition, cognition, and use?' in S.T. Gries and D. Divjak (eds.) *Frequency Effects in Language Learning and Processing*, Berlin: Mouton de Gruyter, pp. 7–34.

Erling, E.J. (2002) ' "I learn English since ten years": The global English debate and the German university classroom', *English Today* 18(2): 8–13.

European Commission. (2006) 'Europeans and their languages', *Special Eurobarometer* 243. http://ec.europa.eu/commfrontoffice/publicopinion/archives/ebs/ebs_243_sum_en.pdf

European Council for Cultural Co-operation. (2001) *Common European Framework of Reference for Languages: Learning, Teaching, Assessment*, Cambridge: Cambridge University Press.

Even-Zohar, I. (1990a) 'The position of translated literature within the literary polysystem', *Poetics Today* 11(1): 45–51.

Even-Zohar, I. (1990b) 'Laws of literary interference', *Poetics Today* 11(1): 53–72.

Faarlund, J.T. (1989) 'Pragmatics and syntactic change', in L.E. Breivik and E.H. Jahr (eds.) *Language Change: Contributions to the Study of Its Causes*, Berlin: Mouton de Gruyter.

Faez, F. (2011) 'Are you a native speaker of English? Moving beyond a simplistic dichotomy', *Critical Inquiry in Language Studies* 8(4): 378–99.

Farrar, K. (1999) 'Explanations for word order change in modern German', *Zeitschrift für Dialektologie und Linguistik* 66(1): 1–30.

Ferguson, A. (1767/1995) *An Essay on the History of Civil Society*, F. Oz-Salzburger (ed.), Cambridge: Cambridge University Press.

Ferguson, C.A. (1971) 'Absence of copula and the notion of simplicity: A study of normal speech, baby talk, foreigner talk and pidgins', in D. Hymes (ed.) *Pidginization and Creolization of Languages*, Cambridge: Cambridge University Press, pp. 141–50.

Ferguson, C.A. (1982/1992) 'Foreword to the first edition', in B.B. Kachru (ed.) *The Other Tongue: English Across Cultures*, 2nd edn, Urbana: University of Illinois Press, pp. xiii–xvii.

Ferguson, G. (2007) 'The global spread of English, scientific communication and ESP: Questions of equity, access and domain loss', *Ibérica: Revista de la Asociación Europea de Lenguas para Fines Específicos* 13: 7–38.

Ferguson, G. (2009) 'Issues in researching English as a lingua franca: A conceptual enquiry', *International Journal of Applied Linguistics* 19(2): 117–35.

Ferguson, G. (2012) 'The practice of ELF', *Journal of English as a Lingua Franca* 1(1): 177–80.

Ferguson, G., Pérez-Llantada, C. and Plo, R. (2011) 'English as an international language of scientific publication: A study of attitudes', *World Englishes* 30(1): 41–59.

Filppula, M. (2003) 'The quest for the most "parsimonious" explanations: Endogeny vs. contact revisited', in R. Hickey (ed.) *Motives for Language Change*, Cambridge: Cambridge University Press, pp. 161–73.

Filppula, M., Klemola, J. and Paulasto, H. (2008) *English and Celtic in Contact*, London: Routledge.

Firth, A. (1996) 'The discursive accomplishment of normality: On 'lingua franca' English and conversation analysis', *Journal of Pragmatics* 26(2): 237–59.

Firth, A. (2009) 'The lingua franca factor', *Intercultural Pragmatics* 6(2): 147–70.

Firth, A. and Wagner, J. (1997) 'On discourse, communication, and (some) fundamental concepts in SLA research', *Modern Language Journal* 81(3): 285–300.

Fish, S. (1981) 'Literature in the reader: Affective stylistics', in *Is There a Text in This Class? The Authority of Interpretive Communities*, Cambridge, MA: Harvard University Press, pp. 21–57.

Fishman, J.A. (1982) 'Whorfianism of the third kind: Ethnolinguistic diversity as a worldwide societal asset', *Language in Society* 11(1): 1–14.

Foucault, M. (1972/2002) *The Archaeology of Knowledge*, trans. A.S. Smith, London: Routledge.

Fowler, H.W. and Crystal, D. (2009) *A Dictionary of Modern English Usage*, Oxford: Oxford University Press.

Furiassi, C., Pulcini, V. and Rodríguez González, F. (eds.) (2012) *The Anglicization of European Lexis*, Amsterdam: John Benjamins.

Gallitelli, E. (2013) 'Il ruolo delle traduzioni letterarie dall'inglese nell'italia unita. Analisi diacronica delle tendenze traduttive e studio di casi', unpublished *Dottorato di Ricerca in Letterature Comparate*, Milan: Libera Università di Lingue e Comunicazione IULM.

García, O. and Wei, L. (2014) *Translanguaging: Language, Bilingualism and Education*, Basingstoke: Palgrave Macmillan.

Gardner, J. (2016) 'Misused English words and expressions in EU publications', European Court of Auditors, Secretariat General Translation Directorate, Luxembourg, www.eca.europa.eu/Other%20publications/EN_TERMINOLOGY_PUBLICATION/EN_TERMINOLOGY_PUBLICATION.pdf

Gardner-Chloros, P. (1991) *Language Selection and Switching in Strasbourg*, Oxford: Clarendon Press.

Gass, S.M., Behney, J. and Plonsky, L. (2013) *Second Language Acquisition: An Introductory Course*, 4th edn, London: Routledge.

Gazzola, M. and Grin, F. (2007) 'Assessing efficiency and fairness in multilingual communication: Towards a general analytical framework', in A. Carli and U. Ammon (eds.) *Linguistic Inequality in Scientific Communication Today, AILA Review*, Amsterdam: John Benjamins, 20: 87–105.

Gazzola, M. and Grin, F. (2013) 'Is ELF more effective and fair than translation? An evaluation of the EU's multilingual regime', *International Journal of Applied Linguistics* 23(1): 93–107.

Gellerstam, M. (2005) 'Fingerprints in translation', in G. Anderman and M. Rogers (eds.) *In and Out of English: For Better, for Worse?* Clevedon: Multilingual Matters, pp. 201–13.

Giles, H., Coupland, N. and Coupland, J. (1991) 'Accommodation theory: Communication, context, and consequence', in H. Giles, N. Coupland and J. Coupland (eds.) *Contexts of Accommodation*, Cambridge: Cambridge University Press, pp. 1–68.

Givón, T. (1985) 'Iconicity, isomorphism and non-arbitrary coding in syntax', in J. Haiman (ed.) *Iconicity in Syntax*, Amsterdam: John Benjamins, pp. 187–220.

Givón, T. (1994) 'Isomorphism in the grammatical code: Cognitive and biological considerations', in R. Simone (ed.) *Iconicity in Language*, Amsterdam: John Benjamins, pp. 47–76.

Goethe, J.W. von. (1813/1977) '*Zu brüderlichem Andenken Wielands*' [In fraternal memory of Wieland], trans. by A. Lefevere as 'In praise of the translator', in A. Lefevere (ed.) *Translating Literature: The German Tradition From Luther to Rosenzweig*, Assen: Van Gorcum, pp. 38–9.

Goethe, J.W. von. (1819/2004) 'Notes and queries for a better understanding', in *West—Eastern Diwan* [*West-östlicher Divan*], trans. by S. Sloan as 'Translations', in L. Venuti (ed.) *The Translation Studies Reader*, 2nd edn, London: Routledge, pp. 64–6.

Goethe, J.W. von. (1828/1921) 'Relations to other countries' [*Bezüge nach Aussen*, from *Über Kunst und Alterthum*, Vol. 6, Part 2], in 'Goethe's theory of a world literature', in J.E. Springarn (ed. and trans.) *Goethe's Literary Essays*, New York: Harcourt, Brace, pp. 89–99.

Goethe, J.W. von. (1827/1850) *Conversations of Goethe With Eckermann and Soret, Vol. I*, trans J. Oxenford, London: Smith, Elder.

Görlach, M. (ed.) (2001) *A Dictionary of European Anglicisms: A Usage Dictionary of Anglicisms in Sixteen European Languages*, Oxford: Oxford University Press.

Görlach, M. (2002) *Still More Englishes*, Amsterdam: John Benjamins.

Görlach, M. (ed.) (2002) *English in Europe*, Oxford: Oxford University Press.

Graddol, D. (1997) *The Future of English?* London: British Council.

Graddol, D. (2006) *English Next*, London: British Council.

Grin, F. (2005) *L'enseignement des langues étrangères comme politique publique*, Paris: Haut Conseil de l'évaluation de l'école, Rapport no 19.

Grin, F. (2008) 'Intercompréhension, efficience et équité', in V. Conti and F. Grin (eds.) *S'entendre entre langues voisines: vers l'intercompréhension*, Chêne-Bourg: Georg, pp. 79–109.

Grin, F. (2017) 'Translation and language policy in the dynamics of multilingualism', *International Journal of the Sociology of Language* 243: 155–81.

Grosjean, F. (1995) 'A psycholinguistic approach to code-switching: The recognition of guest words by bilinguals', in L. Milroy and P. Muysken (eds.) *One Speaker, Two Languages: Cross-Disciplinary Perspectives on Code-Switching*, Cambridge: Cambridge University Press, pp. 259–75.

Grosjean, F. (2008) 'The bilingual's language modes', in *Studying Bilinguals*, Oxford: Oxford University Press, pp. 37–66.

Grosjean, F. (2010) *Bilingual: Life and Reality*, Cambridge, MA: Harvard University Press.

Grosman, M. (2000) 'Non-mother tongue translation', in M. Grosman, M. Kadric, I. Kovačič and M. Snell-Hornby (eds.) *Translation into Non-Mother Tongues in Professional Practice and Training*, Tübingen: Stauffenburg, pp. 21–34.

Gunter, B. (2014) 'Discovering theoretical models to explain mediated influences on language', *Journal of Sociolinguistics* 18(2): 262–71.

Gut, U. (2011) 'Studying structural innovations in New English varieties', in J. Mukherjee and M. Hundt (eds.) *Exploring Second-Language Varieties of English and Learner Englishes: Bridging a Paradigm Gap*, Amsterdam: John Benjamins, pp. 104–24.

Hagège, C. (2012) *Contre la pensée unique*, Paris: Odile Jacob.

Haiman, J. (1985) *Natural Syntax: Iconicity and Erosion*, Cambridge: Cambridge University Press.

Hakuta, K., Bialystok, E. and Wiley, E. (2003) 'Critical evidence: A test of the critical period hypothesis for second-language acquisition', *Psychological Science* 14(1): 31–8.

Hall, E.T. (1977) *Beyond Culture*, New York: Anchor.

Halliday, M.A.K. (1968) 'The users and uses of language', in J. Fishman (ed.) *Readings in the Sociology of Language*, The Hague: Mouton, pp. 139–69.

Halliday, M.A.K. and Martin, J.R. (1993) *Writing Science: Literacy and Discursive Power*, London: The Falmer Press.

Hamel, R.E. (2007) 'The dominance of English in the international scientific periodical literature and the future of language use in science', in A. Carli and U. Ammon (eds.) *Linguistic Inequality in Scientific Communication Today, AILA Review* 20: 53–71.

Hamers, J.F. and Blanc, M.H.A. (1989) *Bilinguality and Bilingualism*, Cambridge: Cambridge University Press.

Harissi, M., Otsuji, E. and Pennycook, A. (2012) 'The performative fixing and unfixing of subjectivities', *Applied Linguistics* 33(5): 524–43.

Harris, A.C. and Campbell, L. (1995) *Historical Syntax in Cross-Linguistic Perspective*, Cambridge: Cambridge University Press.

Harris, R. (1990) ‘On redefining linguistics’, in H. Davis and T. Taylor (eds.) *Redefining Linguistics*, London: Routledge, pp. 18–52.

Hartsuiker, R.J., Pickering, M.J. and Veltkamp, E. (2004) ‘Is syntax separate or shared between languages? Crosslinguistic syntactic priming in Spanish—English bilinguals’, *Psychological Science* 15(6): 409–14.

Haspelmath, M. (1998) ‘How young is Standard Average European?’ *Language Sciences* 20(3): 271–87.

Haspelmath, M. (1999a) ‘Optimality and diachronic adaptation’, *Zeitschrift für Sprachwissenschaft* 18(2): 180–205.

Haspelmath, M. (1999b) ‘Why is grammaticalization irreversible?’ *Linguistics* 37(6): 1043–68.

Haspelmath, M. (2001) ‘The European linguistic area: Standard Average European’, in M. Haspelmath, E. König, W. Oesterreicher and W. Raible (eds.) *Language Typology and Language Universals*, Berlin: Mouton de Gruyter, pp. 1492–1510.

Hawkins, J.A. (2004) *Efficiency and Complexity of Grammars*, Oxford: Oxford University Press.

Hawkins, J.A. (2012) ‘The drift of English toward invariable word order from a typological and Germanic perspective’, in T. Nevalainen and E.C. Traugott (eds.) *The Oxford Handbook of the History of English*, Oxford: Oxford University Press, pp. 622–32.

Hawkins, J.A. (2014) *Cross-Linguistic Variation and Efficiency*, Oxford: Oxford University Press.

Heine, B. and Kuteva, T. (2005) *Language Contact and Grammatical Change*, Cambridge: Cambridge University Press.

Heine, B. and Kuteva, T. (2006) *The Changing Languages of Europe*, Cambridge: Cambridge University Press.

Herder, J.G. (1767–8/1977) ‘Fragments on recent German literature’, in A. Lefevere (ed. and trans.) *Translating Literature: The German Tradition From Luther to Rosenzweig*, Assen: Van Gorcum, pp. 31–4.

Herdina, P. and Jessner, U. (2002) *A Dynamic Model of Multilingualism: Perspectives of Change in Psycholinguistics*, Clevedon: Multilingual Matters.

Hermans, W.F. (1966/1997) *Nooit Meer Slapen*, Amsterdam: De Bezige Bij.

Hermans, W.F. (2006) *Beyond Sleep*, trans. I. Rilke, London: Harvill Secker.

Hickey, R. (ed.) (2012) *Standards of English: Codified Varieties Around the World*, Cambridge: Cambridge University Press.

Hickey, R. (2013) ‘English as a contact language in Ireland and Scotland’, in D. Schreier and M. Hundt (eds.) *English as a Contact Language*, Cambridge: Cambridge University Press, pp. 88–105.

Hilpert, M. (2013) *Constructional Change in English: Developments in Allomorphy, Word Formation and Syntax*, Cambridge: Cambridge University Press.

Hinds, J. (1983) ‘Contrastive rhetoric: Japanese and English’, *Text* 3(2): 183–95.

Hinds, J. (1987) ‘Reader versus writer responsibility: A new typology’, in U. Connor and R.B. Kaplan (eds.) *Writing Across Languages: Analysis of L2 Text*, Reading, MA: Addison-Wesley, pp. 141–52.

Hinds, J. (1990) ‘Inductive, deductive, quasi-inductive: Expository writing in Japanese, Korean, Chinese, and Thai’, in U. Connor and A.M. Johns (eds.) *Coherence in Writing: Research and Pedagogical Perspectives*, Alexandria, VA: TESOL, pp. 87–110.

Hinrichs, L. and Szmrecsanyi, B. (2007) 'Recent changes in the function and frequency of Standard English genitive constructions: A multivariate analysis of tagged corpora', *English Language and Linguistics* 11(3): 437–74.
Hinrichs, L., Szmrecsanyi, B. and Bohmann, A. (2015) '*Which*-hunting and the Standard English relative clause', *Language* 91(4): 806–36.
Hoey, M. (2005) *Lexical Priming*, London: Longman.
Holliday, A. (2005) *The Struggle to Teach English as an International Language*, Oxford: Oxford University Press.
Holliday, A. (2006) 'Native-speakerism', *ELT Journal* 60(4): 385–7.
Hopper, P.J. (1988) 'Emergent grammar and the a priori grammar postulate', in D. Tannen (ed.) *Linguistics in Context: Connecting Observation and Understanding*, Norwood, NJ: Ablex, pp. 117–34.
Hopper, P.J. (1998) 'Emergent grammar', in M. Tomasello (ed.) *The New Psychology of Language: Cognitive and Functional Approaches to Linguistic Structure*, Englewood Cliffs, NJ: Lawrence Erlbaum, pp. 155–75.
Hopper, P.J. and Traugott, E.C. (2003) *Grammaticalization*, 2nd edn, Cambridge: Cambridge University Press.
Horrocks, G. (2010) *Greek: A History of the Language and Its Speakers*, 2nd edn, Oxford: Wiley-Blackwell.
House, J. (1981) *A Model for Translation Quality Assessment*, Tübingen: Gunter Narr.
House, J. (2013) 'English as a lingua franca and translation', in Y. Gambier and L. van Doorslaer (eds.) *Handbook of Translation Studies, Vol. 4*, Amsterdam: John Benjamins, pp. 59–62.
Hughes, G. (2000) *A History of English Words*, Oxford: Wiley-Blackwell.
Hulstijn, J.H. (2015) *Language Proficiency in Native and Non-Native Speakers: Theory and Research*, Amsterdam: John Benjamins.
Humboldt, W. von. (1820/1904) 'Über das vergleichende Sprachstudium in Beziehung auf die verschiedenen Epochen der Sprachentwicklung', in A. Leitzmann (ed.) *Wilhehm von Humboldts Werke, Band 4, 1820–1822*, Berlin: B. Behr, pp. 1–34.
Hundt, M. (1998) *New Zealand English Grammar, Fact or Fiction?* Amsterdam: John Benjamins.
Hundt, M. (2013) 'The diversification of English: Old and new and emerging epicentres', in D. Schreier and M. Hundt (eds.) *English as a Contact Language*, Cambridge: Cambridge University Press, pp. 182–203.
Hundt, M. and Vogel, K. (2011) 'Overuse of the progressive in ESL and learner Englishes—fact or fiction?' in J. Mukherjee and M. Hundt (eds.) *Exploring Second-Language Varieties of English and Learner Englishes: Bridging a Paradigm Gap*, Amsterdam: John Benjamins, pp. 145–66.
Hyltenstam, K. and Abrahamsson, N. (2000) 'Who can become native-like in a second language? All, some, or none? On the maturational constraints controversy in second language acquisition', *Studia Linguistica* 54(2): 150–66.
Hyltenstam, K. and Abrahamsson, N. (2003) 'Maturational constraints in second language acquisition', in C. Doughty and M. Long (eds.) *Handbook of Second Language Acquisition*, Oxford: Wiley-Blackwell, pp. 539–88.
Hymes, D. (1972) 'On communicative competence', in J.B. Pride and J. Holmes (eds.) *Sociolinguistics*, Harmondsworth: Penguin, pp. 269–93.
Ioup, G., Boustagui, E., El Tigi, M. and Moselle, M. (1994) 'Reexamining the critical period hypothesis: A case study in a naturalistic environment', *Studies in Second Language Acquisition* 16(1): 73–98.

Ishiguro, K. (1982) *A Pale View of Hills*, London: Faber & Faber.

Ishiguro, K. (1986) *An Artist of the Floating World*, London: Faber & Faber.

Ishiguro, K. (2008) *Conversations With Kazuo Ishiguro*, B.W. Shaffer and C.F. Wong (eds.), Jackson: University Press of Mississippi.

Jakobson, R. (1938/1962) 'Sur la théorie des affinités phonologiques des langues', in *Selected Writings 1: Phonological Studies*, s-Gravenhage: Mouton, pp. 234–46.

Jakobson, R. (1959/2004) 'On linguistic aspects of translation, in L. Venuti (ed.) *The Translation Studies Reader*, 2nd edn, London: Routledge, pp. 138–44.

James, A.R. (2000) 'English as a European lingua franca: Current realities and existing dichotomies', in J. Cenoz and U. Jessner (eds.) *English in Europe: The Acquisition of a Third Language*, Clevedon: Multilingual Matters, pp. 22–38.

Janin, P. (2008) 'L'intercompréhension dans une politique francophone du plurilinguisme', in V. Conti and F. Grin (eds.) *S'entendre entre langues voisines: vers l'intercompréhension*, Chêne-Bourg: Georg, pp. 53–77.

Jarvis, S. and Pavlenko, A. (2009) *Crosslinguistic Influence in Language and Cognition*, London: Routledge.

Jenkins, J. (2000) *The Phonology of English as an International Language*, Oxford: Oxford University Press.

Jenkins, J. (2005) 'Teaching pronunciation for English as a lingua franca: A sociopolitical perspective', in C. Gnutzmann and F. Intemann (eds.) *The Globalisation of English and the English Language Classroom*, Tübingen: Gunter Narr, pp. 145–58.

Jenkins, J. (2006) 'Current perspectives on teaching World Englishes and English as a lingua franca', *TESOL Quarterly* 40(1): 157–81.

Jenkins, J. (2007) *English as a Lingua Franca: Attitude and Identity*, Oxford: Oxford University Press.

Jenkins, J. (2013) *English as a Lingua Franca in the International University: The Politics of Academic English Language Policy*, London: Routledge.

Jessner, U. (2006) *Linguistic Awareness in Multilinguals: English as a Third Language*, Edinburgh: Edinburgh University Press.

Johnstone, B. (1996) *The Linguistic Individual: Self-Expression in Language and Linguistics*, Oxford: Oxford University Press.

Jørgensen, J.N. (2008) 'Polylingual languaging around and among children and adolescents', *International Journal of Multilingualism* 5(3): 161–76.

Kachru, B.B. (1983) *The Indianization of English: The English Language in India*, New Delhi: Oxford University Press.

Kachru, B.B. (1985) 'Standards, codification, and sociolinguistic realism: The English language in the outer circle', in R. Quirk and H.G. Widdowson (eds.) *English in the World: Teaching and Learning the Language and Literatures*, Cambridge: Cambridge University Press, pp. 11–30.

Kachru, B.B. (1991) 'Liberation linguistics and the Quirk concern', *English Today* 7(1): 3–13.

Kachru, B.B. (1992a) 'Models for non-native Englishes', in B.B. Kachru (ed.) *The Other Tongue: English Across Cultures*, 2nd edn, Urbana: University of Illinois Press, pp. 48–74.

Kachru, B.B. (1992b) 'Teaching World Englishes', in B.B. Kachru (ed.) *The Other Tongue: English Across Cultures*, 2nd edn, Urbana: University of Illinois Press, pp. 355–65.

Kachru, B.B. (1994) 'Englishization and contact linguistics', *World Englishes* 13(2): 135–54.

Kachru, Y. (1995) 'Contrastive rhetoric in World Englishes', *English Today* 11(1): 21–31.

Kachru, Y. and Smith, L.E. (2008) *Cultures, Contexts, and World Englishes*, London: Routledge.

Kaplan, R.B. (1972) 'Cultural thought patterns in intercultural education', in K. Croft (ed.) *Readings on English as a Second Language*, Cambridge, MA: Winthrop, pp. 245–62.

Kaplan, R.B. (1987) 'Cultural thought patterns revisited', in U. Connor and R.B. Kaplan (eds.) *Writing Across Languages: Analysis of L2 Text*, Reading, MA: Addison-Wesley, pp. 9–21.

Kasper, G. (1997) ' "A" stands for acquisition: A response to Firth and Wagner', *The Modern Language Journal* 81(3): 307–12.

Kasper, G. and Blum-Kulka, S. (1993) 'Interlanguage pragmatics: An introduction', in G. Kasper and S. Blum-Kulka (eds.) *Interlanguage Pragmatics*, New York: Oxford University Press, pp. 3–17.

Kecskes, I. and Papp, T. (2000) *Foreign Language and Mother Tongue*, Mahwah, NJ: Lawrence Erlbaum.

Keller, R. (1994) *On Language Change: The Invisible Hand in Language*, trans. B. Nerlich, London: Routledge.

Kellerman, E. and Sharwood Smith, M. (eds.) (1986) *Crosslinguistic Influence in Second Language Acquisition*, Oxford: Pergamon.

Kersaudy, G. (2001) *Langues sans frontières: À la découverte des langues de l'Europe*, Paris: Autrement.

Kerswill, P. (1996) 'Children, adolescents and language change', *Language Variation and Change* 8(2): 177–202.

Kerswill, P., Cheshire, J., Fox, S. and Torgersen, E. (2013) 'English as a contact language: The role of children and adolescents', in D. Schreier and M. Hundt (eds.) *English as a Contact Language*, Cambridge: Cambridge University Press, pp. 258–82.

Kharkhurin, A.V. (2016) 'Multi-competence as a creative act: Ramifications of the multi-competence paradigm for creativity research and creativity fostering education', in V.J. Cook and L. Wei (eds.) *The Cambridge Handbook of Linguistic Multi-Competence*, Cambridge: Cambridge University Press, pp. 420–44.

King, R. (2000) *The Lexical Basis of Grammatical Borrowing: A Prince Edward Island Case Study*, Amsterdam: John Benjamins.

Kirkpatrick, A. (2007) *World Englishes: Implications for International Communication and English Language Teaching*, Cambridge: Cambridge University Press.

Kirkpatrick, A. (2010) *English as a Lingua Franca in ASEAN: A Multilingual Model*, Hong Kong: Hong Kong University Press.

Kirkpatrick, A. (2014) 'English in Southeast Asia: Pedagogical and policy implications', *World Englishes* 33(4): 426–38.

Kirkpatrick, A. and Xu, Z. (2012) *Chinese Rhetoric and Writing: An Introduction for Language Teachers*, Fort Collins, CO: Parlor Press.

Kortmann, B., Burridge, K., Mesthrie, R., Schneider, E.W. and Upton, C. (eds.) (2004) *A Handbook of Varieties of English, Volume 2: Morphology and Syntax*, Berlin: Mouton de Gruyter.

Kortmann, B. and Lunkenheimer, K. (eds.) (2013) *The Electronic World Atlas of Varieties of English*, Leipzig: Max Planck Institute for Evolutionary Anthropology. http://ewave-atlas.org

Kovačič, I. (2000) 'Translating via English as a relay language: The case of subtitling', in M. Grosman, M. Kadric, I. Kovačič and M. Snell-Hornby (eds.) *Translation into Non-Mother Tongues in Professional Practice and Training*, Tübingen: Stauffenburg, pp. 49–60.

Kretzschmar, W.A. Jr. (2009) *The Linguistics of Speech*, Cambridge: Cambridge University Press.

Kretzschmar, W.A. Jr. (2015) *Language and Complex Systems*, Cambridge: Cambridge University Press.

Kroll, J.F. and de Groot, A.M.B. (1997) 'Lexical and conceptual memory in the bilingual: Mapping form to meaning in two languages', in A.M.B. de Groot and J. Kroll (eds.) *Tutorials in Bilingualism: Psycholinguistic Perspectives*, Hillsdale, NJ: Lawrence Erlbaum, pp. 169–99.

Kubota, R. (1999) 'Japanese culture constructed by discourses: Implications for applied linguistics research and English language teaching', *TESOL Quarterly* 33(1): 9–35.

Kubota, R. (2002) 'The impact of globalization on language teaching in Japan', in D. Block and D. Cameron (eds.) *Globalization and Language Teaching*, London: Routledge, pp. 13–28.

Kubota, R. and Lehner, A. (2004) 'Toward critical contrastive rhetoric', *Journal of Second Language Writing* 13(1): 7–27.

Kuhn, T.S. (1962/2012) *The Structure of Scientific Revolutions*, Chicago: University of Chicago Press.

Kuhn, T.S. (1977) *The Essential Tension*, Chicago: University of Chicago Press.

Kuhn, T.S. (2000) *The Road Since Structure*, Chicago: University of Chicago Press.

Labov, W. (1966) *The Social Stratification of English in New York City*, Cambridge: Cambridge University Press.

Labov, W. (1972) *Sociolinguistic Patterns*, Philadelphia: University of Pennsylvania Press.

Labov, W. (1982) 'Building on empirical foundations', in W.P. Lehmann and Y. Malkiel (eds.) *Perspectives on Historical Linguistics*, Amsterdam: John Benjamins, pp. 17–92.

Labov, W. (1989) 'The exact description of the speech community: Short *a* in Philadelphia', in R.W. Fasold and D. Schiffrin (eds.) *Language Change and Variation*, Washington, DC: Georgetown University Press, pp. 1–57.

Labov, W. (1994) *Principles of Linguistic Change, Volume 1: Internal Factors*, Oxford: Wiley-Blackwell.

Labov, W. (2001) *Principles of Linguistic Change, Volume 2: Social Factors*, Oxford: Wiley-Blackwell.

Ladmiral, J.R. (1979) *Traduire: Théorèmes pour la traduction*, Paris: Payot.

Langacker, R.W. (1987) *Foundations of Cognitive Grammar, Volume 1: Theoretical Prerequisites*, Stanford: Stanford University Press.

Lantolf, J. and Thorne, S. (2006) *Sociocultural Theory and the Genesis of Second Language Development*, Oxford: Oxford University Press.

Larsen-Freeman, D. (1997) 'Chaos/complexity science and second language acquisition', *Applied Linguistics* 18(2): 141–65.

Larsen-Freeman, D. and Cameron, L. (2008) *Complex Systems and Applied Linguistics*, Oxford: Oxford University Press.

Lass, R. (1980) *On Explaining Language Change*, Cambridge: Cambridge University Press.

Lass, R. (1990) 'How to do things with junk: Exaptation in language evolution', *Journal of Linguistics* 26(1): 79–102.

Lass, R. (1997) *Historical Linguistics and Language Change*, Cambridge: Cambridge University Press.

Laufer, B. (2003) 'The influence of L2 on L1 collocational knowledge and on L1 lexical diversity in free written expression', in V.J. Cook (ed.) *Effects of the Second Language on the First*, Clevedon: Multilingual Matters, pp. 19–31.

Le Page, R.B. and Tabouret-Keller, A. (1985) *Acts of Identity: Creole-Based Approaches to Language and Ethnicity*, Cambridge: Cambridge University Press.

Leech, G., Hundt, M., Mair, C. and Smith, N. (2012) *Change in Contemporary English: A Grammatical Study*, Cambridge: Cambridge University Press.

Leech, G. and Smith, N. (2006) 'Recent grammatical change in written English 1961–1992: Some preliminary findings of a comparison of American with British English', in A. Renouf and A. Kehoe (eds.) *The Changing Face of Corpus Linguistics*, Amsterdam: Rodopi, pp. 185–204.

Lefevere, A. (1992) *Translation, Rewriting and the Manipulation of Literary Fame*, London: Routledge.

Lehmann, C. (2002) *Thoughts on Grammaticalization*, 2nd revised edn, Erfurt: Arbeitspapiere des Seminars für Sprachwissenschaft der Universität Erfurt, No. 9.

Lenneberg, E.H. (1967) *Biological Foundations of Language*, New York: Wiley-Blackwell.

Lévi, B-H. (2006a) *American Vertigo*, Paris: Grasset.

Lévi, B-H. (2006b) *American Vertigo: Traveling America in the Footsteps of Tocqueville*, trans. C. Mandel, New York: Random House.

Lewis-Kraus, G. (2016) 'The great A.I. awakening', *New York Times Magazine*, www.nytimes.com/2016/12/14/magazine/the-great-ai-awakening.html

Li, X. (2008) 'From contrastive rhetoric to intercultural rhetoric: A search for collective identity', in U. Connor, E. Nagelhout and W. Rozycki (eds.) *Contrastive Rhetoric: Reaching to Intercultural Rhetoric*, Amsterdam: John Benjamins, pp. 11–24.

Lieberman, E., Michel, J-B., Jackson, J., Tang, T. and Nowak, M.A. (2007) 'Quantifying the evolutionary dynamics of language', *Nature* 449 (7163) (October 11): 713–16.

Lightfoot, D.W. (1991) *How to Set Parameters: Arguments From Language Change*, Cambridge, MA: MIT Press.

Lightfoot, D.W. (2003) 'Grammaticalization: Cause or effect?' in R. Hickey (ed.) *Motives for Language Change*, Cambridge: Cambridge University Press, pp. 99–123.

Lightfoot, D.W. (2006) *How New Languages Emerge*, Cambridge: Cambridge University Press.

Lillis, T. and Curry, M.J. (2010) *Academic Writing in a Global Context: The Politics and Practices of Publishing in English*, London: Routledge.

Liu, J. (1999) 'Nonnative English speaking professionals in TESOL', *TESOL Quarterly* 33(1): 85–102.

Llurda, E. (ed.) (2005) *Non-Native Language Teachers: Perceptions, Challenges and Contributions to the Profession*, New York: Springer.

Lodge, A. (1998) 'French is a logical language', in L. Bauer and P. Trudgill (eds.) *Language Myths*, London: Penguin, pp. 23–31.

Long, M.H. (1990) 'Maturational constraints on language development', *Studies in Second Language Acquisition* 12(3): 251–85.

Long, M.H. (1997) 'Construct validity in SLA research: A response to Firth and Wagner', *The Modern Language Journal* 81(3): 318–23.

Lüdi, G., Höchle, K. and Yanaprasart, P. (2010) 'Patterns of language use in polyglossic urban areas and multilingual regions and institutions: A Swiss case study', *International Journal of the Sociology of Language* 205: 55–78.

MacKenzie, I. (2012) 'Fair play to them: Proficiency in English and types of borrowing', in C. Furiassi, V. Pulcini and F. Rodrígucz González (eds.) *The Anglicization of European Lexis*, Amsterdam: John Benjamins, pp. 27–42.

MacKenzie, I. (2014a) 'As if—Vaihinger, translation, and other useful fictions', *Paralleles* 26, www.paralleles.unige.ch/tous-les-numeros/numero-26/mackenzie/Paralleles_26_dec2014_mackenzie.pdf

MacKenzie, I. (2014b) *English as a Lingua Franca: Theorizing and Teaching English*, London: Routledge.

MacKenzie, I. (2014c) 'Lexical innovation: Cromulently embiggening a language', *Alicante Journal of English Studies* 27: 91–105. https://rua.ua.es/dspace/bitstream/10045/46815/1/RAEI_27_06.pdf

Mackey, A., Abbuhl, R. and Gass, S.M. (2012) 'Interactionist approach', in S.M. Gass and A. Mackey (eds.) *The Routledge Handbook of Second Language Acquisition*, London: Routledge, pp. 7–23.

MacWhinney, B. (1987a) 'Applying the competition model to bilingualism', *Applied Psycholinguistics* 8(4): 315–27.

MacWhinney, B. (1987b) 'The competition model', in B. MacWhinney (ed.) *Mechanisms of Language Acquisition*, Hillsdale, NJ: Lawrence Erlbaum, pp. 249–308.

MacWhinney, B. (2008) 'A unified model', in P. Robinson and N.C. Ellis (eds.) *Handbook of Cognitive Linguistics and Second Language Acquisition*, London: Routledge, pp. 341–71.

Mahboob, A. (ed.) (2010) *The NNEST Lens: Nonnative English Speakers in TESOL*, Newcastle, UK: Cambridge Scholars Press.

Mair, C. (2006) *Twentieth-Century English: History, Variation and Standardization*, Cambridge: Cambridge University Press.

Mair, C. and Leech, G. (2006) 'Current changes in English syntax', in B. Aarts and A. McMahon (eds.) *The Handbook of English Linguistics*, Malden, MA: Wiley-Blackwell, pp. 318–42.

Makoni, S. and Pennycook, A. (2007) 'Disinventing and reconstituting languages', in S. Makoni and A. Pennycook (eds.) *Disinventing and Reconstituting Languages*, Clevedon: Multilingual Matters, pp. 1–41.

Matras, Y. (2009) *Language Contact*, Cambridge: Cambridge University Press.

Matthey, M. (2008) 'Comment communiquer sans parler la langue de l'autre?' in V. Conti and F. Grin (eds.) *S'entendre entre langues voisines: vers l'intercompréhension*, Chêne-Bourg: Georg, pp. 113–29.

Maurais, J. (2003) 'Towards a new global linguistic order', in J. Maurais and M.A. Morris (eds.) *Languages in a Globalising World*, Cambridge: Cambridge University Press, pp. 13–36.

Mauranen, A. (1993) *Cultural Differences in Academic Rhetoric*, Frankfurt am Main: Peter Lang.

Mauranen, A. (2006a) 'Signalling and preventing misunderstanding in English as lingua franca communication', *International Journal of the Sociology of Language* 177: 123–50.

Mauranen, A. (2006b) 'Speaking the discipline', in K. Hyland and M. Bondi (eds.) *Academic Discourse Across Disciplines*, Bern: Peter Lang, pp. 271–94.

Mauranen, A. (2012) *Exploring ELF: Academic English Shaped by Non-Native Speakers*, Cambridge: Cambridge University Press.

Mauranen, A., Hynninen, N. and Ranta, E. (2010a) 'English as an academic lingua franca: The ELFA project', *English for Specific Purposes* 29(3): 183–90.

Mauranen, A. and Kujamäki, P. (2004) 'Introduction', in A. Mauranen and P. Kujamäki (eds.) *Translation Universals: Do They Exist?* Amsterdam: John Benjamins, pp. 1–11.

Mauranen, A., Perez-Llantada, C. and Swales, J.M. (2010b) 'Academic Englishes—a standardized knowledge?' in A. Kirkpatrick (ed.) *The Routledge Handbook of World Englishes*, London: Routledge, pp. 634–52.

McArthur, T. (1998) *The English Languages*, Cambridge: Cambridge University Press.

McCagg, P. (1996) 'If you can lead a horse to water, you don't have to make it drink: Some comments on reader and writer responsibilities', *Multilingua* 15(3): 239–56.

McLaughlin, M. (2011) *Syntactic Borrowing in Contemporary French: A Linguistic Analysis of News Translation*, London: Legenda/MHRA.

McWhorter, J.H. (2007) *Language Interrupted: Signs of Non-Native Acquisition in Standard Language Grammars*, Oxford: Oxford University Press.

McWhorter, J.H. (2011) *Linguistic Simplicity and Complexity: Why Do Languages Undress?* Berlin: De Gruyter Mouton.

McWhorter, J.H. (2014) *The Language Hoax*, Oxford: Oxford University Press.

Medgyes, P. (1994) *The Non-Native Teacher*, London: Palgrave Macmillan.

Medgyes, P. (2011) 'Review of Braine (2010) *Nonnative Speaker English Teachers: Research, Pedagogy, and Professional Growth*', *English Language Teaching Journal* 65(2): 190–2.

Medgyes, P. (2012) 'Review of Mahboob (ed.) (2010) *The NNEST Lens: Non-native English speakers in TESOL*', *English Language Teaching Journal* 66(1): 122–4.

Meierkord, C. (2012) *Interactions Across Englishes: Linguistic Choices in Local and International Contact Situations*, Cambridge: Cambridge University Press.

Meillet, A. (1912/1958) 'L'évolution des formes grammaticales', in *Linguistique historique et linguistique générale, Volume 1*, Paris: Champion, pp. 130–48.

Meisel, J.M. (1983) 'Transfer as a second language strategy', *Language and Communication* 3(1): 11–46.

Meissner, F-J. (2008) 'La didactique de l'intercompréhension à la lumière des sciences de l'apprentissage', in V. Conti and F. Grin (eds.) *S'entendre entre langues voisines: vers l'intercompréhension*, Chêne-Bourg: Georg, pp. 229–50.

Mesthrie, R. and Bhatt, R.M. (2008) *World Englishes: The Study of New Linguistic Varieties*, Cambridge: Cambridge University Press.

Meyerhoff, M. and Niedzielski, N. (2003) 'The globalisation of vernacular variation', *Journal of Sociolinguistics* 7(4): 534–55.

Milroy, J. (1992) *Linguistic Variation and Change*, Oxford: Wiley-Blackwell.

Milroy, J. (2003) 'On the role of the speaker in language change', in R. Hickey (ed.) *Motives for Language Change*, Cambridge: Cambridge University Press, pp. 143–60.

Milroy, J. and Milroy, L. (1985) 'Linguistic change, social network and speaker innovation', *Journal of Linguistics* 21(2): 339–84.

Misgeld, D. and Nicholson, G. (1992) *Hans-Georg Gadamer on Education, Poetry, and History: Applied Hermeneutics*, Albany NY: SUNY Press.

Montgomery, S.L. (2000) *Science in Translation: Movements of Knowledge Through Cultures and Time*, Chicago: University of Chicago Press.

Montgomery, S.L. (2013) *Does Science Need a Global Language?* Chicago: University of Chicago Press.

Mougeon, R. and Beniak, E. (1991) *Linguistic Consequences of Language Contact and Restriction: The Case of French in Ontario, Canada*, Oxford: Clarendon Press.

Mounin, G. (1955/1994) *Les Belles Infidèles*, Lille: Presses Universitaires de Lille.

Moussu, L. and Llurda, E. (2008) 'Non-native English-speaking English language teachers: History and research', *Language Teaching* 41(3): 315–48.

Mufwene, S.S. (2001) *The Ecology of Language Evolution*, Cambridge: Cambridge University Press.

Mufwene, S.S. (2010) 'Globalization and the spread of English: What does it mean to be Anglophone?' *English Today* 26(1): 57–9.

Mufwene, S.S. (2012) 'English as a lingua franca: Myths and facts', *Journal of English as a Lingua Franca* 1(2): 365–70.

Mukherjee, J. and Hundt, M. (eds.) (2011) *Exploring Second-Language Varieties of English and Learner Englishes: Bridging a Paradigm Gap*, Amsterdam: John Benjamins.

Müller, M. (1870) 'Darwinism tested by the science of language', *Nature* 1(10) (January 6): 256–9.

Musacchio, M.T. (2005) 'The influence of English on Italian', in G. Anderman and M. Rogers (eds.) *In and Out of English: For Better, for Worse?* Clevedon: Multilingual Matters, pp. 71–96.

Myard, J. et al. (eds.) (2000) *La langue française en colère: Manifeste pour une résistance*! Troyes: Librairie Bleue.

Myers-Scotton, C. (2002) *Contact Linguistics: Bilingual Encounters and Grammatical Outcomes*, Oxford: Oxford University Press.

Nation, I.S.P. (2001) *Learning Vocabulary in Another Language*, Cambridge: Cambridge University Press.

Nemser, W. (1971) 'Approximative systems of foreign language learners', *IRAL: International Review of Applied Linguistics in Language Teaching* 9(2): 115–24.

Nesselhauf, N. (2009) 'Co-selection phenomena across New Englishes: Parallels (and differences) to foreign learner varieties', *English World-Wide* 30(1): 1–26.

Nida, E. (1964/2004) *Toward a Science of Translating: With Special Reference to Principles and Procedures Involved in Bible Translating*, Leiden: Brill; extracted in L. Venuti (ed.) *The Translation Studies Reader*, 2nd edn, London: Routledge, pp. 153–67.

Niederhoffer, K.G. and Pennebaker, J.W. (2002) 'Linguistic style matching in social interaction', *Journal of Language and Social Psychology* 21(4): 337–60.

Nord, C. (2005) *Text Analysis in Translation*, trans. C. Nord and P. Sparrow, Amsterdam: Rodopi.

Norris, J. and Ortega, L. (2000) 'Effectiveness of L2 instruction: A research synthesis and quantitative meta-analysis', *Language Learning* 50(3): 417–528.

Norton Peirce, B. (1995) 'Identity, investment, and language learning', *TESOL Quarterly* 29(1): 9–31.

Odlin, T. (1989) *Language Transfer: Cross-Linguistic Influence in Language Learning*, Cambridge: Cambridge University Press.

Ortega y Gasset, J. (1937/1992) 'The misery and the splendor of translation', trans. E.G. Millar, in R. Schulte and J. Biguenet (eds.) *Theories of Translation: An Anthology of Essays From Dryden to Derrida*, Chicago: University of Chicago Press, pp. 93–112.

Ostler, N. (2005) *Empires of the Word: A Language History of the World*, London: HarperCollins.

Ostler, N. (2010) *The Last Lingua Franca: English Until the Return of Babel*, London: Allen Lane.

Otheguy, R., García, O. and Reid, W. (2015) 'Clarifying translanguaging and deconstructing named languages: A perspective from linguistics', *Applied Linguistics Review* 6(3): 281–307.

Owen, S. (1990) 'What is World Poetry?' *New Republic* (November 19): 28–32.

Paradis, M. (1997) 'The cognitive neuropsychology of bilingualism', in A.M.B. de Groot and J. Kroll (eds.) *Tutorials in Bilingualism: Psycholinguistic Perspectives*, Hillsdale, NJ: Lawrence Erlbaum, pp. 331–54.

Park, J.S-Y. and Wee, L. (2012) *Markets of English: Linguistic Capital and Language Policy in a Globalizing World*, London: Routledge.

Parks, T. (2007) *Translating Style*, Manchester: St Jerome.

Parks, T. (2014) *Where I'm Reading From: The Changing World of Books*, London: Harvill Secker.

Pavlenko, A. (2009) 'Conceptual representation in the bilingual lexicon and second language vocabulary learning', in A. Pavlenko (ed.) *The Bilingual Mental Lexicon: Interdisciplinary Approaches*, Clevedon: Multilingual Matters, pp. 125–60.

Pavlenko, A. (2011) 'Introduction: Bilingualism and thought in the 20th century', in A. Pavlenko (ed.) *Thinking and Speaking in Two Languages*, Bristol: Multilingual Matters, pp. 1–28.

Pavlenko, A. and Lantolf, J. (2000) 'Second language learning as participation and the (re)construction of selves', in J.P. Lantolf (ed.) *Sociocultural Theory and Second Language Learning*, Oxford: Oxford University Press, pp. 155–77.

Peal, E. and Lambert, W.E. (1962) 'The relation of bilingualism to intelligence', *Psychological Monographs* 76: 1–23.

Pei, M. (1967) *The Story of the English Language*, London: George Allen & Unwin.

Pennycook, A. (1998) *English and the Discourses of Colonialism*, London: Routledge.

Phillipson, R. (1992) *Linguistic Imperialism*, Oxford: Oxford University Press.

Phillipson, R. (2003) *English-Only Europe? Challenging language Policy*, London: Routledge.

Phillipson, R. (2008) '*Lingua franca* or *lingua frankensteinia*? English in European integration and globalisation', *World Englishes* 27(2): 250–67.

Phillipson, R. (2009) *Linguistic Imperialism Continued*, London: Routledge.

Pickering, M.J. and Branigan, H. (1999) 'Syntactic priming in language production', *Trends in Cognitive Sciences* 3(4): 136–41.

Pickering, M.J. and Garrod, S. (2004) 'Toward a mechanistic psychology of dialogue', *Behavioral and Brain Sciences* 27(2): 169–225.

Piirainen, E. (2016) *Lexicon of Common Figurative Units: Widespread Idioms in Europe and Beyond, Volume II*, New York: Peter Lang.

Pinker, S. (1994) *The Language Instinct*, London: Penguin.

Plag, I. (2003) *Word-Formation in English*, Cambridge: Cambridge University Press.

Platt, J., Weber, H. and Ho, M.L. (1984) *The New Englishes*, London: Routledge & Kegan Paul.

Pool, J. (2010) 'Panlingual globalization', in N. Coupland (ed.) *Handbook of Language and Globalization*, Oxford: Wiley-Blackwell, pp. 142–61.

Poplack, S. and Levey, S. (2010) 'Contact-induced grammatical change: A cautionary tale', in P. Auer and J.E. Schmidt (eds.) *Language and Space—An International Handbook of Linguistic Variation: Volume 1—Theories and Methods*, Berlin: De Gruyter Mouton, pp. 391–419.

Poplack, S., Zentz, L. and Dion, N. (2012a) 'Phrase-final prepositions in Quebec French: An empirical study of contact, code-switching and resistance to convergence', *Bilingualism: Language and Cognition* 15(2): 203–25.

Poplack, S., Zentz, L. and Dion, N. (2012b) 'What counts as (contact-induced) change', *Bilingualism: Language and Cognition* 15(2): 247–54.

Pride, J. (ed.) (1982) *New Englishes*, Rowley, MA: Newbury House.

Prodromou, L. (2008) *English as a Lingua Franca: A Corpus-Based Analysis*, London: Continuum.

Proshina, Z.G. et al. (2016) 'Russian English linguaculture', in Z.G. Proshina and A.A. Eddy (eds.) *Russian English: History, Functions, and Features*, Cambridge: Cambridge University Press, pp. 35–80.

Pullum, G.K. (2009) '50 years of stupid grammar advice', *The Chronicle of Higher Education* 55(32) (April 17).

Pym, A. (1995) 'Schleiermacher and the problem of "Blendlinge"', *Translation and Literature* 4(1): 5–30.

Rampton, B. (2005) *Crossing: Language and Ethnicity Among Adolescents*, 2nd edn, Manchester: St. Jerome.

Ranta, E. (2006) 'The "attractive" progressive—Why use the *-ing* form in English as a lingua franca?' *Nordic Journal of English Studies* 5(2): 95–116.

Regan, V. (1996) 'Variation in French interlanguage: A longitudinal study of sociolinguistic competence', in D. Preston and R. Bayley (eds.) *Variation in Second Language Acquisition*, Amsterdam: John Benjamins, pp. 177–201.

Rehbein, J., Ten Thije, J.D. and Verschik, A. (2011) 'Lingua Receptiva (LaRa)—Remarks on the quintessence of receptive multilingualism', *International Journal of Bilingualism* 16(3): 248–64.

Rehder, R. (2009) 'The Gam', in *First Things When*, Manchester: Carcanet Press, pp. 75–8.

Remnick, D. (2005) 'The translation wars', *New Yorker*, November 7, www.newyorker.com/magazine/2005/11/07/the-translation-wars

Richards, J.C. (1972) 'Social factors, interlanguage, and language learning', *Language Learning* 22(2): 159–88.

Riley, P. (2015) 'Book Review of V. Muni Toke (ed.) *Le locuteur natif*, numéro thématique de la revue *Histoire Épistémologie Langage* 35(2) (2013)', *Journal of English as a Lingua Franca* 4(2): 391–6.

Ringbom, H. (2001) 'Lexical transfer in L3-production', in J. Cenoz, B. Hufeisen and U. Jessner (eds.) *Cross-Linguistic Influence in Third Language Acquisition: Psycholinguistic Perspectives*, Clevedon: Multilingual Matters, pp. 59–68.

Rivarol, A. de. (1784) *Discours sur l'universalité de la langue française*, Paris: Académie de Berlin.
Rivarol, A. de. (1785) 'Avertissement', in Dante Alighieri, *L'Enfer*, trans. A. Rivarol, Paris: Didot.
Robinson, P. (1995) 'Attention, memory, and the "noticing" hypothesis', *Language Learning* 45(2): 283–331.
Rohdenburg, G. (2003) 'Cognitive complexity and *horror aequi* as factors determining the use of interrogative clause linkers in English', in G. Rohdenburg and B. Mondorf (eds.) *Determinants of Grammatical Variation in English*, Berlin: Mouton de Gruyter, pp. 205–50.
Rollason, C. (2005) 'Unequal systems: On the problem of Anglicisms in contemporary French usage', in G. Anderman and M. Rogers (eds.) *In and Out of English: For Better, for Worse?* Clevedon: Multilingual Matters, pp. 39–56.
Romaine, S. (1995) *Bilingualism*, 2nd edn, Oxford: Wiley-Blackwell.
Ross, M.D. (1996) 'Contact-induced change and the comparative method: Cases from Papua New Guinea', in M. Durie and M.D. Ross (eds.) *The Comparative Method Reviewed: Regularity and Irregularity in Language Change*, New York: Oxford University Press, pp. 180–217.
Ross, M.D. (2003) 'Diagnosing prehistoric language contact', in R. Hickey (ed.) *Motives for Language Change*, Cambridge: Cambridge University Press, pp. 174–98.
Ross, M.D. (2007) 'Calquing and metatypy', *Journal of Language Contact* 1(1): 116–43.
Salager-Meyer, F. (2008) 'Scientific publishing in developing countries: Challenges for the future', *Journal of English for Academic Purposes* 7(2): 121–32.
Sankoff, G. (2002) 'Linguistic outcomes of language contact', in J.K. Chambers, P. Trudgill and N. Schilling-Estes (eds.) *The Handbook of Language Variation and Change*, Oxford: Blackwell, pp. 638–68.
Santos, B. de S. (1998) 'The fall of the *Angelus Novus*: Beyond the modern game of roots and options', *Current Sociology* 46(2): 81–118.
Sapir, E. (1949) *Selected Writings in Culture, Language and Personality*, D.G. Mandelbaum (ed.), Berkeley: University of California Press.
Saussure, F. de. (1916/1986) *Course in General Linguistics*, C. Bally and A. Sechehaye (eds.), R. Harris (trans.), Chicago: Open Court.
Sayers, D. (2014) 'The mediated innovation model: A framework for researching media influence in language change', *Journal of Sociolinguistics* 18(2): 185–212.
Schlegel, A.W. von. (1818) *Observations sur la langue et littérature provençales*, Paris: La Librairie Grecque-Latine-Allemande.
Schleiermacher, F. (1813/2004) 'On the different methods of translating', trans. S. Bernofsky, in L. Venuti (ed.) *The Translation Studies Reader*, 2nd edn, London: Routledge, pp. 43–63.
Schmidt, R.W. (1990) 'The role of consciousness in second language learning', *Applied Linguistics* 11(2): 129–58.
Schmidt, R.W. (1993) 'Awareness and second language acquisition', *Annual Review of Applied Linguistics* 13: 206–26.
Schmied, J. (1991) *English in Africa: An Introduction*, London: Longman.
Schneider, E.W. (2007) *Postcolonial English: Varieties Around the World*, Cambridge: Cambridge University Press.

Schneider, E.W. (2012) 'Exploring the interface between World Englishes and second language acquisition—and implications for English as a Lingua Franca', *Journal of English as a Lingua Franca* 1(1): 57–91.

Schoonbaert, S., Hartsuiker, R.J. and Pickering, M.J. (2007) 'The representation of lexical and syntactic information in bilinguals: Evidence from syntactic priming', *Journal of Memory and Language* 56(2): 153–71.

Schreuder, R. and Weltens, B. (eds.) (1993) *The Bilingual Lexicon*, Amsterdam: John Benjamins.

Schrijver, P. (2014) *Language Contact and the Origins of the Germanic Languages*, London: Routledge.

Schütze, F. (1975) *Sprache soziologisch gesehen*, München: Wilhelm Fink.

Schwyter, J.R. (2011) '"Me talk funny": A stroke patient's personal account', *English Today* 27(4): 49–52.

Scollon, R. and Scollon, S.W. (1997) 'Point of view and citation: Fourteen Chinese and English versions of the "same" news story', *Text* 17(1): 83–125.

Scovel, T. (1988) *A Time to Speak: A Psycholinguistic Inquiry Into the Critical Period for Human Speech*, Rowley, MA: Newbury House.

Seidlhofer, B. (2001) 'Closing a conceptual gap: The case for a description of English as a lingua franca', *International Journal of Applied Linguistics* 11(2): 133–58.

Seidlhofer, B. (2003) *A Concept of "International English" and Related Issues: From "Real English" to "Realistic English"?* Strasbourg: Council of Europe, www.coe.int/t/dg4/linguistic/Source/SeidlhoferEN.pdf

Seidlhofer, B. (2009) 'Common ground and different realities: World Englishes and English as a lingua franca', *World Englishes* 28(2): 236–45.

Seidlhofer, B. (2011) *Understanding English as a Lingua Franca*, Oxford: Oxford University Press.

Selinker, L. (1972) 'Interlanguage', *IRAL: International Review of Applied Linguistics in Language Teaching* 10(3): 209–31.

Selvi, A.F. (2014) 'Myths and misconceptions about nonnative English speakers in the TESOL (NNEST) movement', *TESOL Quarterly* 5(3): 573–611.

Sharwood Smith, M. (1993) 'Input enhancement in instructed SLA: Theoretical bases', *Studies in Second Language Acquisition* 15(2): 165–79.

Sinclair, J. (2004) *Trust the Text: Language, Corpus and Discourse*, London: Routledge.

Sinclair, J. and Mauranen, A. (2006) *Linear Unit Grammar*, Amsterdam: John Benjamins.

Singer, M. (2002) 'Words fool me', in *Mr. Personality: Profiles and Talk Pieces From The New Yorker*, New York: Mariner, 2005, pp. 182–219.

Singleton, D. (2016) 'A critical reaction from second language acquisition research', in V.J. Cook and L. Wei (eds.) *The Cambridge Handbook of Linguistic Multi-Competence*, Cambridge: Cambridge University Press, pp. 502–20.

Slobin, D.I. (1996) 'From "thought and language" to "thinking for speaking"', in J. Gumperz and S. Levinson (eds.) *Rethinking Linguistic Relativity*, Cambridge: Cambridge University Press, pp. 70–96.

Smith, A. (1759/1853) 'Considerations concerning the first formation of languages and the different genius of original and compounded languages', in *The Theory of Moral Sentiments, New Edition*, London: Henry G. Bohn.

Smith, A. (1776/1909) *An Inquiry Into the Nature and Causes of the Wealth of Nations*, New York: Cosimo.

Smith, A. (2016) *Autumn*, London: Hamish Hamilton.

Sorace, A. (1993) 'Incomplete vs. divergent representations of unaccusativity in non-native grammars of Italian', *Second Language Research* 9(1): 22–47.

Sperber, D. and Wilson, D. (1986/1995) *Relevance: Communication and Cognition*, Oxford: Wiley-Blackwell.

Spolsky, B. (2004) *Language Policy*, Cambridge, Cambridge University Press.

Sridhar, K.K. and Sridhar, S.N. (1992) 'Bridging the paradigm gap: Second language acquisition theory and indigenized varieties of English', in B.B. Kachru (ed.) *The Other Tongue: English Across Cultures*, 2nd edn, Urbana: University of Illinois Press, pp. 91–107.

Stamm, P. (1999) *Blitzeis, Erzählungen*, Zürich & Hamburg: Arche-Verlag.

Stamm, P. (2006) *In Strange Gardens and Other Stories*, trans. M. Hofmann, New York: Other Press.

Steiner, G. (1998) *After Babel: Aspects of Language and Translation*, 3rd edn, Oxford: Oxford University Press.

Strunk, W. and White, E.B. (1999) *The Elements of Style*, 4th edn, New York: Longman.

Swales, J.M. (1997) 'English as *Tyrannosaurus rex*', *World Englishes* 16(3): 373–82.

Szmrecsanyi, B. (2005) 'Creatures of habit: A corpus-linguistic analysis of persistence in spoken English', *Corpus Linguistics and Linguistic Theory* 1(1):113–49.

Szmrecsanyi, B. (2009) 'Typological parameters of intralingual variability: Grammatical analyticity vs. syntheticity in varieties of English', *Language Variation and Change* 21(3): 319–53.

Szmrecsanyi, B. (2012) 'Analyticity and syntheticity in the history of English', in T. Nevalainen and E.C. Traugott (eds.) *The Oxford Handbook of the History of English*, Oxford: Oxford University Press, pp. 654–65.

Szmrecsanyi, B. and Kortmann, B. (2009) 'Vernacular universals and Angloversals in a typological perspective', in M. Filppula, J. Klemola and H. Paulasto (eds.) *Vernacular Universals and Language Contacts: Evidence From Varieties of English and Beyond*, London: Routledge, pp. 33–53.

Tadmor, U. (2009) 'Loanwords in the world's languages: Findings and results', in M. Haspelmath and U. Tadmor (eds.) *Loanwords in the World's Languages: A Comparative Handbook*, Berlin: De Gruyter Mouton, pp. 55–75.

Talmy, L. (1985) 'Lexicalization patterns: Semantic structure in lexical forms', in T. Shopen (ed.) *Language Typology and Syntactic Description, Volume 3: Grammatical Categories and the Lexicon*, Cambridge: Cambridge University Press, pp. 57–149.

Talmy, L. (2000) *Toward a Cognitive Semantics: Concept Structuring Systems*, Cambridge, MA: MIT Press.

Talmy, S. (2014) 'Toward an interpretivist turn in L2 studies: Reflexivity, the cognitive-social divide, and beyond', in J.H. Hulstijn et al., 'Bridging the gap: Cognitive and social approaches to research in second language learning and teaching', *Studies in Second Language Acquisition* 36(3): 361–421, (pp. 383–9).

Tarone, E. (2000) 'Still wrestling with "context" in interlanguage theory', *Annual Review of Applied Linguistics* 20: 182–98.

Taylor, I. and Taylor, M.M. (2014) *Writing and Literacy in Chinese, Korean, and Japanese*, Revised edn, Amsterdam: John Benjamins.

Thomas, L. (1983) 'Humanities and science', in *Late Night Thoughts on Listening to Mahler's Ninth Symphony*, New York: Viking, pp. 143–55.

Thomason, S.G. (2001) *Language Contact: An Introduction*, Edinburgh: Edinburgh University Press.

Thomason, S.G. (2007) 'Language contact and deliberate change', *Journal of Language Contact* 1(1): 41–62.

Thomason, S.G. (2008) 'Social and linguistic factors as predictors of contact-induced change', *Journal of Language Contact* 2(1): 42–56.

Thomason, S.G. (2013) 'Innovation and contact: The role of adults (and children)', in D. Schreier and M. Hundt (eds.) *English as a Contact Language*, Cambridge: Cambridge University Press, pp. 283–97.

Thomason, S.G. and Kaufman, T. (1988) *Language Contact, Creolization, and Genetic Linguistics*, Berkeley: University of California Press.

Toury, G. (1995) *Descriptive Translation Studies and Beyond*, Amsterdam: John Benjamins.

Tristram, H.L.C. (1999) *How Celtic Is Standard English?* Saint Petersburg: Nauka.

Trudgill, P. (1983) *On Dialect: Social and Geographical Perspectives*, Oxford: Wiley-Blackwell.

Trudgill, P. (1984) 'Standard English in England', in P. Trudgill (ed.) *Language in the British Isles*, Cambridge: Cambridge University Press, pp. 32–44.

Trudgill, P. (1986) *Dialects in Contact*, Oxford: Wiley-Blackwell.

Trudgill, P. (1989) 'Contact and isolation in linguistic change', in L.E. Breivik and E.H. Jahr (eds.) *Language Change: Contributions to the Study of Its Causes*, Berlin: Mouton de Gruyter, pp. 227–37.

Trudgill, P. (1995) 'Linguistic oppression and the non-native speaker', *Journal of Pragmatics* 24(3): 314–7.

Trudgill, P. (2001) 'Contact and simplification: Historical baggage and directionality in linguistic change', *Linguistic Typology* 5(2/3): 371–74.

Trudgill, P. (2002) *Sociolinguistic Variation and Change*, Edinburgh: Edinburgh University Press.

Trudgill, P. (2004) *New-Dialect Formation: The Inevitability of Colonial Englishes*, Edinburgh: Edinburgh University Press.

Trudgill, P. (2005) 'Native speaker segmental phonological models and the English Lingua Franca Core', in K. Dziubalska-Kolaczyk and J. Przedlacka (eds.) *English Pronunciation Models: A Changing Scene*, Bern: Peter Lang, pp. 77–98.

Trudgill, P. (2008) 'Colonial dialect contact in the history of European languages: On the irrelevance of identity to new-dialect formation', *Language in Society* 37(2): 241–80.

Trudgill, P. (2010) *Investigations in Sociohistorical Linguistics: Stories of Colonisation and Contact*, Cambridge: Cambridge University Press.

Trudgill, P. (2011) *Sociolinguistic Typology: Social Determinants of Language Complexity*, Oxford: Oxford University Press.

Trudgill, P. (2014a) 'Before ELF: GLF from Samarkand to Sfakia', *Journal of English as a Lingua Franca* 3(2): 387–93.

Trudgill, P. (2014b) 'Diffusion, drift, and the irrelevance of media influence', *Journal of Sociolinguistics* 18(2): 214–22.

Trudgill, P. and Hannah, J. (2008) *International English: A Guide to the Varieties of Standard English*, 5th edn, London: Hodder Arnold.

Uzuner, S. (2008) 'Multilingual scholars' participation in core/global academic communities: A literature review', *Journal of English for Academic Purposes* 7(2): 250–63.

Vaihinger, H. (1924) *The Philosophy of 'As If': A System of the Theoretical, Practical and Religious Fictions of Mankind*, trans. C.K. Ogden, London: Routledge & Kegan Paul.

Van Coetsem, F. (1988) *Loan Phonology and the Two Transfer Types in Language Contact*, Dordrecht: Foris.

Van Coetsem, F. (2000) *A General and Unified Theory of the Transmission Process in Language Contact*, Heidelberg: Universitätsverlag Winter.

Van der Auwera J. (1998) 'Conclusion', in J. van der Auwera (ed.) *Adverbial Constructions in the Languages of Europe*, Berlin: Mouton de Gruyter, pp. 813–36.

Van Hell, J. and De Groot, A.M.B. (1998) 'Conceptual representation in bilingual memory: Effects of concreteness and cognate status in word association', *Bilingualism: Language and Cognition* 1(3): 193–211.

Van Parijs, P. (2011) *Linguistic Justice for Europe and for the World*, Oxford: Oxford University Press.

Van Rooy, B. (2011) 'A principled distinction between error and conventionalized innovation in African Englishes', in J. Mukherjee and M. Hundt (eds.) *Exploring Second-Language Varieties of English and Learner Englishes: Bridging a Paradigm Gap*, Amsterdam: John Benjamins, pp. 189–208.

Vennemann, T. (2003) *Europa Vasconica—Europa Semitica*, P.N.A. Hanna (ed.), Berlin: Mouton de Gruyter.

Vennemann, T. (2010) 'Contact and prehistory: The Indo-European Northwest', in R. Hickey (ed.) *Handbook of Language Contact*, Oxford: Wiley-Blackwell, pp. 380–405.

Venuti, L. (1998) *The Scandals of Translation: Towards an Ethics of Difference*, London: Routledge.

Venuti, L. (ed.) (2004) *The Translation Studies Reader*, 2nd edn, London: Routledge.

Venuti, L. (2008) *The Translator's Invisibility: A History of Translation*, 2nd edn, London: Routledge.

Venuti, L. (2013) *Translation Changes Everything*, London: Routledge.

Vosberg, U. (2003) 'The role of extractions and *horror aequi* in the evolution of *-ing* complements in modern English', in G. Rohdenburg and B. Mondorf (eds.) *Determinants of Grammatical Variation in English*, Berlin: Mouton de Gruyter, pp. 305–28.

Vygotsky, L.S. (1934/1962) *Thought and Language*, trans. E. Hanfmann and G. Vakar, Cambridge, MA: MIT Press.

Weaver, W. (1949) 'Recent contributions to the mathematical theory of communication', in C.C. Shannon and W. Weaver (eds.) *The Mathematical Theory of Communication*, Urbana: University of Illinois Press.

Weinreich, U. (1953) *Languages in Contact: Findings and Problems*, The Hague: Mouton.

Weinreich, U., Labov, W. and Herzog, M. (1968) 'Empirical foundations for a theory of language change', in W.P. Lehmann and Y. Malkiel (eds.) *Directions for Historical Linguistics*, Austin, TX: University of Texas Press, pp. 95–189.

Wells, J.C. (2005) 'Goals in teaching English pronunciation', in K. Dziubalska-Kolaczyk and J. Przedlacka (eds.) *English Pronunciation Models: A Changing Scene*, Bern: Peter Lang, pp. 101–10.

Wenger, E. (1998) *Communities of Practice: Learning, Meaning and Identity*, Cambridge: Cambridge University Press.

White, L. and Genesee, F. (1996) 'How native is near-native? The issue of ultimate attainment in adult second language acquisition', *Second Language Research* 12(3): 233–65.

Whorf, B.L. (1956) *Language, Thought, and Reality: Selected Writings of Benjamin Lee Whorf*, J.B. Carroll (ed.), Cambridge, MA: MIT Press.

Widdowson, H. G. (1994) 'The ownership of English', *TESOL Quarterly* 28(2): 377–89.

Widdowson, H.G. (2003) *Defining Issues in English Language Teaching*, Oxford: Oxford University Press.

Wierzbicka, A. (2006) *English: Meaning and Culture*, New York: Oxford University Press.

Wierzbicka, A. (2014) *Imprisoned in English: The Hazards of English as a Default Language*, Oxford: Oxford University Press.

Wilks, Y. (2009) *Machine Translation: Its Scope and Limits*, New York: Springer.

Williams, J. (1987) 'Non-native varieties of English: A special case of language acquisition', *English World-Wide* 8(2): 161–99.

Williams, J.M. (1975) *Origins of the English Language: A Social and Linguistic History*, New York: Free Press.

Wilson, D. and Sperber, D. (1988) 'Representation and relevance', in R.M. Kempson (ed.) *Mental Representations: The Interface Between Language and Reality*, Cambridge: Cambridge University Press, pp. 133–54.

Winford, D. (2003) *An Introduction to Contact Linguistics*, Oxford: Wiley-Blackwell.

Wray, A. (2002) *Formulaic Language and the Lexicon*, Cambridge: Cambridge University Press.

Wray, A. and Grace, G.W. (2007) 'The consequences of talking to strangers: Evolutionary corollaries of socio-cultural influences on linguistic form', *Lingua* 117(3): 543–78.

Wright, L. (2013) 'The contact origins of standard English', in D. Schreier and M. Hundt (eds.) *English as a Contact Language*, Cambridge: Cambridge University Press, pp. 58–74.

Wright, S. (2006) 'French as a lingua franca', *Annual Review of Applied Linguistics* 26: 35–60.

Zamel, V. (1997) 'Toward a model of transculturation', *TESOL Quarterly* 31(2): 341–52.

Zipf, G.K. (1935) *The Psycho-Biology of Language: An Introduction to Dynamic Philology*, New York: Houghton-Mifflin.

Zipf, G.K. (1949) *Human Behavior and the Principle of Least Effort*, Cambridge, MA: Addison-Wesley.

Zobl, H. (1992) 'Prior linguistic knowledge and the conservatism of the learning procedure: Grammaticality judgements of unilingual and multilingual learners', in S.M. Gass and L. Selinker (eds.) *Language Transfer in Language learning*, Amsterdam: John Benjamins, pp. 176–96.

Index